HEAD AND HEART

HEAD
AND *Heart*

PERSPECTIVES
FROM RELIGION
and PSYCHOLOGY

EDITED BY

Fraser Watts and Geoff Dumbreck

TEMPLETON PRESS

Templeton Press
300 Conshohocken State Road, Suite 500
West Conshohocken, PA 19428
www.templetonpress.org

Unless otherwise noted, the Scripture quotations contained herein are
from the New Revised Standard Version Bible, copyright © 1989 by the
Division of Christian Education of the National Council of Churches
of Christ in the U.S.A. Used by permission. All rights reserved.

Scripture quotations marked KJV are from the King James Version
of the Bible.

Designed and typeset by Gopa & Ted2, Inc.

Library of Congress Cataloging-in-Publication Data

Head and heart : perspectives from religion and psychology / edited
by Fraser Watts, Geoff Dumbreck.
    pages cm
  Includes bibliographical references and index.
  ISBN 978-1-59947-439-7 (pbk.)
1. Psychology, Religious. I. Watts, Fraser N. II. Dumbreck, Geoff.
  BL53.H365 2013
  200.1'9—dc23

Printed in the United States of America

13 14 15 16 17 18   10 9 8 7 6 5 4 3 2 1

Table of Contents

Preface

It is a rare pleasure to be able to edit a book with a team of colleagues who were already working closely together before the book was even conceived. This book arises from the work of the Psychology and Religion Research Group in Cambridge, and came to birth when we noticed that almost everyone in the research group was engaged in one way or another with issues about head and heart in religion. Ten of the twelve chapters are written by current or former members of the research group, and the other two by people with whom we have collaborated.

Head and heart are concepts that have been used quite extensively in the religious and philosophical literatures, and the first section of the book approaches things in that way. Others of us have approached head and heart psychologically, focusing on empirical or theoretical work in the psychology of religion (even though "head" and "heart" are more concepts in folk psychology than in contemporary academic psychology). Yet others in the research group have focused on issues about head and heart from an applied perspective, especially the concern that personal transformation needs to occur at both head and heart levels to be deep and enduring. Finally, some of us have found the concepts of head and heart to be fruitful ones to bring into work on the interface between psychology and theology.

We hope that this book shows how it is fruitful to approach an important topic like the relationship between head and heart in an interdisciplinary way, drawing on both theology and scientific psychology. At the same time we would like to think that it provides a methodological model for how to approach a specific topic on the interface between theology and psychology. It is an interface that has been relatively neglected in the more general field of work on theology and science, and we hope that this book illustrates the scope and richness of what remains to be done in that field.

I am grateful to all the contributors for their willingness to share in this project, and especially to my present and former colleagues in the Psychology and Religion Research Group. I am more grateful than I can adequately express for the opportunity to work with such admirable and delightful young colleagues, who carry such promise for the future of the field. I am also most grateful to the John Templeton Foundation for funding various projects of the research group and contributing a substantial share of our funding over a number of years. Finally, I am enormously grateful to Geoff Dumbreck for shouldering the burden of coediting this book and for the graciousness, high intelligence, and remarkable diligence that he has brought to that task.

Fraser Watts

Head and Heart

Introduction

GEOFF DUMBRECK AND FRASER WATTS

Charles Dickens's *Hard Times for These Times* (1854) opens with a stark pedagogical vision that would prompt even the most hardened rationalist to question their cause:

> *Now, what I want is, Facts. Teach these boys and girls nothing but Facts. Facts alone are wanted in life. Plant nothing else, and root out everything else. You can only form the minds of reasoning animals upon Facts. (I.1)*

The outlook of the speaker, the fictional headmaster Mr. Thomas Gradgrind, represents the ultimate triumph of the head. He will not allow children to consider anything that cannot be established by rational or empirical means. Feelings, sentiments, imaginings, and aesthetic sensibilities are strictly forbidden. His two younger sons are even named after leading rationalist intellectuals: Adam Smith and Thomas Malthus.

Over the course of the novel, it becomes clear that Mr. Gradgrind's position is untenable. He is forced to consider the heart as well as the head when his daughter, Louisa, has a breakdown. Trapped in a loveless marriage to another staunch rationalist, she protests to her father:

> *How could you give me life, and take from me all the inappreciable things that raise it from the state of conscious death?*

Where are the graces of my soul? Where are the sentiments of my heart? What have you done, O father, what have you done, with the garden that should have bloomed once, in this great wilderness here! (II.12)

The consequences of the narrow education that Louisa has received slowly dawn on Mr. Gradgrind, and he begins to recognize that his neglect of the heart is partly responsible for her intense unhappiness:

"Some persons hold," he pursued, still hesitating, "that there is a wisdom of the Head, and that there is a wisdom of the Heart. I have not supposed so; but, as I have said, I mistrust myself now. I have supposed the head to be all-sufficient. It may not be all-sufficient; how can I venture this morning to say it is!" (III.1)

Mr. Gradgrind is, of course, a caricature. But while few would take rationalism to the extreme extent depicted at the start of Dickens's novel, it is commonplace for scholars to privilege the head over the heart, even in a religious context. Take, for example, recent critiques of religion by the so-called "New Atheists." In his best-selling book, *The God Delusion* (2006), Richard Dawkins identifies seven groupings or "milestones" on the spectrum of religious belief. Describing the two theistic groupings, he writes as though religious convictions depend on rational calculations:

1. Strong theist. 100 per cent probability of God. In the words of C. G. Jung, "I do not believe, I know."

2. Very high probability but short of 100 per cent. De facto theist. "I cannot know for certain, but I strongly believe in God and live my life on the assumption that he is there." (Dawkins 2006, 50)

The intractability of disagreements surrounding religious belief suggests that religious conviction is much more than an assessment of probability. John Cottingham (2005) helpfully compares the religious worldview with a self-reinforcing net. This net may consist of rational judgments in part, but also includes praxis, symbols, narratives, moral commitments, and so forth. The subjective, affective elements are just as important to the integrity of the net as the objective, propositional strands. In other words, the insights of the heart are just as necessary as the deliberations of the head.

Cottingham is a philosopher, but his findings are mirrored in both theology and psychology. At least since Pascal, religious figures have often distinguished between religion of the head and religion of the heart, even if few have stopped to explain what the terms "head" and "heart" actually denote. Cognitive psychologists and neurologists have rarely adopted the same vocabulary, but they have made a very similar distinction between two different modes of cognition. "Head" and "heart" is thus a highly fruitful—though neglected—topic of research on the interface between science and religion.

Head and Heart in Recent Research

The dearth of published material on this subject is surprising given the mounting interest in the affective dimension of religious life, as reflected in general publications like *The Oxford Handbook of Religion and Emotion* (Corrigan 2008). John Corrigan's edited book *Religion and Emotion* (2004) brings together essays on the place of emotion in religion, but focuses on specific settings (from Bengal to sixteenth-century Jewish mysticism). His monograph, *Business of the Heart*, is likewise specific to nineteenth-century America. Although this historical perspective is important, Corrigan is not primarily concerned with the contemporary theological and psychological questions that we address here.

A smaller number of texts have considered the distinction between "heart" and "head" or "mind" directly. Peter Borys has written two books on the subject: *Transforming Heart and Mind: Learning from the Mystics* (2006) and the self-published *Unity of the Heart: Transforming Consciousness to an Enlightened Humanity* (2008). Both are aimed at the self-help market. Andrew Tallon's *Head and Heart: Affection, Cognition, Volition as Triune Consciousness* (1997) is an academic text and draws extensively on the phenomenological tradition of Husserl, Heidegger, Sartre, Scheler, and others. Several of these figures have been important for theology, but Tallon's book is not primarily concerned with religion.

Wayne Proudfoot's *Religious Experience* (1985) also has some bearing on this topic, because it draws extensively on psychological research on emotion. He dismisses the concept of unmediated experience, which he finds particularly evident in the writings of Schleiermacher, Otto, and James. Yet Proudfoot's book is over twenty-five years old, and the psychological experiments he relies on are now somewhat dated. The present volume takes account of more recent research and has a more applied focus.

Cottingham's *The Spiritual Dimension* and Mark Wynn's *Emotional Experience and Religious Understanding* (2005) have done much to clarify the relationship between affect and mind and are specifically concerned with religion. In a similar vein, William Wainwright's *Reason and the Heart: A Prolegomenon to a Critique of Passional Reason* (1995) draws extensively on two religious figures, Jonathan Edwards and John Henry Newman, who will be considered in the second chapter of this book. We hope to take the discussions that they have begun further in the present volume, drawing more heavily on psychological literature, and placing far more weight on the practical ramifications of this research.

Michael Polanyi has also explored what might be seen as the knowing of the heart in his well-known book on *Personal Knowledge* (1958), a mode of knowing that clearly has implications for religion. In psychology, there has been a small but steady stream of books on intuition, such as Eugene Sadler-Smith's *Inside Intuition* (2008). However, "intuition" is not quite synonymous with the affective understanding of the heart (though it overlaps with it), and the psychology of intuition has not generally been much applied to religion. A related stream of psychological work, led by Eugene Gendlin, more closely related to therapeutic psychology, concerns "felt meanings" (1978), a concept quite close to the understanding of the heart, though again its implications for religion have not been much explored. However, Watts and Williams (1988, chapter 5) have explored the similarities between religious knowing and various forms of more intuitive knowing such as aesthetics, empathy, and self-understanding.

It is the assumption of this book that it will be fruitful to bring together theological reflection on "head" and "heart" with strands of psychology that are concerned with similar phenomena under a variety of other headings. Though there is something inherently elusive about the intuitive, affective mode of understanding associated with the "heart," there is a strong and recurrent intuition that it is of considerable human importance. We share that intuition and hope that this interdisciplinary project will help to elucidate the nature of head and heart.

Defining Head and Heart

One of the greatest conceptual difficulties facing research on "head" and "heart" concerns the terms themselves. Although most people are familiar with the distinction, few could clearly define the scope of each term. Interpreted most literally, "head" could denote the brain, while "heart" could denote the organ that pumps blood around the body. Yet nobody would seriously claim that the intuitions ascribed to the "heart" develop in that organ, and likewise the deliberations of the "head" need not be strictly limited to the brain (they could involve, for example, the nervous system). Both terms are used figuratively. That is not, of course, to deny that there is a different physiological basis to head and heart cognition. Head cognition is probably particularly associated with the dominant left brain, whereas heart cognition is perhaps more associated with the nondominant right brain, which is in turn much more closely connected with the rest of the body (including the heart). The understanding of the heart is thus a more thoroughly embodied mode of cognition.

One option would be to adopt a particular definition of "head" and "heart" for use throughout the present volume. But this would be to impose an arbitrary limit, which could not take into account the diversity of usage in everyday English. Instead, we have chosen to treat "head" and "heart" as multifaceted terms, the various meanings of which have a family resemblance (and not necessarily a strict equivalence). Some of the theories and models considered in the chapters use these terms explicitly, while others express a similar distinction in different ways.

What, then, do the terms "head" and "heart" usually convey? There is an important distinction to be made between process, content, and origin. To consider process first, "head" cognition usually refers to a relatively abstract, intellectual, and propositional mode of cognition; it is most frequently associated with reason, rationality, or detached understanding. The head is primarily concerned with facts, logical arguments, and propositions. In a religious context, this could include theistic proofs, creeds, doctrine, and scripture (especially when it is interpreted literally). Head knowledge of religion can be easily taught and learned; preaching and catechizing both facilitate that process.

In contrast, "heart" cognition refers to a more felt, intuitive mode of cognition. It is usually connected with feelings, emotions, instincts, sentiments, intuitions, and dispositions. It is also linked to life-changing beliefs, but not with beliefs that are merely held in abstract. Some authors have associated it with the imagination (albeit ascribing a far greater role to the latter than make-believe). For James Hillman, much influenced here by Henry Corbin, the defining feature of the heart is the link with imagination (Hillman 1992). The key principle is "that the heart is the seat of imagination, that imagination is the authentic voice of the heart" (Hillman 1992, 4). In a religious context, the heart has been variously understood as the dwelling place of the Holy Spirit and as the ground of the religious worldview. It has also been used to differentiate personal conviction from the dogma of organized religion. Heart cognition is a "gleam in the eye," what we know "deep-down," in our "guts."

It is easier to be articulate about head cognition, which is itself an articulate mode of cognition. It is much harder to be articulate about the more intuitive heart cognition, and one is almost inevitably left gesturing and hand-waving. There is also more diversity in what people mean by "heart" cognition. People largely agree about what "head" cognition is, but "heart" cognition can be an ill-defined "something more," something other than the abstract, articulate cognition we associate with the head. This is true of the way "heart" is used in most of the chapters of this book. Although chapters 5 and 6 tie their analysis to psychological models of cognition, with "head" and "heart" representing different levels of cognition or parts of the brain, most use "heart" in a far broader sense. It indicates those dimensions of human existence, both secular and religious, that cannot be reduced to a series of factual propositions. To return to the example of Dickens's *Hard Times for These Times*, it covers the very aspects of life that the rationalistic Gradgrind neglects: sentiments, feelings, and the experience of relatedness and being.

For others, the distinction is not so much between two different *ways* of knowing things as about the different *content* of what we understand with head and heart; it is about the difference between what we know with our heads and what we know with our hearts. Much of the psychological research discussed in chapters 4 and 7 is about content rather than process (for example, the distinction between what people know they are supposed to believe about God and what they actually think about God). To phrase things like that is also to introduce ideas about the origin of head and heart cognition, and to suggest that head cognition is learned from external sources: that it is part of semantic memory, while heart cognition has a more personal, experiential basis.

THE PSYCHOLOGY AND RELIGION RESEARCH GROUP AT CAMBRIDGE

The present volume is rooted in the work of the University of Cambridge's Psychology and Religion Research Group, and all but one of the chapters are contributed by current or former members of the research group. The group brings together three distinct approaches to the interface between psychology and religion: the dialogue between theology and psychology (part of the wider dialogue between theology and science), the study of religion in psychological theory and research, and the application of religion to further religious life and practice. These three ways of relating psychology and religion provide three different perspectives on the relationship between head and heart in religion.

The first approach is interdisciplinary, examining the interface between psychology and theology. This lies behind the historical accounts of the "heart" offered in chapters 1 and 2, and the assessment of contemporary philosophy of religion found in chapter 3. It also informs chapters 9 and 10, which seek to integrate psychological and theological approaches to head and heart, with particular reference to wisdom, hope, optimism, and forgiveness.

The second approach is more directly grounded in psychological theory and research. This is the focus of chapter 4, which centers on empirical research on head and heart in religion; also of chapter 5, which relates head and heart in religion to broader psychological theorizing about two different modes of cognition, which seem to correspond, at least approximately, to what has often been meant by head and heart.

The third approach is explicitly concerned with the religious application of psychological theory and research. Chapters 6, 7, and 8 consider the ramifications of the distinction between head and heart for religious deradicalization, for pastoral work with people whose God concepts are in some way dysfunctional, and for a mode of religious education that works with the head as well as the heart.

Overview of Chapters

Part 1 of this volume is concerned with conceptualizations of head and heart in disciplines other than psychology. Chapter 1 traces the development of the theological distinction. Pascal proves to be a pivotal figure here, for he draws a much sharper distinction between head and heart than earlier writers. Yet his insistence that religious faith must transform the whole person, and not only the intellect, has clear biblical and patristic precedents. Moreover, it is a central theme for many later theologians, from Wesley and Edwards in the eighteenth century, to Schleiermacher, Bushnell, and Newman in the nineteenth, to Rahner and the charismatic movement in the twentieth. Dumbreck offers a critical comparison of these writers and their critics, sketching the historical background of the debates covered in later chapters.

While chapter 1 takes a primarily theological approach, chapter 2 engages with literature, exploring the Romantic conceptualization of poetic imagination as a means of apprehending truth. Guite examines a passage of Shakespeare, which distinguishes between apprehension and comprehension. The chapter relates these two ways of knowing to heart and head knowledge, focusing on Coleridge's desire "to keep alive the heart in the head." It points to imaginative apprehension as a way of knowing that balances and integrates heart and head, involving a dynamic interchange between the active and the passive, the reflective and the participative. Moving to more recent writers, the chapter explores how Barfield revived and refined some of Coleridge's insights, characterizing knowledge as an evolving series of "participations." It ends by considering the work of the contemporary Welsh poet

Gwyneth Lewis, who seeks to bridge the divide between the heart and the hard sciences.

In chapter 3, we turn to a branch of philosophy that is more commonly associated with the head than the heart: analytical philosophy of religion. From its outset, its proponents sought to analyze and evaluate the often imprecise and emotive claims that are characteristic of religious discourse in terms of the precision and rigor of the head. Yet the latter half of the twentieth century saw something of a "turn to the heart," with the recognition that religious discourse is unavoidably, and unproblematically, embedded in contexts of religious practices. More recently still, much work in analytical philosophy of religion has been characterized by a desire to move beyond the rationalist/expressionist either/or, embracing both head and heart as mutually reinforcing aspects of the rationality of religious discourse. Here Re Manning endorses this approach, defending an account of the rationality of religious discourse of the discernment of the transcendent in nature—a theme central to natural theology—as both inferential and experiential.

Whereas part 1 draws on material from a range of disciplines, part 2 focuses on the latest psychological research. Chapter 4 examines empirical findings about "head" and "heart" distinctions in believers' interpretations of religion. It differentiates between two kinds of knowledge: knowledge *about* God in terms of propositional knowledge, or a set of theological assertions about the nature of God ("head knowledge"), and knowledge *of* God in terms of experiential knowledge, or a set of experiences the believer attributes to direct, personal knowledge of God ("heart knowledge"). Zahl, Sharp, and Gibson assess the strengths and weaknesses of three measurement techniques: self-report questionnaires, qualitative methods, and cognitive methods. They suggest that these methodologies may be improved in order to more accurately measure the religious heart. Finally, they consider findings from three fields of empirical research addressing the religious heart: representations of God, relationships with and closeness to God, and emotions toward God. These findings offer a base of information that will be beneficial for developing clinical interventions and formulating and addressing further questions about the religious heart.

Chapter 5 relates the folk distinction between head and heart to the growing acceptance in psychology of the idea that humans (and perhaps only humans) have two different cognitive systems, two different ways of understanding the world, two ways of making meanings. There is not yet any agreement within psychology about how best to formulate these two systems, but there is widespread agreement that some such two-system formulation is needed. Watts suggests that two-system cognitive theory psychology is elucidating what has traditionally been indicated more informally by the distinction between head and heart. The chapter then goes on to explore the role of these two systems in religion. In many ways, the more intuitive, affective heart cognition seems especially important in religion, and many religious practices seem designed to give the heart a prominent role. However, it is the scope for interplay between head and heart cognition that gives religious life its full richness.

The type of practical considerations seen at the end of chapter 5 come to the fore in part 3. Chapter 6 tackles the topical problem of religious radicalization. While radicalization may be perceived as an overemotional form of religion, this chapter proposes that the manifold nature of religious radicalization is rooted not in overemotionalism but in a separation of head from heart. This represents an intensification of a broader bias toward head-centered religion and culture in the Western, globalized world. Ironically, being split off from reasons of the heart leads toward greater aggression in order to defend sacred values. In this chapter, Savage builds on the empirically assessed prevention method that she developed with Liht, adding the lens of recent neuroscience. This goes a long way to explain why it is easy for well-meaning people to become radicalized, but also offers insights into deradicalization. Picking up on a key theme of chapter 4, and drawing on the work of McGilchrist, particular attention is paid to the tension between the left and right hemispheres of the brain.

Chapter 7 offers a pastoral perspective on some of the issues raised by chapter 5. Pastoral counselors and mental health professionals often hear clients discuss differences between their head understandings of God and their heart understandings of God. These clients report discrepancies between what they intellectually believe about God (God concepts) and how they emotionally experience God (God images). God images are the personal, emotional, relational understandings of God, whereas God concepts are the abstract, intellectual, and theological understandings of God. This chapter will begin by reviewing theory and research on God image development and change. Moriarty then describes an easy-to-use pastoral assessment tool, which may help counselors differentiate between head and heart understandings of God. Finally, he discusses several possible interventions, helping the reader to utilize dynamic, cognitive, and narrative techniques in shifting harmful God images.

In chapter 8, Myers addresses faith development and religious education. Theological education is concerned both with passing on the faith as it is received, and reinterpreting, if not re-visioning, that faith for the present generation. That can lead to a tension between religious training, which involves the submission of the heart in the service of predetermined religious intellectual propositions, and holy learning, which requires the engagement, respect, and nurturing of the whole human. Here, Myers explores the implications of taking the heart seriously in theological education, arguing that growth of instinct, intuition, and intellect must be combined for spiritual and theological development. Only together can they facilitate the paradigm shift required to move from one established religious framework to another.

In the final part, we return to the interface between psychology and theology. Chapter 9 attempts to relate the two in relation to wisdom. Accounts of wisdom from both disciplines concur that it is inclusive of, but not adequately captured by, the notion of intellectual or theoretical knowing. This chapter explores three ways of conceptualizing wisdom: one which emphasizes head knowing, one which emphasizes heart knowing, and another which describes a kind of wisdom that requires an integration of both head and heart modes of knowing. Wiseman argues that all three modes represent distinct kinds of wisdom, each of which has situationally appropriate validity. A broad and rich tapestry of wisdom draws upon kinds of knowing that, depending on one's context, require an emphasis on the head, the heart, or some iterative balancing of the two.

Chapter 10 looks at head and heart in relation to hope and forgiveness. In the first part of this chapter, knowledge of the head and heart are examined in relation to a conceptual distinction between optimism and hope. Whereas optimism can be rooted in estimates of probability, Gulliford maintains that the final ground of hope involves the heartfelt confidence of trust, which is sustained in communion with other agents. In the second section, head and heart knowledge are distinguished in relation to the experience of forgiveness. Here too, without dismissing forgiveness of the head, Gulliford argues that truly transformative forgiveness is likely to involve forgiveness of the heart.

In the conclusion, Watts reflects on general issues arising from theology and psychology's characteristic approaches to head and heart and gauges the strengths and weaknesses of what each discipline has to offer. He also asks how the division between head and heart can be overcome and considers how an effective harmonization of head and heart in an integrated religious life can be achieved.

References

Borys, Peter. 2006. *Transforming Heart and Mind: Learning from the Mystics.* New York: Paulist Press.

———. 2006. *Unity of the Heart: Transforming Consciousness to an Enlightened Humanity.* Minneapolis: Mill City Press.

Corrigan, John, ed. 2004. *Religion and Emotion: Approaches and Interpretations.* Oxford: Oxford University Press.

———. 2008. *The Oxford Handbook of Religion and Emotion.* Oxford: Oxford University Press.

Cottingham, John. 2005. *The Spiritual Dimension: Religion, Philosophy and Human Value*. Cambridge: Cambridge University Press.

Dawkins, Richard. 2006. *The God Delusion*. London: Bantam Press.

Dickens, Charles. 1854. *Hard Times for These Times*. London: Bradbury & Evans.

Gendlin, Eugene T. 1978. *Focusing*. New York: Everest House.

Hillman, James. 1992. *The Thought of the Heart [and] The Soul of the World*. Dallas, TX: Spring Publications.

Polanyi, Michael. 1958. *Personal Knowledge: Towards a Post-Critical Philosophy*. London: Routledge and Kegan Paul.

Proudfoot, Wayne. 1985. *Religious Experience*. Berkeley: University of California Press.

Sadler-Smith, Eugene. 2008. *Inside Intuition*. New York: Routledge.

Tallon, A. 1997. *Head and Heart: Affection, Cognition, Volition as Triune Consciousness*. New York: Fordham University Press.

Wainwright, William J. 1995. *Reason and the Heart: A Prolegomenon to a Critique of Passional Reason*. Ithaca, NY: Cornell University Press.

Watts, Fraser N., and Mark Williams. 1988. *The Psychology of Religious Knowing*. Cambridge: Cambridge University Press.

Wynn, Mark. 2005. *Emotional Experience and Religious Understanding: Integrating Perception, Conception and Feeling*. Cambridge: Cambridge University Press.

PART 1

Theology

Head and Heart in Christian Theology 1

GEOFF DUMBRECK

In the introduction, we noted the ubiquity of the distinction between "head" and "heart." Many assume, without any serious reflection, that this has been a feature of Christian thought since the early church. In fact, the biblical authors and the church fathers saw little difference between the "heart" and what we might now call "mind." The distinction owes far more to comparatively recent theologians like Pascal, Wesley, Edwards, and the Romantics. We will consider several of these "theologians of the heart" in more detail here, focusing on the unique or innovative features of their accounts. Yet we will also point to some common themes, considering their continuity with other important strands of the Christian tradition. This will inevitably provide an incomplete series of "snapshots" rather than a comprehensive picture, but it should set the scene for the rest of this volume.

BACKGROUND

Given that the Bible is of crucial importance to the theologians considered here, it is important to begin with scriptural references to the "heart." The Old Testament is replete with figurative references to *lev*.[1] This is roughly equivalent to the English term "heart," but is usually used to mean "intellect." Take, for example, this proverb, as translated in the King James Version:

Wisdom resteth in the heart of him that hath understanding: but that which is in the midst of fools is made known. (Proverbs 14:33)[2]

Because, in modern English, we associate thoughts with our "heads" or "minds," many recent editions translate *lev* as "mind" when it is used in this sense. The author of this proverb does not mean that wisdom belongs to the heart as opposed to the mind; he simply uses the word for "heart" to denote what we would usually call the "mind." Although this seems counterintuitive, there is a parallel in the English phrase, "to learn by heart."

Elsewhere, *lev* is used to denote a range of human experiences. It may denote the will (for example, 2 Chronicles 12:14 or Job 11:13), the conscience (1 Samuel 24:5), or personal character (Jeremiah 12:3 or Isaiah 38:3). In a few cases it is used, as we now frequently find it, to symbolize emotions and feelings (Judges 16:25). But, more importantly, *lev* may also denote the whole person. Thus Solomon prays to the God of Israel, who keeps "covenant and steadfast love for your servants who walk before you with all their heart" (1 Kings 8:23).

We find a similar picture in the New Testament. The Greek word for heart, καρδία, is also used to denote the mind (Matthew 13:15), conscience (1 John 3:19–20), and emotion (John 14:1). There are instances where "heart" and "mind" are in the same sentence, which might suggest that the authors were drawing a distinction between the two. For example, in Matthew's Gospel, Jesus identifies the greatest commandment as, "You shall love the Lord your God with all your heart, and with all your soul, and with all your mind" (Matthew 22:37). This appears to be a paraphrase of a verse in Deuteronomy: "You shall love the Lord your God with all your heart, and with all your soul, and with all your might" (Deuteronomy 6:5).

Instead of "and with all your might," Matthew includes the phrase "and with all your mind," even though he has already referred to the "heart." The equivalent passages in the Gospels of Mark (12:30) and

Luke (10:27) also introduce a reference to the mind, while retaining the reference to strength. Yet there is an explanation that suggests there is no real distinction between "heart" and "mind" in these passages. The presence of both terms may stem from a conflation of the original Hebrew, which refers to heart, soul, and might, and the Greek of the Septuagint, which refers to mind (διανοίασ), soul, and power (see Allen 1912). If this is the case, "heart" and "mind" are not opposed, but identical.

Notably, in the epistles, Paul identifies the "heart" as the location of the Holy Spirit within Christian believers. Thus he observes, "hope does not disappoint us, because God's love has been poured into our hearts through the Holy Spirit that has been given to us" (Romans 5:5). Paul is not afraid to draw an ontological distinction between Christians and non-Christians, describing the former group as being "in the Spirit" or "in Christ." At the same time, he emphasizes the limitations of the "head" in religious matters. In this life, we cannot hope for anything more than a distorted picture of God:

> For now we see through a glass, darkly; but then face to face: now I know in part; but then shall I know even as also I am known. (1 Corinthians 13:12, KJV)

Biblical language about the heart unsurprisingly found its way into the works of major early Christian theologians. Perhaps the most prominent example is St. Augustine of Hippo (AD 354–430). Augustine shared Paul's belief that the heart is God's "land" or dwelling place within us, and in his autobiographical work, the *Confessions* (republished 1998), he declares to God: "I was seeking you outside myself, and I failed to find 'the God of my heart'" (VI.i,1). This stance is informed by his conception of divine grace. Humans cannot find God by themselves. Rather, he penetrates our hearts, and we discover him there.

Like the Old and New Testament writers, Augustine uses the word "heart" (*cor*) to denote the intellect, the will, and the emotions. Yet he is adamant that religion is not rooted in a passing attitude, momentary determination of will, or fleeting passion. It requires firmly held conviction:

> *My love for you, Lord, is not an uncertain feeling but a matter of conscious certainty. With your word you pierced my heart, and I loved you. (X.vi,8)*

Notably, when Augustine makes this claim that God has pierced his heart, he does not mean that God has pierced his mind alone, or will alone, or emotion alone. His point is that God penetrates every aspect of our inner life, and that our love of God should likewise encompass every aspect of our inner life. As with Christ's commandment to love God with all one's heart, soul, and mind, Augustine's focus is on the *unity* of the different facets of the human person in response to God.

This central point is emphasized by Augustine's treatment of what we have called the "head." Augustine elucidates the limitations and capabilities of unaided reason in his treatise *On the Holy Trinity* (republished 1887). On the one hand, God created us with powers of reason, which teach us that the immortal is preferable to the mortal, the righteous to the unrighteous, the good to the evil, and so forth (XV.iv,6). On the other, God remains incomprehensible. Augustine reiterates St. Paul's claims that we can only glimpse God as a distorted image in the present world (XV.8,14), and that Christians are distinguished by faith (XV.18,32). This faith must be underpinned by love, which is not attributed to the head or heart, or indeed any natural human faculty, but is portrayed as a gift of the Holy Spirit.

SHARPENING THE DISTINCTION

The French theologian, philosopher, and mathematician Blaise Pascal (1623–1662) is central to any discussion of theology and the heart. He shares St. Paul and St. Augustine's emphasis on faith and divine grace, but he draws a much sharper distinction between the heart and the intellect than we find in the Bible or church fathers. In the *Pensées* (republished 1950), he famously declares that "the heart has its own reasons which Reason does not know; a thousand things declare it" (§626). Crucially, although he claims that God "plants" religion in both the mind, "by argument," and the heart, "by grace" (*Apology* §1), he ultimately identifies faith as a matter for the heart. As he puts it, "'tis the heart, not reason, that feels God. This is Faith: God felt by the heart, not by reason" (§627).

This is not to say that Pascal was averse to rational argument.[3] His famous wager is an argument for religious belief. He asks us to consider the consequences of nonbelief in a God who actually exists, and belief in a God who does not. Since an existent God would have the power to grant eternal life, it is better to wager that He exists, for then "if you win, you win all; if you lose, you lose naught" (§223). Later, Pascal outlines several proofs for religion, Christianity, and Judeo-Christian scripture. He argues that, of the three routes to belief (reason, habit, and revelation), Christianity alone has reason (§243). More generally, he praises human thought as the basis of "man's greatness" (§169).

Yet Pascal admits that proofs of Christianity "are not of such a kind that we can declare them to be absolutely convincing" (§643). They point toward religion, but they do not constitute religion, and acceptance of proofs does not, in itself, make someone religious. That requires a change of heart:

> And therefore those upon whom God has bestowed religion by cordial feeling are very fortunate, and are quite fairly convinced. But to those who lack religion we can only give it by process of reason, waiting till God makes it felt by the heart, without which faith is but human, and unavailing for salvation. (§630)

Pascal has the same attitude toward prophecies and miracles. While these provide stronger evidence for Christianity than for any other religion, showing the error of nonbelief, they are not responsible for belief (§643). Christianity is, in this sense, both "wise" and "foolish." On the one hand, "it is the most learned, and the best established through miracles and prophecies." On the other, "that is not what makes us Christians." Reason shows the error of nonbelief, but the ground of belief is "the Cross" (§245).

In these passages, Pascal emphasizes that religion is God-given. It is bestowed upon the heart of each believer, and upon humanity through the cross. As such, although one might assume that a religion of the "heart" would be individualistic and anthropocentric, that is not Pascal's position; one cannot truly experience religion without God's grace. By contrast, philosophy is characterized by egotism. Although philosophers claim "God alone is worthy of love and admiration," their real desire is "to be loved and admired by men" (§281).

The same distinction between philosophy and Christianity is found in the "memorial"—a document found sewn into Pascal's coat after his death. It is an account of a mystical experience that he underwent on November 23, 1654, and differentiates between the God of Judeo-Christian faith and the abstract God of philosophical enquiry:

> *From about half past ten at night until about half past twelve, /*
> *Fire. / God of Abraham, God of Isaac, God of Jacob / not of the*
> *philosophers and the learned. / Certitude, certitude; feeling,*
> *joy, peace. (Adversaria §2)*

Pascal's recollection of this striking experience doubtless reinforced his view that the critics of Christianity were misguided. As he explains in the *Pensées*, they failed to understand "the nature of the religion they attack before attacking it." They demanded evidence for God, even though Christians profess that he is hidden. Without denigrating reason, Pascal firmly challenged these rationalists, acclaiming the heart as a superior authority in religious matters.

Like Pascal, Wesley (1703–91, the founder of Methodism) underwent a life-changing religious experience. He described it in his journal as a change within his heart:

> *In the evening I went very unwillingly to a society in Alders-*
> *gate Street, where one was reading Luther's preface to the*
> *Epistle to the Romans. About a quarter before nine, while*
> *the leader was describing the change which God works in*
> *the heart through faith in Christ, I felt my heart strangely*
> *warmed. I felt I did trust in Christ alone for salvation; and an*
> *assurance was given me that He had taken away my sins, even*
> *mine, and saved me from the law of sin and death. (Wesley,*
> *republished 1981)*

Because of this emphasis on feeling, and because he was critical of the rationalism of his day, Wesley is often portrayed as hostile to reason and knowledge. Even in his lifetime, the Cambridge theologian Thomas Rutherford protested that Methodists thought "human learning was rather an impediment than otherwise."[4] Certainly, Wesley was attuned to the limits of human reason; in a sermon on St. Paul's remark that "we know in part," he asks God to "open our own eyes to discern our own ignorance" (1985–87, Sermon 69).

However, we ought not to interpret such polemical proclamations out of context, as an indiscriminate condemnation of reason. For Wesley's uncompromising rhetoric often masks a more nuanced position. In one sermon, for example, he rages against thinkers with a positive view of the human heart, insisting that the heart of "every natural man" is wicked—no less today than four thousand years ago (Sermon 128). Yet he balances this, observing that God purifies the hearts of the faithful, conquering their sin without destroying it completely. The believer's heart is transformed by God from a state of wickedness to one of "righteousness and true holiness."

Similarly, in "The Case of Reason Impartially Considered," he balances his clear warning that reason can lead us astray by bemoaning the number of critics of reason within the church. By Wesley's estimation, "never was there a greater number of these in the Christian Church, at least in Britain, than at this day" (Sermon 70). In this sermon, Wesley tries to identify a middle way between those who dismiss reason and those whose excessive confidence in reason leads them to dismiss the truths expressed in revelation.

Before offering his solution, however, he defines the word "reason" more closely. First, it is a synonym for "argument"; one might, for instance, be asked to give a reason for one's actions or beliefs. Second, and more importantly, it is used as a synonym for "understanding" (including the powers of apprehension, judgment, and discourse). Understood in this second sense, reason is essential to many earthly pursuits, but its religious value is less immediately obvious.

Reason is certainly not the basis of Christianity. Wesley is unequivocal that "true religion stands upon the oracles of God"—namely, the prophets, apostles, and Christ himself. Yet we need reason in order to interpret and communicate their words. With the aid of the Holy Spirit, reason helps us to comprehend the scriptural accounts of God's attributes, the nature of faith and repentance, our duties toward others, and so forth. For Wesley, as for Pascal, it is a "precious gift" from God, "fixed in our souls for excellent purposes." To denigrate reason is to do a disservice to God.

That said, reason has a crucial limitation. It produces neither faith (defined here as a "conviction of things not seen"), nor the hope that derives from faith, nor the love of God that derives from both, nor the love of man that derives from all three. Wesley claims to have discovered this through bitter personal experience. Having collected together rational arguments for God's existence, he found himself unable to reach certainty on *any* matter and "was ready to choose strangling rather than life."

He elaborates on the nature of faith in a further sermon, stressing that the faith required for salvation entails more than the acceptance of propositions:

> *It is such a divine conviction of God, and of the things of God, as, even in its infant state, enables every one that possesses it to "fear God and work righteousness." (Sermon 106)*

In other words, saving faith involves an entire reorientation of life. This is not initiated by the believer's powers of reason, but by the same divine transformation of the heart that was described above, and which Wesley believed himself to have experienced on Aldersgate Street.

Wesley was contemporary with the American Protestant theologian Jonathan Edwards (1703–58). In *Religious Affections* (republished 1959), Edwards seeks to answer a question arising from his belief in predestination: "What are the distinguishing qualifications of those that are in favor with God, and entitled to his eternal rewards?" In his view, the activity of Satan makes it all the more difficult to judge whether someone has these qualifications, by bringing about "the mixture of counterfeit religion with true." His short answer is that "true religion, in great part, consists in holy affections" (I).

Edwards begins his general observations with a definition of the affections as "the more vigorous and sensible exercises of the inclination and will" (I.i). "Inclination" and "will" denote the first of two faculties. When the mind is described in connection with this faculty, it may also be termed the "heart." The other faculty encompasses perception, speculation, discernment, and judgment; it is termed the "understanding." Thus, in Edwards's view, true religion is not primarily a rationalistic enterprise, but entails "vigorous and lively actings of the inclination and will of the soul, or the fervent exercises of the heart" (I.ii.1).

Edwards appeals to the Bible to justify this claim. He assumes that the biblical authors used the term "heart" as he has just defined it and points to the command to "love the Lord your God with all your heart." Although we have seen that *lev* and καρδία actually have a range of meanings, Edwards is correct that the scriptures emphasize many emotions, not least godly fear, hope, and love. He cites, in particular, St. Paul's famous remark to the Corinthians: "faith, hope, and love abide, these three; and the greatest of these is love" (1 Corinthians 13:13).

In the second part of *Religious Affections*, Edwards notes twelve signs that might be thought to indicate that religious affections are genuine (or "gracious"), but which are in fact no guarantee (II). Nothing can be confirmed by their quantity, their effect on the body, their impact on religious discourse, their source in the individual's own strength, or their accompaniment by recall of scripture. We cannot be sure just because there is "an appearance of love in them," because they have multiple forms, or because they follow "awakenings and convictions of conscience." Regular worship offers no assurance; neither does the tendency to "praise and glorify God," nor an ability to impress the "truly godly."

Turning to part three, which enumerates accompanying characteristics that *do* indicate gracious religious affections, Edwards offers an important qualification (III.Int.1). He does not envisage his list as a simple test by which we might judge other people; such judgment is reserved for God. Yet, as we read further, it becomes easy to see how readers might fall into this trap. Edwards himself squabbled with his congregation, suspicious that many converts fell short of the mark (Stein 2007).

The first and most notable characteristic of gracious religious affections is that they are God-given, arising from "spiritual, supernatural, and divine" influences upon the heart (III.i). Again, Edwards looks to the New Testament for support. He notes in particular St. Paul's distinction between those who are in the Spirit and those who are of the flesh. He points to the first letter to the Corinthians, as evidence that we cannot generate the Spirit ourselves:

> *And we speak of these things in words not taught by human wisdom but taught by the Spirit, interpreting spiritual things to those who are spiritual. Those who are unspiritual do not receive the gifts of God's Spirit, for they are foolishness to them, and they are unable to understand them because they are discerned spiritually. (1 Corinthians 2:13–14)*

For this reason, gracious affections are devoid of self-interest (III.ii). They are, rather, "founded on the loveliness of the moral excellency of divine things" (III.iii).

Notably, the mind grasps these divine things through God's stimulation of the understanding: "gracious affections do arise from the mind's being enlightened, richly and spiritually to understand or apprehend divine things" (III.iv). While it is possible for certain affections to occur without understanding, genuine religious affections cannot. Yet we must not mistake the "understanding" he describes here for *natural* human understanding, which he earlier associated with perception, speculation, discernment, and judgment. Edwards is speaking of a divinely bestowed *spiritual* understanding, which is primarily "a sense of heart." This is not merely speculative, but sensible or felt. Religious affections do not arise from the amassing new conceptual knowledge, but from "giving the mind a new taste or relish of beauty and sweetness" (III.iv).

This is not simply a matter for individual judgment; the convictions that give rise to Christian affections should be based on evidence, which can be found within the gospel itself (III.v). Moreover, they should be accompanied by a sense of humility (III.vi) and bring about a change in the convert's nature (III.vii). They should promote Christlike virtues (III.viii) and a tender spirit (III.ix). Finally, they should be balanced (III.x), arouse ever greater desire for "spiritual attainments" (III.xi), and come to fruition in the believers' actions (III.xii).

Despite their differences, there is much common ground between Pascal, Wesley, and Edwards. Pascal continued to advance rational arguments for the existence of God, and yet he emphasized that faith is a matter for the heart, drawing on his own mystical experience. Wesley's ministry is similarly unimaginable without the incident on Aldersgate Street: the transformation of the "heart" that he felt at that point equates to the transformation of life that is required of Christians. We find a similar theme in Edwards, who claims that religious affections, grounded in a God-given spiritual understanding, must bring about a real change in the convert. Although all three have a sharper distinction between the heart and reason or understanding than the biblical authors or church fathers, they do not diverge entirely. Crucially, in emphasizing the heart, they do not wish to prioritize transitory feelings, but to argue that the *whole person* is transformed by Christian faith.

ROMANTICISM

Although Friedrich Schleiermacher (1768–1834) stands in the same Reformed Protestant tradition as Edwards, he is far more liberal in outlook. His early work was strongly influenced by his relationship to the Berlin Romantics; he lived with Friedrich Schlegel and was a close friend of Henrietta Herz, the Jewish founder of a Berlin literary salon. His mature account of feeling is most clearly elucidated in the introduction of *The Christian Faith* (republished 1999).[5] Notably, he does not consider his observations on feeling to belong to theology itself, but describes them as propositions "borrowed" from ethics. Ethics is not understood here in its normative sense but as "that speculative presentation of reason" that seeks to establish an abstract "concept of the church" (§2, postscript 2).

Schleiermacher begins by distinguishing between knowing, doing, and feeling. He uses "feeling" in a narrow sense, so that it is equivalent to the "immediate self-consciousness" (§3.2). This means that it is neither unconscious nor "mediated by self-contemplation." He also distinguishes between abiding-in-self and passing-beyond-self, arguing that our lives alternate between the two (§3.3). When one does something, one passes-beyond-self. When one thinks or feels, one abides-in-self. Feeling is the only *pure* abiding-in-self, and it is therefore antithetical to thought and action. One might conclude that this strict division is a crude form of faculty psychology, implying a still sharper distinction between head (knowing) and heart (feeling) than Pascal, Wesley, or Edwards would countenance, let alone Augustine or the biblical authors. In fact, as we shall see, Schleiermacher's understanding of human consciousness assumes far greater unity than these passages suggest.

Writing in the wake of Kant, who had refuted the traditional metaphysical arguments for the existence of God, Schleiermacher had strong apologetic reasons to deny that religion is *in essence* a matter for the head. If piety were a form of knowledge, the individual's piety would be measured by his level of knowledge, or the strength of his conviction. It cannot be measured by the former, as the "most perfect master of Christian Dogmatics" need not be the most pious (§3.3). Nor can it be measured by the latter—in other disciplines, conviction is gauged by the clarity and completeness of the thought involved, but these qualities of thought are unnecessary for piety.

Equally, the essence of religion cannot be action; otherwise, an individual's level of piety would be determined by the content, motive, or goal of his actions (§3.4). It cannot be determined by the content, for "not only the most admirable but also the most abominable, not only the most useful but also the most inane and meaningless things, are done as pious and out of piety." Nor can it be determined by the goal, for "no one will pronounce an action more or less pious because of the greater or less degree of completeness with which the intended result is achieved." It might be determined by the motive, but motives are not actions.

Since the essence of religion cannot be knowledge or action, it must "belong" to feeling. This does not mean that piety is *unconnected* to knowledge and action—on the contrary, as feeling and immediate self-consciousness, piety is the "mediating link between those moments in which knowing predominates and those in which doing predominates." But knowledge and action are always secondary—they pertain to piety only "inasmuch as the stirred up Feeling sometimes comes to rest in a thinking which fixes it, sometimes discharges itself in an action which expresses it" (§3.4).

In order to get a more accurate understanding of what Schleier-macher means by "feeling," we must first examine his account of human self-consciousness. He argues that self-consciousness is comprised of two elements, naming the first "self-caused" (or "being") and the second "non-self-caused" (or "having-by-some-means-come-to-be"). The self-caused element corresponds to the individual's spontaneous activity and to the "feeling of freedom." The non-self-caused element corresponds to the individual's receptivity and to the "feeling of dependence."

When humans interact with the world, both elements of self-consciousness are involved, because every self-caused action has a non-self-caused object (§4.3). As such, in relation to the temporal world, there can be no pure activity or pure receptivity, and no feelings of absolute freedom or absolute dependence. The feeling of absolute dependence does in fact occur, but only in relation to God. It is the constant self-consciousness that "the whole of our spontaneous activity comes from a source *outside* of us." In this unique feeling, God is *given* to us.

At this point Schleiermacher introduces a crucial qualification, which emphasizes the fundamental unity of consciousness. The feeling of absolute dependence is the highest level of self-consciousness, but while it may be distinguished from other levels of self-consciousness, it cannot occur in isolation. As he puts it:

What we have thus described constitutes the highest grade of human self-consciousness; but in its actual occurrence it is never separated from the lower. (§5)

This helps to explain the variety of religious belief. The feeling of absolute dependence is universal, but the religious consciousness of an individual varies according to the moment of the sensible self-consciousness with which the feeling of absolute dependence combines. Since doctrine develops from reflection on the "religious affections," it is the product of three different aspects of consciousness—the God-given feeling of absolute dependence, the mundane sensible self-consciousness, and rational thought. In other words, academic theology is the head's attempt to give propositional expression to matters of the heart.

Schleiermacher had not always been so sympathetic toward academic theology. In his earliest major work, the *Speeches on Religion* (republished 1996), his apologetic instinct led him to draw a sharper divide between faith, which is grounded in feeling, and systematic religious thought. He rejects the "cold argumentation" of theological discourse, objecting that "the high and noble has strayed from its vocation and has lost its freedom in order to be held in a despicable slavery by the scholastic and metaphysical spirit of barbaric and cold times" (Schleiermacher 1996, 13).

Karl Barth, the influential twentieth-century theologian, shared Schleiermacher's concerns about the use of philosophy. But he was equally suspicious of Schleiermacher's emphasis on feeling. Despite Schleiermacher's insistence that the feeling of absolute dependence has a transcendent "whence," Barth accused him of reducing religion to a human concern. He characterized the *Glaubenslehre* as a "deep, extensive, and palpable" distortion of Protestant theology and called instead for a renewed focus on revelation. Barth's popularity has doubtless damaged Schleiermacher's legacy.

Yet Schleiermacher is far from the most extreme example. The

American Congregationalist minister Horace Bushnell (1802–76) takes this antipathy toward religion of the head to a new level. In a lecture entitled *Dogma and Spirit* (1867), first delivered in 1848, Bushnell characterizes dogma as an opinion that is held "as a rule to the opinions, the faith, or the Christian experience, whether of ourselves or of others." These dogmatic opinions belong to the "head," but true Christian knowledge belongs to the heart:

> *What is loftiest and most transcendent in the character of God, his purity, goodness, beauty and gentleness, can never be sufficiently apprehended by mere intellect, or by any other power than a heart configured to these divine qualities. (1867, 302)*

Bushnell draws upon the scriptural claim that divine gifts cannot be understood or described by human wisdom, but only by another divine gift: the Spirit that dwells within believers (1867, 304). He emphasizes that Christ was the scourge of the theologians of his day, the Pharisees, and that the disciples were motivated to follow Christ by faith, not reason (1867, 282). Similarly, he portrays the early church as "an age, not of dogmas or speculations, but of gifts, utterances, and mighty works, and, more than all, of inspiration, insight, freedom and power" (1867, 284).

Bushnell admits that the early church produced written expressions of their faith, but insists that they were undogmatic. He points to the Apostles' Creed, traditionally believed to have been dictated by the Twelve Apostles after Pentecost (1867, 287). We might question whether this text is as purely historical as he claims, given that it ends with professions of belief in "the communion of saints; the forgiveness of sins; the resurrection of the body; and the life everlasting." Nevertheless, it includes considerably less theological interpretation than the Nicene and Athanasian Creeds, which are also widely accepted and recited by contemporary Christians.

Consider, for example, the claims that the Apostles' Creed makes about Jesus's conception and birth. It declares simply that he "was conceived by the Holy Ghost" and "born of the Virgin Mary." The Nicene Creed mentions the same events, but it adds that Jesus is "the only-begotten Son of God, Begotten of his Father before all worlds, God of God, Light of Light, Very God of very God, Begotten, not made, Being of one substance with the Father, By whom all things were made." This carefully worded explanation of Jesus's relationship to the Father was intended to preclude heresies like Arianism,[6] but Bushnell dismisses such theological elaborations as the product of human wisdom, which will ultimately "stifle the breath of religion" (1867, 287).

Bushnell sees himself as an heir to the Reformation. He praises Luther for his emphasis on scripture, but complains that Luther did not do enough to rid Christianity of dogmatic theology:

> *The great and most fatal defect of Luther's reformation was that he left the reign of dogma or speculative theology untouched. He did not restore the ministration of the Spirit. Opinions were left to rule the church, with just as much of consequence as they had before. (1867, 290)*

Bushnell allows that theological propositions serve a practical purpose, being useful for teaching, apologetics, and dialogue with other disciplines. And yet, considered in themselves, he regards them as "no more entitled to a Christian standing than our speculations in geology" (1867, 310). In this respect, Bushnell is far more extreme than Schleiermacher, who attached sufficient value to dogmatic statements to compose his own systematic theology.

Perhaps unsurprisingly, given his conversion to Roman Catholicism, Newman (1801–90) places far more weight on church teaching than either Schleiermacher or Bushnell. Yet Newman shares their conviction that religion cannot be captured in a series of abstract claims, and chose "cor ad cor loquitur" (heart speaks unto heart) as his motto. His celebrated *An Essay in Aid of a Grammar of Assent* offers a detailed account of rational processes, including assent, inference, and the so-called "illative sense" (republished 1979). Yet it is his important distinction between notional and real assent that warrants particular consideration here (1979, chapter 4).

Every assent is unconditional, but notional assent takes several forms. Newman elucidates them in order of decreasing passivity (1979, 52–76). Profession is the most passive; it includes halfhearted claims of political allegiance or musical taste based on family background or social trends. Credence is the type of assent that we give to the "professed facts" that we stumble across in everyday life—in conversation, for example, or light reading. Opinion is similar to credence, but requires the individual to consider the probability of the fact in question, rather than accepting it at face value. Presumption is the assent to first principles, while speculation (defined here in a technical sense) is the fully conscious acceptance of a proposition's truth.

Real assent differs from all these forms of notional assent, as Newman illustrates with a series of examples. One concerns the abolition of dueling:

> *When Mr. Wilberforce, after succeeding in the slave question, urged the Duke of Wellington to use his great influence in discontinuing duelling, he could only get from him in answer, "A relic of barbarism, Mr. Wilberforce;" as if he accepted a notion without realising a fact: at length, the growing intelligence of the community, and the shock inflicted upon it by the tragical circumstances of a particular duel, were fatal to that barbarism. The governing classes were roused from their dreamy acquiescence in an abstract truth, and recognised the duty of giving it practical expression. (1979, 78)*

In this example, the Duke of Wellington gives notional assent to Wilberforce's criticism of barbarism but nothing more. He accepts Wilberforce's point of view at an intellectual level but is not minded to act. An especially appalling duel provides the catalyst for change. It stirs the powerful to give *real* assent to the criticisms of dueling, and they bring the practice to an end. Many similar examples can be found in modern life—for instance, an individual's notional assent to the importance of wearing a seat belt might be upgraded to real assent after the experience of a road accident.

Assent to dogmatic propositions may be either notional or real, but whereas real assent is an act of religion, notional assent is an act of mere theology (Newman 1979, 73). As Newman explains in an extended quotation from an earlier work, philosophers who speak of Christianity in the abstract, without reference to actual experience, have missed the point:

> *They sit at home, and reach forward to distances which astonish us; but they hit without grasping, and are sometimes as confident about shadows as about realities. They have worked out by a calculation the lie of a country which they never saw, and mapped it by means of a gazetteer. (1979, 90)*

Continuing with a savage attack on the attempt to prove religious beliefs from first principles, Newman adds:

> *But if we commence with scientific knowledge and argumentative proof, or lay any great stress upon it as the basis of personal Christianity, or attempt to make man moral and religious by libraries and museums, let us in consistency take chemists for cooks, and mineralogists for our masons. (1979, 91)*

Real assent to dogmatic propositions requires experience, but not necessarily mystical experience. We do not have to perceive God through the senses to give real assent to his oneness; our pangs of conscience lead us beyond mere notions of God to an image of the "One to whom we are responsible, before whom we are ashamed, whose claims upon us we fear" (1979, 101). Newman does not intend such images to

GEOFF DUMBRECK

replace theological notions. Indeed, while theology is impoverished when devoid of experience, religion "cannot maintain its ground at all" without theological underpinning.

This indicates a significant divergence from Schleiermacher. While the German pastor locates the ground of doctrine in the feeling of absolute dependence, Newman insists that "knowledge must ever precede the exercise of the affections," such that "devotion falls back upon dogma" (1979, 109). Newman is still further removed from Bushnell, one telling point of divergence being their reading of the Athanasian Creed. They agree that religion cannot be reduced to rational argument, but whereas Bushnell dismisses this creed in a deluge of antidogmatic polemic, Newman lauds "the antithetical form of its sentences" (1979, 118). By eluding human comprehension, dogmatic propositions can lead us into mystery.

The Neoscholastic Backlash

Newman's *Essay* was completed in 1870, the same year that the First Vatican Council was adjourned. The decisions of the third session include a striking endorsement of proofs for the existence of God:

> *If anyone says that the one, true God, our creator and lord, cannot be known with certainty from the things that have been made, by the natural light of human reason: let him be anathema. (Canon 2.1)*

While this does not contradict Newman's comments on proofs, which criticize those who demand proofs as a *basis* for religious belief, the difference in emphasis is clear. There is an even stronger (though hardly surprising) divergence between the council and Schleiermacher, who assumed that Immanuel Kant's critique of the traditional proofs was insurmountable.

Contemporary developments in philosophy seem to have caused the

Roman Catholic Church increasing concern.[7] In the encyclical *Aeterni Patris* (1879), Pope Leo XIII blames contemporary philosophy for many of the modern world's problems, noting that false opinions lead to wrong action. Yet he does not question the legitimacy of philosophical theology *per se*. As well as commending its apologetic and polemical applications, he reaffirms Vatican I's conclusion that philosophy "demonstrates that God is" (§4).

For philosophical theology to be acceptable, it should take the form established by the church fathers. They were faced with a plethora of opinions from the ancient philosophers, but they were able to distinguish the true from the false. This is because they never doubted the revealed truth of Christianity, which stems from God rather than the human intellect: "that, according to divine plan, the restorer of human science is Christ, who is the power and the wisdom of God, and in whom are hid all the treasures of wisdom and knowledge" (§10). Justin Martyr and Augustine are held up as examples, but the highest praise is reserved for Thomas Aquinas. "Single handed," the encyclical states, "he victoriously combated the errors of former times, and supplied invincible arms to put those to rout which might in after-times spring up" (§18).

Aquinas is contrasted with the Enlightenment philosophers, who approached their subject "without any respect for faith." The fact that they have reached so many conflicting conclusions is held up as evidence of their flawed methodology. The pope's main concern, however, is that they have influenced Catholic thought:

> But as men are apt to follow the lead given them, this new pursuit seems to have caught the souls of certain Catholic philosophers, who, throwing aside the patrimony of ancient wisdom, chose rather to build up a new edifice. (§24)

Aquinas's works are not, in themselves, wholly opposed to the "heart" tradition of that great Catholic heart theologian, Blaise Pascal. For Pascal accepted the Thomist claim that now seems most controversial: that

Christianity's truth can be demonstrated by reason. Moreover, Aquinas accepted that such proofs are unnecessary for faith; in the *Summa Contra Gentiles*, he maintains that the truth of reason and the truth of Christianity are compatible, but denies that it is irrational to accept religious claims through faith (1.7). Yet, in promoting the scholastic method, *Aeterni Patris* precluded any attempt to realign religion with feeling in place of metaphysics. It is difficult to see how one could accept this document while drawing Pascal's sharp distinction between the God of faith and the God of the philosophers. It is all but impossible to reconcile it with Schleiermacher, as it effectively ignores the Kantian problem that he aimed to solve.

While *Aeterni Patris* gave papal endorsement to a particular form of "head" theology, "heart" theology had a renaissance in the form of the Catholic modernists. Like Schleiermacher, their prime concern was to make Christianity palatable to modern thinkers, yet Pius X's encyclical *Pascendi Dominici Gregis* (1907) explicitly condemned their approach. From the very outset, it warns against dangerous philosophical innovations and notes the papacy's duty to refute them:

> *The office divinely committed to Us of feeding the Lord's flock has especially this duty assigned to it by Christ, namely, to guard with the greatest vigilance the deposit of the faith delivered to the saints, rejecting the profane novelties of words and oppositions of knowledge falsely so called. (§1)*

This highly polemical document takes a "them and us" approach to secular philosophy. It leaves no room for modernist ideas in Roman Catholic teaching, and modernist priests and theologians are accused of poisoning their own church from within. The solution is clear: Roman Catholics must follow the conclusions of *Aeterni Patris*, taking scholastic theology as "the basis of the sacred sciences" (§45). The bishops must forbid the publication of modernist texts and prevent access to those already published (§50).

The most interesting feature of *Pascendi* for our present discussion, besides its severe tone, is its condemnation of the modernist principle of "vital immanence." It claims that modernist philosophy breaches Canon 2.1 of the First Vatican Council, quoted above, by denying that God's existence can be known by human reason. Instead, the modernists appeal to a human sentiment, or "movement of the heart," which stems from a "need of the divine" and can be considered as a form of revelation. This is not the place to ask whether *Pascendi* gives an accurate account of modernist teachings; it is enough to note the papacy's specific objection to this "religion of the heart," which they associate entirely with philosophical innovation, and their rigorous defense of a neoscholastic "religion of the head."

THE LATE TWENTIETH CENTURY

In this chapter, we have focused on the period from Pascal until the end of the long nineteenth century. We have seen that theologians who emphasize the heart are not without their critics in both Roman Catholic and Protestant circles. Yet it is worth noting two strands of late twentieth-century thought that suggest a renewed focus on the heart; there are doubtless many others, and some will be examined in later chapters of this volume. The first is in Roman Catholic theology: in spite of its severity, the papal assault on the modernists did not quash further appeals to the heart. The influential Jesuit theologian Karl Rahner (1904–84) is one important example. In a late essay, entitled "The Foundation of Belief Today" (1979), he offers a subtle and compelling analysis of the nature of religious belief. He resists fideism, noting that "the Catholic mind always included respect for human intelligence, for reflection and for intellectual reasoning and argument" (1979, 3–4). Yet he also rejects rationalism, complaining that "current theology does not pay enough attention to the internal" (1979, 4).

Taking a notably different line from *Aeterni Patris* and *Pascendi*

Dominici Gregis, Rahner recognizes the need to bring both head and heart to religious matters. His view of the heart is closely tied to his conception of mystery. God is not simply another "thing" in our lives, to be processed by the senses and reason. Rather, the Christian must "accept him as an incomprehensible mystery in silence and adoration, as the beginning and end of his hope" (1979, 14–15). This mystery draws him, with the aid of divine grace, toward fulfilment:

> *From the innermost heart of his experience a Christian knows that he himself is sustained by this mystery in his trust and hope for the fulfilment of his being. So he calls this movement towards God at work within him, "grace," "The Holy Spirit," even if he does not necessarily have to reflect on it and may even repress it, although he cannot destroy it. (1979, 15)*

Notably, Rahner believes that any human can undergo this "interior movement toward God," whether or not they recognize it as such, and whether or not they have accepted Christian teaching. This implies that we may approach God in our "hearts" without first accepting a doctrine of God with our "heads." Individuals cannot be sure how far they have, in fact, advanced on this journey into mystery; hence Rahner's striking claim that one can, at best, "hope to be a Christian."

The distinction between head and heart is made explicit in an earlier but similarly entitled lecture, "Thoughts on the Possibility of Belief Today" (Rahner 1966). Rahner's subject here is "belief in the real sense of the world," which is characterized by personal decision and the potential to "bring about a change of heart" (1966, 3). This is contrasted with "belief arising merely out of middle-class convention and social antecedents." Indeed, Rahner apologizes for the academic tone of the lecture, observing that his message is "something more simple and . . . more important." He trusts that he *is* a Catholic Christian "in his innermost being" (1966, 4). His faith has brought about an ontological change and not merely an intellectual change within him. This reality is ultimately known by God and is quite separate from academic discussion about theology:

> *My faith does not depend on whether exegetes or the Church have or have now already found the correct interpretation of the first Chapter of Genesis.... Such arguments, therefore, are beside the point from the very start. (1966, 5)*

There is clear continuity between Rahner and many of the other figures that we have examined. He is clear that the interior movement toward God is a product of God's grace—just like Pascal's cordial feeling, Wesley's change of heart from wickedness to righteousness, Edwards's religious affections, or Schleiermacher's "feeling of absolute dependence." Like Pascal, Schleiermacher, and Newman, he is known for his philosophical writing, but recognizes that religious truths transcend rational and scientific approaches.

A second strand of late twentieth-century theology that emphasizes the heart is the charismatic movement. Although Karl Barth's criticisms of Schleiermacher's focus on feeling remain influential among Protestant theologians, this movement continues to thrive and places considerable emphasis on feeling. Indeed, charismatics focus on a personal commitment and experience that is often far more concerned with the individual than Schleiermacher's immutable and universal feeling of absolute dependence. This movement owes much to Pentecostalism, but did not begin to develop until the 1960s and has been particularly strong since the 1980s. The first comprehensive charismatic systematic theology appeared with the publication of the first volume of J. Rodman Williams's *Renewal Theology* (1996).

In the introduction to this work, Williams distinguishes between dogmatic and systematic theology (1996, 1:17). While dogmatic theology is tied explicitly to the teaching of the church, systematic theology operates more freely. Williams regards historical documents as one source for his work, but he also appeals to the guidance of the Holy

Spirit, to scripture, to "awareness of the contemporary scene," and "growth in Christian experience" (1996, 1:21–28). The latter, in particular, is associated with an increasingly pure heart. As he explains, the theologian "must see to write, and there is no seeing with clouded eye and impure heart" (1996, 1:28). For Williams as for Schleiermacher, the intellectual output of the theologian cannot be divorced from their innermost consciousness.

Notably, Williams appeals to Augustine's famous claim that his heart was restless until it found itself in God. Although, as we have seen, Augustine does not actually draw a clear distinction between the heart and the mind, Williams takes this passage to mean that "faith is not, as is sometimes suggested, wishful thinking, but the result of God's responding to the searching heart" (1996, 1:48). Williams describes a clear process. God grants knowledge of himself to the believer, who responds with faith. God, in turn, sends the Holy Spirit "into the believer's heart," where it testifies to the truth of that faith. Thus the believer moves from a "conviction of faith" to a "full assurance of faith."

This step-by-step account may appear rather simplistic, leaving little room for the uncertainties that are faced by most believers. Although his reference to the "full assurance of faith" is based on the Epistle to the Hebrews (10:22), it is debatable whether that text depicts a state that has already been realized or an ideal state that Christians should strive toward. Yet Williams's distinction between conviction and full assurance bears some resemblance to Newman's distinction between notional and real assent. Moreover, he implies that Christians are granted knowledge of God that would not be available to them through human reason. It is not that they believe in spite of the evidence, but that God has granted them a new type of evidence that justifies their faith (1996, 1:48).

Williams's position is further clarified in the second volume of *Renewal Theology*, when he addresses the nature of faith. Here he uses Newman's term "assent" to denote the middle stage between knowledge of the gospel and trust. Thus faith begins with knowledge—Williams sees the mystical tendency to stress ignorance as "unbiblical"—but knowledge is insufficient for salvation (1996, 2:29). The believer must assent, not merely to church teachings, but in both "mind and heart to the grace of God in Jesus Christ" (1996, 2:30). The final stage of faith is trust in Jesus Christ, which is no small requirement: "it is the conviction that He is totally trustworthy, that in Him and Him alone is to be found full salvation, and that one must surrender all to Him as Savior and Lord" (1996, 2:31).

As with so many of the theologians we have examined, Williams is convinced that the whole person must be changed in response to God—heart, mind, and will. However, rather than using the changed heart as a sign of the other two, he examines all three in turn. The heart is cleansed of its propensity to cause sin, it is inscribed with God's law, and it is undivided (1996, 2:50–52). The mind is given a new attitude or perspective that is focused on God rather than the individual (1996, 2:52–53). The will is "liberated" from bondage to sin and to Satan (1996, 2:53–54). In this way, the new believer is transformed or "born again"—a central feature of charismatic forms of Christianity.

Conclusion

In this chapter, we have focused on theological attitudes to the heart from Pascal until the beginning of the twentieth century. We have seen that although Pascal, Wesley, and Edwards all draw a sharper distinction between the heart and reason or understanding than Augustine or the biblical authors had, their prime concern remained the same: to emphasize the transformation of the whole person. Schleiermacher stands in the same tradition, prioritizing feeling as the foundation of religious thought and action, but reaffirming the importance of doctrine as an expression of the common feeling of a religious community. Newman's position is similar but reversed: in his system doctrine provides the starting point, but it must be accepted with feeling for the assent to be real.

We also noted that this tradition had come under attack, with Protestant theologians like Barth dismissing Schleiermacher's focus on feeling as anthropocentric, and the papacy dismissing the Catholic modernists for abandoning the scholastic method. Had they considered him, their disapproval of Bushnell would have been still stronger; he stands apart from the others considered here because he advocates the prioritization of the heart to the exclusion of religious thought. It would be exceedingly difficult for members of mainstream organized religions to accept his claims without radically revising their views. In this sense, his work is a manifesto rather than a description.

While individual representatives of the heart tradition have faced strong criticism, I would like to focus on two insights that remain pertinent to this day. First, theoretical arguments and academic discussions about Christianity are often tangential to faith. As Pascal so astutely observed, the God of the philosophers is not always the God of Abraham. Second, faith is better understood in terms of relationships and ontological change. Whether we express this in Pauline terms as being newly located in Christ, or in Rahner's language of "innermost being," or in Williams's language of rebirth, the message remains the same: if a person is truly Christian, that is a fact about their *being* and their relationship to God, and not merely an intellectual stance.

NOTES

1. For an expanded version of this background section, see chapter three of Dumbreck (2012). The sections on Pascal are also based on parts of this book. For an extensive list of definitions of *lev*, see the entry in Briggs et al. (1906).
2. For similar uses, see also Exodus 31:6; Job 37:24; and 1 Kings 10:24.
3. For an excellent discussion of this issue, see Cottingham (2005).
4. Quoted in Haas (1994).
5. For a much fuller account of Schleiermacher's position, including his early works, see part II of Dumbreck (2012).
6. Arians believed that Jesus was created, and thus of a different substance from God.

7. The council report and papal encyclicals cited in this section are available online at http://www.papalencyclicals.net/.

References

Allen, Willoughby C. 1912. *A Critical and Exegetical Commentary on the Gospel According to S. Matthew*. 3rd ed. Edinburgh: T. & T. Clark.

Augustine. 1887. *On the Holy Trinity*. In *Nicene and Post-Nicene Fathers*, First Series, Vol. 3, edited by P. Schaff, 6–476. Peabody, M.A.: Hendrickson.

———. 1998. *Confessions*. Translated by H. Chadwick. Oxford: Oxford University Press.

Briggs, Charles A., Francis Brown, S. R. Driver, and Wilhelm Gesenius. 1906. *A Hebrew and English Lexicon of the Old Testament: With an Appendix, Containing the Biblical Aramaic*. Oxford: Clarendon Press.

Bushnell, Horace. 1867. "Dogma and Spirit; or the True Reviving of Religion." In *God in Christ*, 277–356. Hartford: Wm. James Hamersley.

Cottingham, John. 2005. *The Spiritual Dimension: Religion, Philosophy and Human Value*. Cambridge: Cambridge University Press.

Dumbreck, Geoff. 2012. *Schleiermacher and Religious Feeling*. Leuven: Peeters.

Edwards, Jonathan. 1959. *Religious Affections*. New Haven, CT: Yale University Press.

Haas, J. W. 1994. "John Wesley's Views on Science and Christianity: An Examination of the Charge of Anti-science." *Church History* 63:378–92.

Newman, J. H. 1979. *An Essay in Aid of a Grammar of Assent*. Notre Dame: University of Notre Dame Press.

Pascal, Blaise. 1950. *Pensées*. Translated by H. F. Stewart. London: Routledge and Kegan Paul.

Rahner, K. 1966. "Thoughts on the Possibility of Belief Today." In *Theological Investigations*, Vol. 5, 3–22. London: Darton, Longman and Todd.

———. 1979. "The Foundation of Belief Today." In *Theological Investigations*, Vol. 16, 3–23. London: Darton, Longman and Todd.

Schleiermacher, Friedrich D. E. 1996. *On Religion: Speeches to its Cultured Despisers*. Translated by R. Crouter. Cambridge: Cambridge University Press.

———. 1999. *The Christian Faith*. Translated by H. R. Mackintosh and J. S. Stewart. Edinburgh: T&T Clark.

Stein, Stephen J. 2007. *The Cambridge Companion to Jonathan Edwards*. Cambridge: Cambridge University Press.

Wesley, John. 1985–87. *The Works of John Wesley: Sermons.* Edited by A. C. Outler. Vols. 2 and 4. Nashville, TN: Abingdon Press.

Wesley, John, and Charles Wesley. 1981. *John and Charles Wesley: Selected Prayers, Hymns, Journal Notes, Sermons, Letters and Treatises.* New York: Paulist Press.

Williams, J. Rodman. 1996. *Renewal Theology: Systematic Theology from a Charismatic Perspective.* 3 vols. Grand Rapids, MI: Zondervan.

"Keeping Alive the Heart in the Head" 2

Poetic Imagination as a Way of Knowing

MALCOLM GUITE

This exploration of the role of the poetic imagination in mediating between head knowledge and heart knowledge will begin with some of Coleridge's observations about "heart and head." It will then go on to investigate the workings of the poetic imagination through a close reading of a passage in Shakespeare, which was itself a source for some of Coleridge's own insights, before returning to a deeper consideration of Coleridge's teaching about "Imagination" in light of the concerns of this book. Finally we will turn to the work of contemporary poet Gwyneth Lewis for an example of the actual outworking of the poetic imagination when it seeks to heal the "divide" between head and heart in our own time, particularly as that divide is manifested in a division between art and science.

In the course of the *Biographia Literaria*, the great work of self-analysis and reflection that did so much to lay the foundations of modern literary criticism and to bridge the divide between so-called "subjective" and "objective" approaches to truth, Coleridge pays tribute to the writings of certain mystics (specifically, George Fox and Jacob Boehme) in the following remarkable terms:

> *The writings of these Mystics acted in no slight degree to prevent my mind from being imprisoned within the outline of*

> *any single dogmatic system. They contributed to keep alive*
> *the heart in the head; gave me an indistinct, yet stirring and*
> *working presentiment, that all the products of the mere reflec-*
> *tive faculty partook of death, and were as the rattling twigs*
> *and sprays in winter, into which a sap was yet to be propelled*
> *from some root to which I had not penetrated, if they were to*
> *afford my soul either food or shelter. (1983, 152)*

The distinction between heart knowledge and head knowledge, which is the substance of the present book, was clearly important and real to Coleridge. Yet more important still was the need to integrate or reintegrate them as ways of knowing; neither to reject head knowledge in favor of a series of private fantasies or unexamined romantic intuitions, nor to marginalize or render as "merely subjective," the intuitions of the heart. Rather, Coleridge wanted to see these two modes of knowing as mutually indwelling and interanimating one another. Earlier in the same work, in chapter seven, Coleridge remarks that

> *the faith, which saves and sanctifies, is a collective energy, a*
> *total act of the whole moral being; . . . its living sensorium is*
> *in the heart; and . . . no errors of the understanding can be*
> *morally arraigned unless they have proceeded from the heart.*
> *(1983, 122)*

It is this "collective energy" involved in the act of knowing, this recognition that "the living sensorium of the heart" must sometimes correct the inevitable "errors of the understanding," which animates the best and most fruitful of Coleridge's writings.

So having expressed this desire "to keep alive the heart in the head," he goes on to say that head knowledge is dead without complementary heart knowledge. He expresses this insight by means of a characteristically organic metaphor: products of "the mere reflective faculty" (reason or head knowledge) "partake of death" unless they can be renewed from within by heart knowledge. They are "as the rattling twigs and sprays in winter, into which a sap has yet to be propelled from some root." At this stage in his life Coleridge confesses that he had "not yet penetrated" into this root, but the *Biographia Literaria* goes on to tell the story of how he did penetrate to it in the end and found the root from which this necessary sap must flow, to link and interanimate heart and head knowledge in the mediating power of the "Imagination," both human and divine, and particularly at that point where the human and divine imagination meet.

Before we proceed, however, we must be clear about what Coleridge meant by "Imagination," human and divine, because in the course of his work he develops a new and profound understanding of it. When Coleridge speaks of the "Imagination," he is emphatically not meaning the usual sense of "imagination" and the "imaginary" as referring to things we "make up," our fantasies, some subjective realm of "make-believe." Coleridge uses the "lesser" word "Fancy" to describe our inner fantasies, our temporary and purely private self-chosen mental constructs:

> *The Fancy is indeed no other than a mode of Memory eman-cipated from the order of time and space; while it is blended with, and modified by that empirical phenomenon of the will, which we express by the word CHOICE. (1983, 304–5)*

By contrast, he makes the "Imagination" the "living power and prime agent of all human perception" and distinguishes two important modes of its operation:

> *The IMAGINATION then, I consider either as primary or sec-ondary. The primary IMAGINATION I hold to be the living Power and prime Agent of all human Perception, as a repe-tition in the finite mind of the eternal act of creation in the infinite I AM. The secondary Imagination I consider as an*

> *echo of the former, co-existing with the conscious will, yet still*
> *as identical with the primary in the kind of its agency, and*
> *differing only in degree, and in the mode of its operation. It dis-*
> *solves, diffuses, dissipates, in order to re-create; or where this*
> *process is rendered impossible, yet still at all events it struggles*
> *to idealize and to unify. It is essentially vital, even as all objects*
> *[as objects] are essentially fixed and dead. (1983, 305)*

He is saying three essential things here. Firstly, that the very way we perceive and configure the input of our senses into a series of recognizable and intelligible phenomena, or appearances, is itself a collective and, at this stage, preconscious act of imagination. Perception is as much an active and shaping power as it is a passive response. (We shall see later how he configures the relation between these active and passive elements in our perception of, and knowledge of the world.) Secondly, the "Secondary Imagination," the imagination that is at work in the conscious shaping and interpretation of experience made by the human mind (whether in the modelling of science or the making of art and poetry) is organically related to this primary imaginative perception. Yes, our efforts can degenerate into mere idle fancy, but we can also produce imaginative shaping that is of the same consistency, and that has the same integrity as the world we imaginatively perceive. Finally, Coleridge maintains that this exalted and truth-bearing capacity of the "Secondary Imagination" is made possible because of the relation that exists between the human imagination, which perceives and responds creatively to the world, and the divine imagination, which brings that world, with its human participants, into being in the first place. The human imagination, according to Coleridge, is "a repetition in the finite mind of the eternal act of creation in the infinite I AM" (1983, 304). So, for Coleridge, "Imagination" is a truth-bearing faculty, a cocreative response to the world that arises naturally and organically out of our experience of "I am" consciousness. It finds a correspondence and truth in its shaping of the phenomena of the world because the finite mind, with its consciousness—its possibility of saying "I am"—is itself a repetition and image of the great I Am, out of whom all things arise.

The "Imagination" is therefore comprehensively involved in the knowledge of all things: it is as intimately concerned with the way we configure the comprehensions of our "head" knowledge as it is with the way we shape and express the apprehensions of our heart knowledge; it is as vital to the discovery of the facts of science as it is to the creative expression of the intuitions of art. Indeed, as we shall see, for Coleridge "Imagination" plays a vital role in linking heart knowledge and head knowledge for it is a *reconciling and mediatory power* (1972, 29).

Though Coleridge went on to write works of philosophy and theology, as well as some investigations in the science of his day, the book in which he first clarified these ideas, and from which our opening passage about heart knowledge and head knowledge is taken, is called *Biographia Literaria*, not "Biographia Philosophica," or "Theologica." It was by reflecting on the experience of literary artists, the working of the poetic imagination (especially in Shakespeare but also in his own and Wordsworth's writing) that Coleridge was able to explore more deeply what it might mean to "keep alive the heart in the head."

So let us take a lead from Coleridge and begin with a reflection on a passage in Shakespeare about the work of the poet, a passage that distinguishes between reason and imagination as ways of knowing. This should enable us to see how far the poetic imagination might enable us to keep alive the heart in the head, to penetrate to that root from which sap might flow to bring life again, to the bare branches, "the rattling twigs and sprays" on the tree of knowledge.

In *A Midsummer Night's Dream*, Shakespeare gives his character Theseus a beautiful speech that describes the working of the poetic imagination. Shakespeare frames his description of the poet at work between two symmetrical pairings of the words "apprehend" and "comprehend" as ways of knowing. Imagination, he says, can "apprehend / More than cool reason ever comprehends" (IV.1.5–6) and later: "If it would but apprehend some joy / It comprehends some bringer of that joy" (lines 19–20). Between these two references to our differing faculties of apprehension and comprehension comes this description of the poetic imagination:

> *The poet's eye, in fine frenzy rolling,*
> *Doth glance from heaven to earth, from earth to heaven;*
> *And as imagination bodies forth*
> *The forms of things unknown, the poet's pen*
> *Turns them to shapes and gives to airy nothing*
> *A local habitation and a name.*
> (IV.1.12–16)

Many poets and critics have come to find in Theseus's description of how the poet sets to work the very best embodiment in words of the relation between imagination, poetry, and truth. The work of the poet begins with perception, with the observation of life as he or she sees and feels it. But it is to be a *comprehensive* observation: nothing is to be omitted or excluded as unreal or unearthly. The poet's eye is to "glance from heaven to earth from earth to heaven," not only literally but figuratively as well. The poet's observation is to include the things that earth and heaven here symbolize: visibility and invisibility, imperfection and perfection. For the phrase "from heaven to earth, from earth to heaven" not only expresses the comprehensiveness of all that poets must take into their observation, but also anticipates something of the mystery they will subsequently embody in the shapes and names of their art. The essence of this art is to express heaven in earthly terms and move us through the comprehension of earth to the apprehension of heaven, so we glimpse "heaven in ordinary." How does the poet achieve this? What role does imagination play in the process?

First there is observation, the poet's eye "glancing," but then there is a transformation and a bodying forth. The images the poet has seen enter into and are transformed by the power of imagination. Simple observation is not enough, and in fact never takes place—even in science—without some involvement of the shaping spirit of imagination. What imagination does here is to discern that the outer shapes or forms are in fact pregnant with meaning, to realize that things unknown can be made known by being embodied, not in mere copies of nature, but through imitations of nature, so that the things between heaven and earth presented to our senses are so re-presented in the poet's art that they "body forth" the invisible, that they turn into shape and so into comprehensibility, truth, and experience that would otherwise have been either inaccessible or only accessible once and for a fleeting moment; apprehendable perhaps, but also irretrievable. And here we begin to see the relevance of Shakespeare's "framing" phrases about apprehension and comprehension. The poet takes that experience, that apprehension, that potentially fleeting glimpse, and by exercise of the poetic imagination gives to apprehension's "airy nothingness" a shape, and more than a shape: "a local habitation and a name."

This is the heart of the art; to create a shape that can be sounded, a network of vocables, a nameable name, in which to incarnate insight, so that the remote or uncatchable is caught in the net of sound and has a local habitation and a name that can evoke it forever thereafter. The purpose of imagination in its playfulness, and poetry in particular, is to be a bridge between reason and intuitive apprehension, between head and heart, to find for apprehension just those shapes, those local habitations and names that make for comprehension. We must not distrust the longings of the imagination. When Theseus says, "Such Tricks hath Strong Imagination, / that if it would but apprehend some joy / it comprehends some bringer of that joy" (lines 18–20), he implies that its comprehension is false, but actually it is only by "strong imagination" that we ever enjoy the truths we apprehend at all. For every act of communication—including the most rigorously scientific—is built of language, and language is a vast system of metaphors bequeathed us by the possibilities of imagination and by the work of poets. Indeed, you could argue that all great poetry works by holding these two ways of knowing in creative tension. Poetic force is generated between the apprehension of the hitherto unknowable (which gives it its depth, resonance, and meaning) and the comprehension of the shapes and images in which it bodies forth its apprehensions (which is what allows it to communicate at all). We can see poems failing when they capitulate to either one of these poles: when they are so comprehensible as to lead us nowhere, give us nothing, and remain on a trite surface, or when they are so full of unclothed or unembodied apprehension that they offer us no common bridge in language or picture to the poet's truth, remaining obscure and opaque. But we can equally see, and indeed we know in all the faculties of our soul, when a poem succeeds, when the knowable form of its comprehended image, the glassy surface of its mirror of imitation, is suddenly a window that lets us pass through into the new world the poet has apprehended.

After Theseus has finished his speech ostensibly attacking, but actually describing, the poetic imagination, Hippolyta replies that we can trust to a story as truth-bearing if it "grows to something of great constancy." Her choice of the word "grows" springs naturally from Theseus's choice of the word "bodies." Both imply what Coleridge called "organic" coherence and growth rather than merely "mechanic" construction. The work grows in our minds because its structure and unity are *organic*. The principles of its inner organization, the way all its parts are related to its whole, is like the organization and accommodation of a living thing. Coleridge more than any other critic grasped this principle about art in general—and Shakespeare's art in particular— and developed it very fruitfully,[1] but there is no doubt that the seeds of his critical theory are all here in this exchange between Theseus and Hippolyta. The speech is all the more remarkable when we realize that Shakespeare is giving a sense and power to the word "imagination" that is common to us since Coleridge's time, but in Shakespeare's time was unheard of. In Shakespeare's day, the word "imagination" meant the capacity to hold an interior mental image and no more. Owen Barfield notes this, citing this very passage in his *History in English Words*:

"Phantasia" and "imaginatio" were in use among the School-
men, and fantasy and imagination are both found in Chaucer in
the sense of "a mental image or reflection," or more particularly
"an image of something which either has no existence or does not
yet exist." After the Renaissance Shakespeare suddenly transfig-
ured one of the two words in one of those extraordinary passages
which make us feel that genius is indeed more than earthly:

> *And as imagination bodies forth*
> *The forms of things unknown, the poet's pen*
> *Turns them to shapes and gives to airy nothing*
> *A local habitation and a name.*

In such a passage we seem to behold him standing up, a figure
of colossal stature, gazing at us over the heads of the intervening
generations. He transcends the flight of time and the laborious
building up of meanings, and, picking up a part of the outlook
of an age which is to succeed his by nearly two hundred years,
gives it momentary expression before he lets it drop again. That
mystical conception which the word embodies in these lines—a
conception which would make imagination the interpreter and
part creator of a whole unseen world—is not found again until
the Romantic Movement has begun. (republished 1985, 213–14)

In works like *Poetic Diction* (1928) and *What Coleridge Thought*
(1972), as well as in his own philosophical writings like *Saving the*
Appearances (1957), Barfield himself has made a significant contribution to the debate about the relations between heart and head, and in
particular he has helped us to recognize how the phenomena that are
the object of so much head knowledge have themselves been "figured"
or constructed by the unconscious, but participative, knowledge of
the heart.

So how might this reflection on the specifically poetic imagination help us in our exploration of the relations between heart knowledge and head knowledge and specifically in our quest to "keep alive the heart within the head"?

Firstly, I think the distinction between "apprehend" and "comprehend" is very helpful here. Head knowledge might be seen as being concerned with the content of achieved comprehension and heart knowledge as the repository of those apprehensions that have not yet been sufficiently "bodied forth" to live and move in the realm of comprehension. The role of imagination, then, is to make the link between apprehension and comprehension, so that they may communicate and the one may indwell the other. It is helpful at this point to return to Coleridge and see how he develops some of these ideas in what he has to say about "Imagination." In what follows I am concerned specifically with Coleridge's view of imagination's mediating or unifying role. As we have seen, he also had profound things to say about the nature of imagination itself, as both primary and secondary, as an element of the *Imago Dei* in humanity, and I have explored these elsewhere (Guite 2010, chapter 9). Here, to reiterate, I am concerned specifically with how imagination enables apprehension to become comprehension: how the heart is to be kept alive in the head.

Certainly if we return to Coleridge we will see that he understood imagination, and particularly imaginative "leaps," to play just such a role. The imagination is not "heart knowledge" over against "head knowledge," but is itself the comprehensive and mediating link that allows them to meet and indwell one another.

Engell and Bate's critical introduction to the *Biographia* provides a very helpful summary of how Coleridge understood the role of imagination:

> *Imagination belongs neither to the purely subjective nor to the purely objective, neither to the ideal nor the real, to the spiritual or the concrete. Reconciling and harmonizing these opposites, it partakes of both. (Coleridge 1983, editors' introduction)*

Coleridge makes this reconciling or mediatory role of imagination clear in a fine passage in *The Statesman's Manual*, when he is considering the power of poetic imagery and symbol in scripture, and says that the scriptures contain:

> *the living educts of the imagination; of that reconciling and mediatory power, which incorporating the reason in images of the sense, and organizing (as it were) the flux of the Senses by the permanence and self-circling energies of the Reason, gives birth to a system of symbols, harmonious in themselves and consubstantial with the truths, of which they are the conductors.* *(1972, 29)*

Here we see reason and imagination at work together, the imagination attending to the energies of reason and *incorporating* them (here Coleridge Latinizes Shakespeare's "Imagination *bodies* forth") into images that are not dead ciphers but "living educts." These are harmonious and participating in the truths they represent. In other words, the imagination makes precisely that connection which Coleridge was asking for in our opening quotation, whereby head knowledge can penetrate a root, allowing the sap to flow again, through the "living educt," into the "rattling twigs and sprays in winter" of that desiccated knowledge of the "merely reflective faculty."

So how does the imagination move between reason and sense and "give birth to a system of symbols"? Coleridge reflected on this question deeply and came to feel that the purely passive or reactive model of the mind, simply responding to or recording data, was completely inadequate as an image for how we perceive and read the world. Instead he came to see the imagination, in its mediation between sense-data and reason, as *both* active and passive. We do not, in fact, come to a perception of the world or any understanding of it as a result of a series of logical deductions or calculations of the discursive reason. It is not the case that a certain quantum of data falls as it were, ready-made into the mind through the senses, and then we make the necessary calculations to make sense of it, but rather that our minds and hearts go *out* to embrace the world *imaginatively*. There is a kind of "leap of faith," a sudden shaping and finding of the whole; or rather, there is an alternation between our "passively receiving" the influx of what seems to be there, and "actively shaping" its sense and meaning.

Coleridge himself described the imagination as just such an alternation of looking out and taking in, of leaping forward and being borne along; but given the exclusively passive and deterministic caste of Enlightenment thinking against which he was fighting, his initial image of the "leap" in the following passage, is essential:

> *Let us consider what we do when we leap. We first resist the gravitating power by an act purely voluntary, and then by another act, voluntary in part, we yield to it in order to light on the spot, which we had previously proposed to ourselves. Now let a man watch his mind while he is composing; or, to take a still more common case, while he is trying to recollect a name; and he will find the process completely analogous. Most of my readers will have observed a small water-insect on the surface of rivulets, which throws a cinque-spotted shadow fringed with prismatic colours on the sunny bottom of the brook; and will have noticed, how the little animal wins its way up against the stream, by alternate pulses of active and passive motion, now resisting the current, and now yielding to it in order to gather strength and a momentary fulcrum for a further propulsion. This is no unapt emblem of the mind's self-experience in the act of thinking. There are evidently two powers at work, which relatively to each other are active and passive; and this is not possible without an intermediate faculty, which is at once both active and passive. (In philosophical language, we must denominate this intermediate faculty*

in all its degrees and determinations, the IMAGINATION.)
(1983, 124–25)

There is far more about the imagination in this image than even Coleridge purports to get out of it, containing as it does three of the deepest elements of Coleridge's symbolic language about imagination: the river, the light, and the shadows. He might have made the point about the way in which our acts of perception are alternately active and passive simply by reference to the water-insect, and no more. But by placing his insect upon so vividly imagined a stream, with its surface of rivulets, and the sunlight striking through the water to the bottom of it, he is able to suggest far more than he makes explicit. For example, he implies that however wonderful our imaginative acts of perception might be, we are as yet still only on the surface of things; we move through life on the surface of a stream whose depths we could hardly guess. And yet, we do sometimes glimpse them, for fringing the shadows we cast are prismatic colors, suggestive of the light we have not yet turned to face. As we shall see, this mysterious stream that flows so fluently and independently just beneath the surface of our discourse emerges again as both image and metaphor in Gwyneth Lewis's work *Parables and Faxes*.

If Coleridge is right about imagination, then we should see its connecting and intermediating energy at work especially in those times and places where the poetic imagination is concerned with *both* heart knowledge *and* head knowledge. And that is very much the case. Moving forward from Coleridge, let us look at the work of this contemporary poet, who has had a particular concern to bridge the gap between the head knowledge of the sciences and the heart knowledge of the arts, to keep alive the heart in the head.

Gwyneth Lewis, who was made the first National Poet of Wales in 2005, has been described as a bilingual virtuoso, having published several award-winning collections of poetry in both English and Welsh, and composed the poem combining both languages that is written in letters six feet high over the front of Cardiff's Millennium Centre. However, she is also a bilingual virtuoso in the second sense that her poetry is not confined to the language of only "subjective" inner or "psychological" concerns, although she writes very well about these things. Her poetry is equally fluent in the language of science and technology, mathematics, the nature of perception, neurology, cosmology, and bioethics. Indeed she deals, poetically, with those topics in neuroscience and the study of cognition, which are the subject of other chapters of this book. The acknowledgments at the end of her most recent volume, *A Hospital Odyssey* (2010), begin not with the usual list of arts funding bodies and MA courses in creative writing, but with a list of distinguished scientists in biomedicine and stem cell technology, with thanks to the Wellcome Trust for awards, and with an acknowledgment of her time as poet in residence at Cardiff University's School of Physics and Astronomy. This concern to bridge the gap between the "heart knowledge" of poetry and the "head knowledge" of the hard sciences, to "keep alive the heart in the head," to find metaphor for poetry in science, and remind science that it too is a kind of metaphor and poetry, goes right back to concerns expressed even in the very title of her first volume in English, *Parables and Faxes* (2010).

All the poetry in *Parables & Faxes* explores levels of truth-telling movements out from and back to the literal, movements between image, symbol, and paradigm, but in the "Epilogue," the final poem in the book, she makes some of these concerns explicit. In this poem she asks us to imagine "a saint from the east and a saint from the west" meeting "on opposite banks of a stream / for holy conversation":

> *West was Parable, dazzled by the sun,*
> *crow's feet showing how he used his eyes*
> *to squint and focus, distance and transform*
> *hints from nature into other order*
> *which his imagination could explain.*

East was Fax, straight observation,
simple facts lit from afar,
seen in themselves by long attention
and strict devotion to things as they are—
not Parable's similes, but metaphor.
(Reprinted in Lewis 2005, 75)

In these two verses she bodies forth as image two ways of attending to truth, two ways of attending to nature, a "Western" order that seeks to distance the observer, to squint at things and discern pattern to construct a parallel and explanatory model, and an "Eastern" approach that is more concerned with the intrinsic "is-ness" of things without extracting or imposing pattern, and then she imagines a conversation in which each critiques the other:

Said Fax to Parable: "How can you guess
what all you see can begin to mean?"
And Parable back: "How can you bless
the chaotic surface that resists the sign?"
(Lewis 2005, 76)

This argument is not in itself resolved in the poem; instead she draws our attention to the stream—it is Coleridge's stream—she had mentioned at the outset of the poem: "And still the stream laughed past in a line, / praying its way to the lexicon sea," suggesting that between the two of them runs a reality neither has adequately captured, and indeed she emphasizes this at the end of the poem by saying that each has:

a quenching thirst
which turned them . . .
and sent them home
"to do what they could with provisional praise
and their partial vision, both overcome

> *by a conversation they'd scarcely begun."*
> *(Lewis 2005, 76)*

This "conversation scarcely begun," with which her first book in English ends, is picked up again and developed in her poetry in various ways over the course of the next fifteen years, often in a setting of reflection on theology, science, and on the relation between the deepest feelings and intuitions of the heart and the most recent developments in science. Her next book, *Zero Gravity* (1998), contains a sequence of poems from which the volume takes its title and which she subtitles "A Space Requiem." The sequence tells three distinct stories that are nevertheless interleaved and juxtaposed in a very thought-provoking way. The first is the story of the journey of her cousin Joe Tanner, on board the space shuttle in 1997, to fly out and repair the Hubble telescope. The second is the journey of her sister-in-law through cancer to death, which occurred in the same year, and the third is the journey of the Hale-Bopp comet in its brief crossing of our sight lines before it disappears again into the cold of space. The comet in the poem becomes an emblem of an experience, intense but also brief, and of vanishing love. The power of the sequence to mediate between, to interanimate, heart knowledge and head knowledge lies in the way the images from the space mission, the comet, and the deathbed become intense metaphors for the experience of the heart in both its joy and its grieving, and the way in which—conversely—the account of space and astronomy being given by information from the Hubble telescope is expressed in language that is rich and value-laden rather than purely mathematical and statistical. The two great themes, which unite all three stories, and play back and forth between them, are vision and change. How do we see things? How do we deal with the way they change? How does the way *we* move and change, change the way we see things? And lying behind both these questions, a question for both heart and head: what is the relation of love to time?

The prologue sets this theme:

We watched you go
in glory: Shuttle,
comet, sister-in-law.

The one came back.
The other two
went further. Love's an attack

on time. The whole damn thing
explodes, leaving
us with our count-down days

still more than zero.
My theme is change.
My point of view

ecstatic . . .
. . . Distance
is a matter of seeing;
faith, a science

of feeling faint objects.
(Lewis 1998, 13)

As the sequence unfolds, we come to recognize that just as her cousin goes out to adjust and recalibrate the great mirror of the Hubble telescope so that we can again see, in focus, the "faint objects" of the cosmos—objects that tell us the story of our origins and our place in that cosmos—so too language itself, and especially language shaped and formed by the poetic imagination and the intuitions of the heart, is also a kind of instrument—perhaps just as subtle, delicate, and accurate as the telescope—which also enables us to get a better grip, a clearer view of the true nature of things. This becomes clear in the twelfth poem, after the shuttle has returned. Having celebrated the fact that "the new spectrograph / you've installed in the Hubble to replace the old / makes black holes leap closer, allows us to grasp / back in time through distance, to see stars unfold" (Lewis 1998, 24), the poet turns the poem around and asks for a similar clarification of vision of and for the heart:

> *Give me a gaze*
> *that sees deep into systems through clouds of debris*
> *to the heart's lone pulsar, let me be amazed*
> *by the red shifts, the sheer luminosity*
> *that plays all around us.*
> *(Lewis 1998, 24)*

This new way of seeing, of perceiving the faint objects that purely head knowledge misses, is in fact exemplified a little earlier in the sequence, in the ninth poem, in which the poet speaks directly of her sister-in-law's death in the hospital:

> *Now that she's dead*
>
> *she's wiped herself off*
> *our neural screens.*
> *We no longer reach her.*
> *But Jaqueline—*
>
> *not her body,*
> *not her history,*
> *not our view of her—*
> *now she's free*
>
> *of her rubbish,*
> *explodes on the eye*
> *that perceives faint object*

on an inner sky.
(Lewis 1998, 21)

In the final poem of the sequence, the "Epilogue," which describes a party to welcome home the astronauts, all these different ways of seeing, both outer and inner, on both the vast "macrocosmic" scale and the inner "microcosmic" one, are fused and brought together by means of a series of metaphors in which the narrator is "clothed" with the cosmos, though still aware of "dark matter" both "out there" and "in here," unknowns for both head and heart. In this unified vision even the casual motions of a family playing around a swimming pool become resonant with a universal meaning:

My sense of scale's

exploded. Now I wear
glass beads like planets.
In my ears

are quasars. I have meteorites
for a bracelet, a constellation
necklace so bright

that, despite dark matter
in the heart,
I'm dazzled. "Here" and "there"

have flared together. A nonchalant father
throws Saturn rings.
Dive for them now and find everything.
(Lewis 1998, 28)

Her most recent volume, *A Hospital Odyssey* (2010), a single book-length poem that tells the love story of a wife's desperate search for her husband as he undergoes cancer treatment in a modern NHS hospital, constitutes a continuous interweaving of heart and head knowledge that further develops and even more cogently expresses some of the insights hinted at in her earlier verse. I would like to conclude this exploration of the role of the poetic imagination as a way of knowing, a way that mediates between head and heart knowledge, between "out there" and "in here," by looking at the extraordinary moment toward the end of this poem when the narrator Maris finally finds her husband, Hardy. The scene is imagined in "outer space," a metaphor of the distance Hardy has traveled in his dying. Up until this point in the poem we have seen everything from Maris's point of view. Then suddenly, as they are reunited, everything is turned around and we see things from Hardy's point of view:

> *This is what Hardy saw*
> *from his dying: Maris, bending over him*
> *and, behind her the vibrant, dazzling core*
> *of the sun, rich and red as haemachrome*
> *at fifteen million degrees. He was overcome*
>
> *by the knowledge that everything "out there"*
> *was, in truth, his own body. We're filaments*
> *of light, we're talking with everywhere*
> *at once, and we were never meant*
> *to be thought of as single, lines to be bent*
>
> *in the space-time continuum . . .*
> *That's prose. No, it's more like the drive*
> *of poetry. It's as when I rhyme,*
> *there's always a nano-second before I've*
> *chosen a word when I perceive*
>
> *all its homophones at once*
> *before the end-word's probability wave*

collapses, before I take a chance
on one meaning, when my mind revolves
with the quantum mechanics that makes stars evolve

from the tiniest jitters. We're born
to catastrophe. Galaxies fly
away from each other in identical forms.
Matter never sees fit to die
and if life is the transfer of energy

from one state to another—this poem from me
to you—then this continual exchange
must be our purpose. Infinity's
birdsong continues just beyond the range
of our human hearing. Love is the hinge

on which it all turns.
(Lewis 2010, 145–46)

In this remarkable passage, the storyteller, the poet, suddenly introduces herself into the narrative and helps us to see how both the composition of the poem and our very hearing or reading of the poem are
themselves both outwardly and inwardly "cosmic" events. She reminds
us that the mind "revolves / with the quantum mechanics that makes
stars evolve," she shows how our inner knowledge, the knowledge of
the heart, is as much a part of the "continual exchange" as those outward and visible phenomena that are the object of head knowledge, for
those "objects" of head knowledge are the very images with which and
through which the heart thinks. And it is by having thus "kept alive the
head in the heart," as Coleridge did, and as the mystics had done for
him, that she is able to conclude, as they did, that "Love is the hinge /
on which it all turns."

Notes

1. For a fuller discussion of Coleridge's Shakespeare criticism, see Guite 2010, chapter six.

References

Barfield, Owen. 1928. *Poetic Diction: A Study in Meaning*. London: Faber and Gwyer.

———. 1957. *Saving the Appearances: A Study in Idolatry*. London: Faber and Faber.

———. 1972. *What Coleridge Thought*. London: Oxford University Press.

———. 1985. *History in English Words*. Edinburgh: Floris Books.

Coleridge, Samuel Taylor. 1972. "The Statesman's Manual." In *Lay Sermons*, edited by Reginald James White. Princeton, NJ: Princeton University Press.

———. 1983. *Biographia Literaria, or, Biographical Sketches of My Literary Life and Opinions*. Edited by James Engell and Walter Jackson Bate. Vol. 1, 3–52. London: Routledge & Kegan Paul.

Guite, Malcolm. 2010. *Faith, Hope and Poetry: Theology and the Poetic Imagination*. Farnham: Ashgate.

Lewis, Gwyneth. 1995. *Parables & Faxes*. Newcastle upon Tyne: Bloodaxe.

———. 1998. *Zero Gravity*. Newcastle upon Tyne: Bloodaxe Books.

———. 2005. *Chaotic Angels: Poems in English*. Tarset: Bloodaxe.

———. 2010. *A Hospital Odyssey*. Tarset: Bloodaxe.

"If You Can Keep Your Head When All about You / Are Losing Theirs and Blaming It on You" 3

Head and Heart in Recent Analytical Philosophy of Religion and Natural Theology

Russell Re Manning

Introduction

Analytical philosophy of religion is widely associated with an account of reason that makes a firm distinction between head knowledge and heart knowledge. From its outset, analytical philosophy of religion has tended to analyze and evaluate the often imprecise and emotive claims of the heart, characteristic of religious discourse, in terms of the precision and rigor of the head. The latter half of the twentieth century, however, saw something of a "turn to the heart" in analytical philosophy of religion with the recognition that religious discourse is unavoidably, and unproblematically, embedded in contexts of religious practices. Largely inspired by a particular interpretation of Wittgenstein, this expressivist approach tended to prioritize the noncognitive (or at least the nonpropositional) character of religious discourse, but frequently at the expense of a loss of public accountability. More recently, much work in analytical philosophy of religion has been characterized by a desire to move beyond the rationalist/expressivist either/or to embrace both head and heart as mutually reinforcing aspects of the rationality of religious discourse. This chapter endorses such an approach and draws on recent work in the phenomenology of religious experience (as materially mediated) to suggest further areas of fruitful development. In conclusion, the chapter will defend an account of the rationality of religious discourse of the discernment of the transcendent in nature—a theme central to natural theology—as both inferential and experiential. Such an account of the "logic of discernment" will be presented as exemplary for a natural theology characteristic of analytical philosophy of religion that recognizes and holds together both the reason of the head and of the heart.

Keeping a Clear Head: The Origins of Analytical Philosophy of Religion

Analytical philosophy is notoriously unconcerned with historical consciousness in general and with its own historical development in particular, tending to view its enterprise as one of the context-independent evaluation of timeless arguments. Analytical philosophy of religion is no exception to this general tendency, with arguments frequently wrenched out of context into anthologized collections. However, as with any discipline, analytical philosophy of religion has a history and has developed according to a combination of factors, some internal and some external. Here is not the place to recount in full the narrative of the origination and development of analytical philosophy of religion; what I will do instead is to identify three key moments in terms of a notable shift in emphasis within the tradition: from the original ideal of pure logical analysis to a turn away from the merely propositional toward a more expressivist account of religion and finally a more synthetic position in which the situated character of religious thought and its analysis takes center stage. In the terms of this volume, these shifts take the form of an initial insistence upon head knowledge followed by a turn to the heart and then a subsequent recognition of the interdependence of both head and heart. That this narrative itself takes something of a dialectical form is no accident: one of the interesting characteristics of much work in recent analytical philosophy of religion is its openness to more "continental" forms of philosophy and the dismantling of the strict either/or of analytical/continental, along with the binary opposition of head and heart.

Any account of the history of analytical philosophy of religion must begin with Kant and his epoch-making restriction of philosophy to "critique"—that is to say a rejection of speculative metaphysics and a reorientation of philosophy toward epistemological reflection upon its own limits. In this, the philosophy of religion plays a central role: Kant emphatically rejected the whole project of "natural theology" as conceived by his rationalist forebears, such as Leibniz and Wolff, as the exercise of proving the existence and nature of God and instead focused philosophy of religion on the analysis of the idea of God. Of course, Kant had his own "argument" for the existence of God via the moral law and practical reason, but what became central in post-Kantian analytical philosophy of religion was the (frequently misunderstood) idea of "pure reason"—the clear-sighted and unaffected critical analysis of the head.

This Kantian legacy was combined with the influence of the tradition of British empiricism from Locke to Hume (itself, of course, an invention) and the so-called "linguistic turn" to the logical analysis of the underlying structure of language associated with Carnap and Bertrand Russell to produce the first true analytical philosophy of religion in A. J. Ayer's 1936 work, *Language, Truth, and Logic*. This work, while not primarily concerned with religion nor particularly original in its application of logical positivism nonetheless fell like a bombshell into the playground of those philosophers interested in religion. Its key contention was that in talk about religion not only is the truth of theological assertions in doubt but more fundamentally their meaningfulness. In an exemplary stance of clearheadedness, Ayer questioned whether religious language has sufficient cognitive significance to be evaluated as either true or false. For Ayer, it is the task, indeed the responsibility, of the philosopher of religion to subject religious claims to dispassionate analysis; or preferably to find them unsuitable of such analysis and thus remove them from the domain of philosophical reflection. For Ayer, whatever the inclinations of the religious heart may be, the logical head should rule: religious claims are unverifiable and hence meaningless.

From these unpromising beginnings, the approach of analytical philosophy of religion only really took off with an impassioned debate in the University of Oxford in 1950–51 and made available in the 1955 book *New Essays in Philosophical Theology*, edited by two of its leading protagonists, Anthony Flew and Alasdair MacIntyre. Flew set the tone with his famous rendition of John Wisdom's gardener parable and his uncompromising conclusion that religious assertions typically start out making vast cosmological claims but are slowly whittled away by the lack of falsifiable evidence into vacuous statements signifying very little other than a vague inclination on behalf of their utterer. In his famous phrase, they die the "death of a thousand qualifications" (Flew 1955, 97). Flew's respondents, including Basil Mitchell, I. M. Crombie, and John Hick, all took up the challenge of this falsification argument, seeking in their different ways to defend the cognitive proposition status of religious language. For instance, Hick's notion of "eschatological verification" affirms that traditions do exist within which the religious believer may be satisfied of the truth or falsity of their claims—albeit not in this life. This is then, perhaps, the most extreme example of the head-centric character of early analytical philosophy of religion: what is at stake is the question of the truth/falsity of religious language as propositional claims, a question that is the concern of the disembodied rationality of the religious agent.

It is the head that dominates this form of analytical philosophy of religion, and it is an approach that has significant successors in more recent work in this area. The 1960s saw the eclipse of the original logical positivist trauma in the philosophy of religion and the emergence of what became known as "analytical theism" (sometimes confusingly known as "natural theology"). As William Hasker writes in one of the few extant accounts of the history of analytical philosophy of religion:

Sometime in the late 1960s the claim that speech about God is devoid of cognitive import died a quiet death. There was no quick, decisive refutation of this claim, but many of the arguments supporting it had been answered, and the claim simply ceased to be convincing. The philosophical establishment did not, however, greet the newly rediscovered cognitive claims of theology with marked enthusiasm. Many critics moved easily, and with no apparent discomfort, from their earlier complaint that assertions about God were meaningless to the logically incompatible claim that these assertions are false. (The ease with which this transition was made might cause some to wonder whether the earlier claims of incomprehension were entirely genuine.) The objections raised against theism set up a budget of problems that were addressed in subsequent decades. (Wainwright 2005, 427)

Within this new phase of philosophical debate about theism the philosophers Richard Swinburne and J. L. Mackie reenacted Hume's *Dialogues on Natural Religion*, playing the parts of Cleanthes and Philo respectively, albeit with twentieth-century logical rigor and precision. Here what dominates are arguments for and against the existence of God, analysis of the divine attributes, and a set of related questions concerning the viability of claims to religious experience, divine action, and the existence of the soul. These arguments are the mainstream of most analytical philosophy of religion and have occupied the careers of philosophers including William Hasker, William Wainright, William Alston, John Leslie, William Rowe, Graham Oppy, Eleonore Stump, Norman Kretzman, and more recently Brian Leftow, William Lane Craig, Robin LePoidevin, Nick Trakakis, Tim Mawson, and Yujin Nagasawa. This list could, of course, easily be lengthened. What is clear amongst all the disagreements and arguments of such analytical theists (and atheists) is that it is argumentative rigor that is valued above all else. These philosophers ransack the history of ideas and make use of the very latest logical tool kits (often drawing on the philosophy of science) to construct, defend, and critique arguments for and against specific claims about God and/or about arguments about God. As the recent *Blackwell Companion to Natural Theology* clearly demonstrates, this style within analytical philosophy of religion is very much alive and well—and very much in possession of logical rigor. It is also, clearly, unapologetically a highly technical and professional enterprise. For all the popularity of courses in the philosophy of religion, this can be an austere and forbiddingly impersonal body of work; most definitely of and for the head, not the heart.

Before leaving this style of analytical philosophy of religion, it is worth noting one important substantive characteristic of this approach. Just as the work itself is highly intellectualized, so too is the God that it purports to prove or disprove the existence of. This is particularly apparent in the variant of natural theology known as "perfect being theology." This strand takes its cues from Anselm's famous "definition" of God as "*aliquid quo nihil maius cogitari possit*" ("that than which nothing greater can be conceived"), although the real engine is the modal logic of counterfactuals, associated with David Lewis and others, that has given analytical philosophers of religion pause to wonder about the true maximal greatness of God in the light of alternative possible worlds. Unsurprisingly, the idea of God that dominates in this approach is of a supremely rational agent, whose nature consists in the possession of all capabilities and capacities to their maximal extent. Hardly the God of the heart, open to alteration, self-limitation, and responsive love, this is rather very much a reanimation of the abstract and otherworldly God of classical theism. Brian Leftow disagrees, arguing that the God of perfect being theology is "a way to fill out the concretely less determinate description of God given in the Bible," but nonetheless the suspicion remains that all scripture really requires is, in Philip Quinn's phrase, a "pretty impressive being theology" (Leftow 2011, 103, 110) and that the maximalization of perfections belongs more to an *a priori* intellectualization of divinity than it does to the imaginative and hearty religious tradition of which it aims to be evaluative.

"Off with His Head!": The Expressivist Turn

Whilst many philosophers of religion responded to the falsification challenge by attempting to defend the cognitive status of religious claims, a sizable and influential minority opted instead to sidestep the critique by affirming the noncognitive character of religious assertions. From R. M. Hare's notion of noncognitive "bliks" and R. B. Braithwaite's suggestion that religious beliefs are justified not according to their propositional content but their personal and ethical significance in the lives of believers, a strand of analytical philosophy of religion soon developed that sought to locate the core of religion in the nonpropositional practices of believers (Flew and MacIntyre 1955). Rejecting overly intellectualist and narrowly linguistic accounts of the nature of religion, these philosophers turned instead their attention to the ways of life that religion engenders and the worldviews that these are embedded within. Shifting from a concentration on the "heady" propositional content of religious claims and the linguistic competence of religious believers, this "turn to the heart" prioritized the expressive content of religious claims and the pious sincerity of religious believers. What mattered for these thinkers, in short, was not what religious believers know, but what they feel: the philosophy of religion became the analysis not of religious language but of religious sentiment.

Of course the key figure in this "expressivist turn" was Wittgenstein, in particular as interpreted by Rush Rhees and D. Z. Phillips (Hansen 2010). Focusing on the later Wittgenstein, these "Wittgensteinian" philosophers of religion combined various strands of his thought— notably the ideas of language games in *Philosophical Investigations* and his critique of intellectualism in *Remarks on Frazer's* Golden Bough— into an expressivist account of religion. Rather than being interpreted according to a universalist logic of sense, religious claims are, for Rhees and Phillips, understood as part of a particular language game that is "played" in particular contexts. Religious language is "used" by believers not to assert matters of fact, the truth of which is a matter for dispassionate debate; rather religious claims "express" a certain form of life. Just as Wittgenstein denies that what Frazer called primitive magical and ritual behavior can be explained with reference to the prior beliefs of the savages (or that such behavior is simply mistaken), so Rhees and Phillips conclude that contemporary religious language use and religious practice is to be taken at face value on its own terms as expressing religious faith.

The consequences of this move are already apparent in a statement from Rush Rhees in a 1954 essay: "I should want to say something about what it is to 'talk about God,' and how different it is from talking about the moon or talking about our new house or talking about the Queen" (Rhees 1997, 49). By reorienting philosophy of religion from an analysis of the supposedly factual content of religious language to the analysis of the "adequacy conditions" for the "appropriate" use of religious language, this moves analytical philosophy of religion from the head to the heart; from knowledge to sentiment. Indeed, the echo of Hume here is informative: for such an approach religion is "more properly felt than judged of." Accordingly, the role of the philosopher shifts: from being a critical analyst of the truth-value of religious claims, s/he becomes an enabler of the expressiveness of religious claims. For some the temptation is simply too great and the lapse into what Kai Neilsen famously called "Wittgensteinian fideism" is unavoidable (Nielsen and Phillips 2005), notwithstanding that both fideism and its critique are repetitions of exactly what Wittgenstein warned against, namely the tendency to judge religious claims—and the judgment of religious claims—by standards that are simply not relevant. Fideism is only problematic (indeed, is only fideism) from a perspective that is still dominated by "heady" concerns about universal accountability: a properly Wittgensteinian philosophy of religion can no more be fideistic than it can be intellectualist and it is clear that what looks like fideism to the non-Wittgensteinian philosopher of religion is rather a position *within* the practice of religion, such as Phillips' rejection of self-interest within religion and Wittgenstein's own praise for Kierkegaardian understandings of faith (Mulhall 2001; Schönbaumsfeld 2007).

Recently, this Wittgensteinian expressivist approach to the philosophy of religion has waned somewhat, but its impact on late twentieth-century philosophy of religion and philosophical theology was profound. In some important ways, this approach served to eviscerate the philosophy of religion, leaving an increasingly desiccated analytical shell while all the vital metaphysically demanding questions were either put on hold or diverted into philosophical theology. In the work of philosophical theologians such as Donald MacKinnon and Austin Farrer, for example, the business of the analysis of the truth-value of religion was conducted with no less rigor but with far more exposure to the ultimate concern of religion. Theirs, however, was not typical of mainstream analytical philosophy of religion that flip-flopped between Swinburnian intellectualism and Wittgensteinian fideism. Torn then between a mutually destructive choice between head and heart, it comes as no surprise that many looked elsewhere, beyond the confines of analytical philosophy of religion (and its Wittgensteinian antithesis) to continue the philosophical enquiry into religion. Out of this came a new turn in the philosophy of religion, one in which head and heart are reunited in awareness of the situatedness of religion as both rational and nonrational, cognitive and noncognitive, expressive and nonexpressive, sentimental and nonsentimental; in short as both of the head and the heart.

Reasons of the Heart: A New Direction in the Philosophy of Religion

In this section of this chapter, I will consider this new turn to the embeddedness of religious reflection within religious and nonreligious contexts with particular reference to one specific instance of this

new synthesis of head and heart—Mark Wynn's religious phenomenology—before concluding with a brief sketch of my own position
of a renewed natural theology. Both approaches are explicitly located
within the orbit of analytical philosophy of religion, yet all are deci-
sively influenced by philosophical traditions beyond the analytical
mainstream and by theological perspectives that are, as it were, permitted to intrude into the philosophy of religion. To some extent, this
blurs the distinction between philosophy of religion and philosophical
theology, but whereas the latter is properly speaking a subdiscipline
within theology, both positions to be discussed here are located within
the wider enterprise of philosophy. In both cases what emerges is a new
account of the rationality of religious discourse as both inferential and
experiential, in which reason and faith are held distinct but in constant
interdependence.

Throughout his writings, Mark Wynn has been concerned with the
situatedness of natural theology, particularly emphasizing the need to
hold together claims about God and claims about the world. In this,
he contests the common tendency amongst philosophers of religion to
separate out their discussion of religion from what they might wish to
say about the world or nonreligious subjects. For all its enthusiasm for
the methods and rigor of the natural sciences, analytical philosophy of
religion has, in general, been somewhat distanced from the actual contents of scientific enquiry into the natural world, resulting in conceptual discussions (of God and religious belief) that are abstracted from
any recognizable situation. Here, perhaps, we can see something of the
background to the powerful skepticism regarding "official theology"
(and philosophy of religion) amongst those scientists who study the
origins and development of religious cognition, such as Justin Barrett.
Barrett's affirmation of the "unnaturalness" of theology must surely
(amongst other things) be taken as a perceptive condemnation of the
tendency within mainstream analytical philosophy of religion to isolate
religion from its context (Barrett 2010).

It is against this "head-centric" tendency that Mark Wynn has developed his distinctive approach to the philosophy of religion. Remaining very much within the analytical tradition, Wynn nonetheless rejects its otherworldliness. In his 1999 *God and Goodness: A Natural Theological Perspective* he develops a reformulation of the argument from design to support the central contention that "the world exists because it is good that it should exist" (1). In Wynn's hands this argument—as old as Western philosophy itself—is given new life by his insistence that the now standardized form (synonymous with William Paley) be revised in two important respects, such that the argument becomes less a scientific deduction and more an affirmation of the "enchantment" of the world. Firstly, Wynn warns that arguments from design must be weaned off their reliance upon supposedly evaluatively neutral scientific conceptions of the world that prioritize regularity over all other natural phenomena. He writes:

> Unless it is supplemented by other images, this understanding of the import of human experience is ultimately inimical to religious belief, because it diminishes the world, by representing it in merely mechanical (or at any rate in regular and value-free) terms; and hence it diminishes God, who comes to be understood merely as a kind of celestial engineer. (1999, 195)

Secondly, and by invoking a revived medieval conception of God as "subsistent existence," Wynn contests the concentration upon God as fundamentally an individual mind. Instead, he suggests:

> God is not simply a powerful individual whose purposes are good, but a uniquely concentrated expression of what it is to be. (1999, 196)

As such, the argument from design not only gives an indication of God's benevolent purposes, but also an insight into the goodness and beauty of the divine being itself. This "existential" turn is crucial for

Wynn's conception of a philosophy of religion able to respond to an evaluatively rich conception of the world to provide a view of God as not "merely a kind of computing device, of extraordinary powers [but] a reality whose inherent character is made known at the limiting point of our encounter with the attractiveness of the world" (1999, 196).

In his 2005 book, *Emotional Experience and Religious Understanding: Integrating Perception, Conception, and Feeling*, Wynn develops his argument against the "head or heart" either/or by engaging specifically with the topic of the emotions. He quotes from John Macquarrie a common view of the dilemma:

> *The natural sciences were taken to furnish the only basis for assured knowledge, and anything that smacked of religion or mysticism was treated as non-cognitive and banished to the region of "mere emotion."* (2005, ix)

Macquarrie here refers to Russell and Ayer, but the same may reasonably be said of much work in the analytical philosophy of religion, and it is this that Wynn engages with. In this, he develops—but crucially supplements—a move toward an analysis of religious experience initiated by William Alston in his influential 1991 book, *Perceiving God*. The details of the arguments here are complex, but the gist is simple enough. For most analytical philosophy of religion, religious experience is not a suitable topic of interest. As Alston notes, there is a nagging worry for analytical philosophers of religion that:

> *the phenomenal content of mystical perception wholly consists of affective qualities, various ways in which the subject is feeling in reaction to what the subject takes to be the presence of God.* (Alston 1991, 49)

Alston attempts to overcome this suspicion of "pure subjectivity" by arguing that religious experience be thought of as a "direct perception of God," in which the state of consciousness that accompanies the perception is not itself perceived. In effect, he aims to cut through the "affectively toned" character of religious experience to its more "mundane" content. In short, Alston saves religious experience as a topic for the analytical philosophy of religion, but at the expense of neutralizing its affectivity. For Wynn, this is to have thrown the baby out with the bathwater. Instead, he draws on John McDowell to defend the idea that "affectively toned experience can involve something like a 'perception' of 'moral reality' or values 'in the world,'" such that "theistic experience can be understood (in some cases anyway) as a kind of affectively toned sensitivity to the values that 'make up' God's reality" (Wynn 2005, 4, 5).

In his more recent work, Wynn has turned his attention to the mediating role of place in religious experience, developing a religious phenomenology that affirms the possibility—indeed necessity—of places (both natural and constructed) "bodying forth" religious truth (Wynn 2009; 2013). One of the results of this recent work is the relocation of religious experience within the ordinary day-to-day lives of people. This promotes a "messy" complex account of religion as involving both head and heart, in contrast to the purified accounts of both those analytical philosophers of religion who evacuate all affectivity from "pure" direct religious experience and those who follow Wittgenstein or Kierkegaard to defend the "pure" subjectivity of mystical encounters. Instead for Wynn, "suppose[ing] that religious thoughts can be cast in sensory form . . . marks a further way in which everyday perceptual experience can count as a variety of religious experience" (2013, 337).

TOUCHING THEIR HEARTS: ON DISCERNMENT IN NATURAL THEOLOGY

In conclusion, I want to consider briefly the notion of "the discernment of the transcendent in nature" as the operative practice of natural theology, in light of the problematizing of the distinction between head and heart that we have seen in Wynn's work. Wynn refers to John

Henry Newman's 1870 work *Grammar of Ascent* as a precursor of his kind of affectively sensitive natural theology, in contrast to the overly intellectualist reductive approach of William Paley and the mainstream of analytical philosophy of religion. Wynn quotes a passage from Newman that is instructive for contemporary work in the revival of natural theology. Newman writes:

> *Why am I to begin with taking up a position not my own, and unclothing my mind of that large outfit of existing thoughts, principles, likings, desires, and hopes, which make me what I am? If I am asked to use Paley's argument from my own conversion, I say plainly I do not want to be converted by a smart syllogism, if I am asked to convert others by it, I say plainly I do not care to overcome their reason without touching their hearts. I wish to deal, not with controversialists, but with inquirers. (1979, 330)*

Central to recent attempts to reenvision and reinvigorate the tradition of a specifically Christian natural theology is the idea of precisely such inquiry through "discerning the transcendent in nature." For example, in his 2008 work, *The Open Secret: A New Vision for Natural Theology*, after having defended the "persistence of the notion of the transcendent" (59), Alister McGrath goes on to consider the various theoretical approaches that lie behind what he identifies as the widespread belief characteristic of natural theology; "that it is possible to encounter the transcendent from within the ordinary circumstances of natural existence" (2008, 59). He lists four major approaches:

1. *Ascending from nature* to the transcendent. Here nature is seen primarily as a "base camp" for reaching a peak that soars above it.

2. *Seeing through nature* to the transcendent. This approach treats nature as a gateway or pointer toward the transcendent that lies beyond it.

3. *Withdrawing from nature* into the human interior. This approach prioritizes the inner psychological world as the place of encounter with the transcendent.

4. *Discerning in nature* that which is transcendent. Unlike the other three approaches, this does not rest on a dualistic view of nature and the transcendent, nor on the imagery of movement away from nature to something "better." Nature is seen as holding within it the capacity to disclose or be transfigured by the transcendent (2008, 60).

These four approaches are presented as "strategies" or "practices" of, as he puts it, "accessing the transcendent" and are discernible within various types of (natural) theology, as well as many otherwise apparently secular philosophies (McGrath refers here, as elsewhere, to Iris Murdoch, Roy Bhasker, and John Dewey).

All four approaches capture something of the complex and differentiated character of our everyday experiences of the transcendent; ultimately, however, it is the second and fourth that are clearly of most interest to a natural theology concerned to understand nature as making visible the invisible transcendent. Of these two approaches, it is the final way—that of discernment within nature of that which is transcendent—that McGrath most fully endorses as most consistent with the Christian logic of the Incarnation. While "the Christian doctrine of creation provides an intellectual framework for seeing God *through* nature; the doctrine of the incarnation allows us to see God *in* nature, culminating in Christ himself" (2008, 209–10). As McGrath develops it, the doctrine of the incarnation is presented as the claim that God enters into "place and history" rather than merely into "time and space":

> God enters into a world shaped by memory, and invested with value and meaning. . . . Incarnation is thus about God inhabiting the place and history of humanity. It is a cultural and historical, not merely a physical, assertion. God enters and

inhabits the world of human memories, symbols, and languages. (2008, 212)

For McGrath, it is essential for a Christian natural theology, undertaken from a specifically and explicitly Christian perspective, that "the God who is found in nature . . . must be ontologically identical to the God who is known through God's self-revelation" (2008, 213). In other words, McGrath sets as a challenge to any viable Christian natural theology that it be able to give an account of our natural access to the transcendent that does justice to the manner of engagement that characterizes the relation between the transcendent and the natural, and *vice versa*, within the Christian understanding of the economy of salvation. Interestingly, at this point, McGrath refers, briefly, to sacramentology, citing specifically John Macquarrie's "natural theology of sacramentality" and noting the influence of Paul Tillich's "category of the 'symbol'" (2008, 215), as well as referring to the "essentially anthropological question" of the place of symbols and signs in expressing and maintaining community identity and "the semiotic question of how natural signs come to express cultural ideas and values" (2008, 216). Not untypically, he then defers "a full discussion of such questions" to a future volume.

In what follows I will briefly take up these questions, albeit in a preliminary manner. I do this neither explicitly to further McGrath's project nor to offer a supplement or corrective to his enterprise. My own constructive work in natural theology is far less concerned than McGrath is to establish, in effect, the identity of revealed and natural theology from the Christian perspective. By contrast, I am far more interested to explore further those "happenings of theological expression" that take place outside of the sites of religious traditions, with which they are frequently in tension (although, of course, the question of the relations between such natural/cultural theology and what might be called "religious" or "pistic" theology is a central one) (Re Manning 2005; 2013a; 2013b; 2013c). My aim here is simply to acknowledge

McGrath's recognition that for a natural theology to be viable it must defend a robust account of the "mechanism of discernment" and to endorse his suggestion that it is to notions of signs and symbols that we must turn to do so. For this, I turn to three aspects of the "symbol theory" of the Lutheran philosophical theologian of culture, Paul Tillich.

Tillich famously distinguished between what he called "signs" and "symbols." For Tillich both signs and symbols have the fundamental character of pointing beyond themselves to "something" that cannot in itself be grasped directly. However, while signs do so arbitrarily, in that they have no "innate power" and have no "necessary relation" to that to which they point, symbols by contrast "participate in the reality which is symbolised" (Tillich 1957a, 10). As such, for Tillich, it is only symbols and not signs that are truly disclosive of the reality that they represent, which they do so figuratively. Crucially here Tillich insists that symbols are irreplaceable—both in the sense that a symbol cannot be swapped for an alternative symbol without altering the representation and in the sense that it is never possible to provide a nonsymbolic literal alternative. Both senses are important here because, for Tillich, symbols derive their power to represent from their real participation in that which they symbolize and this places significant constraints on the scope of potential symbols. Signs can be assigned in an infinite variety of combinations (traffic lights really could be any color available), but symbols are determined by the potential power of that to which they point to permit such participation. Unlike signs, symbols are not wholly determined by the power of their interpreter (if I determine that a red traffic light means "go," then there is nothing anyone can do to persuade me otherwise), but are, in effect, chosen, or permitted, by that which they symbolize. This, then, explains their opacity to literalizing desymbolization: we interpreters simply have no way of knowing what such a nonsymbolic literal alternative could be, given that we have no control, as it were, over the generation of the symbol and hence no access to what it *really* represents other than that with which we are presented. A final point about the irreplaceability of symbols is that, for Tillich specifically, religious expression is by necessity symbolic, as it is wholly beyond our power to create autonomously religious expressions; these rather must be received, fundamentally through what Tillich calls *Grundoffenbarung*, or our contentless awareness of our conditional dependence.

Clearly, a natural theology of discernment that aims to defend the possibility of encountering the transcendent *in* nature and not simply *through* nature must be careful to attend to Tillich's distinction between sign and symbol. For the transcendent to be discerned in nature is for nature to be conceived of as a symbol that derives its power of representation from its participation in the transcendence. On this view, the model of discernment seems to entail a certain (hopefully virtuous) circularity: the transcendent can be discerned within nature precisely because nature participates in the transcendent. As such, discernment in natural theology is a form of the self-identification of nature; without wanting to sound overly Hegelian, we might say that it is nature's becoming self-conscious of its situatedness—in the transcendent. Thus a natural theology of discernment is not so much about accessing the transcendent as an object within nature, but rather about discerning that the transcendent is a condition of nature's being the way that it is. In this way, a natural theology of discernment can be said to show forth nature as it is, namely as a symbol or figure of that from which it derives its power of being and meaning. Such a natural theology, in short, is about both nature and the transcendent.

The second aspect of Tillich's theory of symbols that I wish to highlight is his, to some troublesome, insistence that genuinely religious symbols—that is to say, symbols that "point to the ultimate power of being and meaning" (Tillich 1961, 11)—must efface themselves in order to point unreservedly to that which transcends all conditions. Notwithstanding its paradoxical character, Tillich repeatedly insists that "the measure of the truth of [religious symbols] is the measure of their self-negation with respect to what they point to, the Holy-itself" (1961, 11).

This self-negation takes two forms: negatively, the symbol must render itself "transparent" to its referent; positively, the material out of which the symbol is constituted—its concreteness—must be "in unity with its ultimacy" (Tillich 1959, 29). Both of these criteria effectively come down to the requirement that the nonobjective representing that characterizes the symbol as a symbol ought completely to predominate over the objectivity of the symbol as an item of our experience. What Tillich intends here, I think, is that true religious symbols are so thoroughly symbolic that they are scarcely noticeable to us as *symbols of* the transcendent but rather that the transcendent itself seems to be present *as* the symbol. It is here that Tillich's remarks about "natural literalism" are instructive. In *Dynamics of Faith* (1957), Tillich distinguishes between "natural" and "reactive" literalism. He writes:

> *The natural stage of literalism is that in which the mythical and the literal are indistinguishable. The primitive period of individuals and groups consists in the inability to separate the creations of symbolic imagination from the fact which can be verified through observation and experiment. This stage has a full right of its own and should not be disturbed . . . up to the moment when man's questioning mind breaks the natural acceptance of the mythological visions as literal. If, however, this moment has come, two ways are possible. The one is to replace the unbroken by the broken myth. It is the objectively demanded way, although it is impossible for many people who prefer the repression of their questions to the uncertainty which appears with the breaking of the myth. They are forced into the second stage of literalism, the conscious one, which is aware of the questions but represses them. . . . The enemy of a critical theology is not natural literalism but conscious literalism with repression of and aggression toward autonomous thought. (Tillich 1957b, 52–53)*

In effect, then, Tillich's insistence on the self-negation of religious symbols is equivalent to a desire to return to a primitive natural literalism in which the disjunction of the symbol and that which it symbolizes is absent (or at least unremarked).

To appropriate such a perspective for a natural theology of discernment seems, at first sight, a rather unpromising proposition. If the requirement of self-negation means that nature's autonomy must be denied in order to be considered as a religious symbol, in Tillich's terms, then it seems that the practice of discerning the transcendent in nature is going to be severely curtailed. In this case discernment will be replaced by McGrath's first strategy, that of ascent. However, it seems that there is something important in Tillich's criteria of self-effacement that can help with the analysis of discernment. In essence, Tillich's requirement is that claims to religious symbolism must not cut, as it were, against the grain of the particularities of the symbol, an approach that seems to fit well with the desire to envision nature as it really is rather than violently imposing nonnatural interpretative schema upon it. Instead of the reactive literalism of reductionist scientific naturalism/materialism, which it seems leads to ever greater technologization of nature, perhaps a discerning natural theology can see nature with the eyes of a primitive, original, natural literalism?

A further, and final, aspect of Tillich's account of symbols is his awareness of the ease with which symbols—and religious symbols in particular—can become corrupted and thereby exert a powerful hold over people who mistake them for genuine "living" symbols. While Tillich's analysis here is complex, in short, he identifies two basic forms of corruption: symbols can die and symbols can become idols. In both cases, what is essential is that the referring function of the symbol is misdirected, such that the symbol is mistakenly held to be self-referential. For Tillich, religious symbols die when they fail to evoke in their interpreter a "being grasped by" of the power of that from which they derive their symbolic nature. It is not so much that they no longer participate in that to which they point (dead symbols are still symbols), but simply that the means to interpret that participation and thus for us to see the symbol as a symbol of that of which it is a symbol are lacking. In a way, it is not that the symbol has died, but that we have lost the ability to interpret it. Like a dead language, the dead symbol still refers, even though no one can read it. By contrast, a symbol becomes an idol when the particularities of the symbol itself are taken to be that to which a symbol points. Idols, in other words, are short-circuited symbols, symbols interpreted as self-referential and hence accorded a power and authority inappropriate to a conditioned thing (be that an object, a person, or an idea).

Clearly, these dangers are highly significant for a natural theology of discernment. To prevent the conception of nature as a religious symbol from petrifying into a dead symbol, the mechanism of discernment must be thought of as a form of intelligible comprehension. To discern, natural theologically, is not to explain nature in terms of the transcendent, but neither is it a refusal of explanation. For discernment to function as an effective mechanism for accessing the transcendent in nature it must make use of all available interpretative resources to help it to "read" the symbolic language of nature. Just as textual exegesis requires close attention to the context, composition, language, etc., as well as an imaginative openness to novel insights, so does a natural theology of discernment. In other words, effective—living—discernment cannot take place in isolation from other forms of enquiry into nature—both scientific and cultural. Similarly, as a tool of natural theology, discernment must be wary of the ever-present danger of viewing nature as a self-referential symbol and shifting from a natural theology to a theological naturalism. Discernment is of the transcendent *in* nature, not of the transcendent *as* nature.

Conclusion

This chapter has briefly surveyed the origins and development of analytical philosophy of religion in order to highlight the importance of a disjunction between head and heart that runs through the core of the enterprise. I identified the mainstream analytical tradition as dominated by a particularly narrow exclusive focus on head knowledge and located the expressivist turn associated with the reception of the later work of Wittgenstein as a form of a movement toward the heart, but all too frequently, at the expense of the head. We then considered a recent attempt within the analytical tradition to synthesize the head and heart into an "affectively toned" philosophy of religion able to invoke Newman's desire to "touch the heart" of inquirers, rather than deal solely with syllogistic controversialists. In the final section we turned to contemporary work in natural theology that aims precisely to straddle the problematized boundary of head and heart via the application of a logic of symbolic discernment drawn from the work of the philosophical theologian Paul Tillich.

What emerges from this narrative, I hope, is the importance within philosophy of religion that stands within the analytical tradition (broadly defined) of a sensitivity to the embeddedness of philosophical work, in particular its situatedness within theological and cultural locations. Philosophy of religion—even analytical philosophy of religion—does not take place in abstraction from the world nor from the religious phenomena that it addresses. In short, analytical philosophy of religion is a thoroughly human enterprise and, as such, simultaneously as mundane and as wonderful.

REFERENCES

Alston, W. 1991. *Perceiving God: The Epistemology of Religious Experience.* Ithaca, NY: Cornell University Press.

Ayer, A. J. 1936. *Language, Truth, and Logic.* London: Gollancz.

Barrett, Justin L. 2010. "The Relative Unnaturalness of Atheism. On Why Geertz and Markusson Are Both Right and Wrong." *Religion* 40:169–72.

Flew, Anthony, and Alasdair MacIntyre, eds. 1955. *New Essays in Philosophical Theology.* Oxford: Blackwell.

Hansen, Stig Børsen. 2010. "The Later Wittgenstein and the Philosophy of Religion." *Philosophy Compass* 5:1013–22.

Leftow, Brian. 2011. "Why Perfect Being Theology?" *International Journal of the Philosophy of Religion* 69:103–18.

McGrath, Alister. 2008. *The Open Secret: A New Vision of Natural Theology.* Oxford: Blackwell.

Mulhall, Stephen. 2001. "Wittgenstein and the Phlosophy of Religion." In *Philosophy of Religion in the 21st Century,* edited by D. Z. Phillips and Timothy Tessin, 95–118. New York: Palgrave Macmillan.

Newman, John Henry. 1979. *An Essay in Aid of a Grammar of Ascent.* Notre Dame, IN: University of Notre Dame Press.

Nielsen, Kai, and D. Z. Phillips. 2005. *Wittgensteinian Fideism.* London: SCM Press.

Re Manning, Russell. 2005. *Theology at the End of Culture: Paul Tillich's Theology of Culture and Art.* Leuven: Peeters.

———, ed. 2013a. *The Oxford Handbook of Natural Theology.* With John Hedley Brooke and Fraser Watts, consultant editors. Oxford: Oxford University Press.

———. 2013b. "A Perspective on Natural Theology from Continental Philosophy." In *The Oxford Handbook of Natural Theology,* edited by Russell Re Manning, 262–75. Oxford: Oxford University Press.

———. 2013c. *New Varieties of Natural Theology: Innovations at the Interface of Religion, Science and the Arts.* Oxford: Oxford University Press.

Rhees, Rush. 1997. "Religion and Language (1954)." In *Rush Rhees on Religion and Philosophy,* edited by D. Z. Phillips, 39–49. Cambridge: Cambridge University Press.

Schönbaumsfeld, Genia. 2007. *A Confusion of the Spheres: Kierkegaard and Wittgenstein on Philosophy and Religion.* Oxford: Oxford University Press.

Tillich, Paul. 1957a. *Systematic Theology III: Existence and the Christ.* London: James Nisbet.

———. 1957b. *Dynamics of Faith.* New York: Harper and Row.

———. 1959. *Theology of Culture.* Edited by Robert Kimball. New York: Oxford University Press.

———. 1961. "The Meaning and Justification of Religious Symbols." In *Religious Experience and Truth,* edited by Sidney Hook, 3–11. New York: New York University Press.

Wainwright, William. 1995. *Reason and the Heart: A Prolegomenon to a Critique of Passional Reason.* Ithaca, NY: Cornell University Press.

———. 2005. *The Oxford Handbook of the Philosophy of Religion*. Oxford: Oxford University Press.

Wynn, Mark R. 1999. *God and Goodness: A Natural Theological Perspective*. London: Routledge.

———. 2005. *Emotional Experience and Religious Understanding: Integrating Perception, Conception and Feeling*. Cambridge: Cambridge University Press.

———. 2009. *Faith and Place: An Essay in Embodied Religious Epistemology*. Oxford: Oxford University Press.

———. 2013. "Religious Experience and Natural Theology." In *The Oxford Handbook of Natural Theology*, edited by Russell Re Manning, 325–39. Oxford: Oxford University Press.

PART 2

Psychology

Empirical Measures of the Religious Heart 4

BONNIE POON ZAHL, CARISSA A. SHARP,
AND NICHOLAS J. S. GIBSON

DEFINING THE "RELIGIOUS HEART"

Psychologists of religion, like theologians, have concerned themselves with the question of "What is God like?" Unlike theologians, who are primarily interested in the truth of God's nature, psychologists of religion are interested in knowledge or *representations* of God *as they exist in the minds of individuals*, irrespective of how theologically true or divinely inspired such representations may be. Psychologists of religion make no truth claims about representations of God in the religious heart; our interests are in how God's characteristics and the individual's relationship with God are represented in the human mind, as well as the effects of such cognitive representations on emotion and behavior, rather than in the degree to which these map onto metaphysical realities.[1]

In this chapter, we present an overview of the theory, measurement, and findings within psychology of religion in the contents of individuals' religious hearts, focusing on three types of content: representations of God's characteristics, relationship with and closeness to God, and emotions toward God. Our work borrows heavily from theories in social and cognitive psychology and assumes that the acquisition and maintenance of religious beliefs, experiences, and emotions can be explained by ordinary psychological processes that are not unique to religion. In the end, we argue that these three strands of research can give an approximation of people's religious hearts and highlight areas for further research.

DISTINGUISHING BETWEEN THE RELIGIOUS "HEAD" AND THE RELIGIOUS "HEART"

While it would be easy to assume that consistency can always be found between people's religious beliefs and experiences, this is not the case. "I know God is loving, but I just don't feel that God loves me" is not an uncommon sentiment expressed by individuals. Theologian and pastor John Packer draws an important distinction between knowledge *about* God versus knowledge *of* God (Packer 1973; 1993) or "head knowledge" versus "heart knowledge" of God. Put in psychological terms, this is the distinction between knowledge that is propositional in quality versus implicational knowledge, which is affect-laden and based on personal experience.

That there should be at least two types of religious content in the mind follows from the application of many commonly accepted, multiple-level models of cognition (e.g., Barnard and Teasdale 1991; Bucci 1997; Epstein 1994) to the study of religion (see Gibson 2006; Hall 2003; Hill and Hood 1999a). One such application makes a distinction between propositional and implicational subsystems, two cognitive processes described in Barnard and Teasdale's model, Interacting Cognitive Subsystems (ICS, Barnard and Teasdale 1991). The propositional subsystem involves affect-free factual knowledge, whereas the implicational subsystem involves our personal interpretations and experiences. In religious terms, this dichotomy may be understood to be between doctrinal or theological knowledge (what someone believes is true about God; head knowledge) and experiential knowledge (what someone believes is true of his or her religious experience; heart knowledge).

Another method of conceptualizing the distinction between head and heart knowledge is to utilize the tripartite distinction of the mind.

This is a distinction between the "mental activities" of cognition ("thought," "knowing"), affect ("feeling"), and motivation ("conation," "volition"), which has historical as well as contemporary significance (Hilgard 1980). Within this framework, we would expect head knowledge of God to correspond to cognition (e.g., "this is what I know about God"), and we would expect heart knowledge of God to correspond more closely to affect (e.g., "this is how I feel about God") and motivation (e.g., "my knowledge of God motivates me to behave in this way").

Additionally, we may understand the distinction between head and heart knowledge as representing different construal levels of psychological distance. High-level construals tend to be more abstract and coherent compared to low-level construals (Trope and Liberman 2010). Moreover, according to the authors, "people use increasingly higher levels of construal to represent an object as the psychological distance from the object increases" (Trope and Liberman 2010, 441). Following from this application of construal theory, we would expect head knowledge of God to be a higher level of construal (e.g., "God is loving"), and thus more psychologically distant, than heart knowledge of God, which is based on personal experience (e.g., "I feel loved by God"). Barrett (1999) has applied a similar distinction to people's religious understanding, positing that people may have differing "theological concepts" (which are more abstract/complex), and "basic concepts" (which are more concrete/simple) in regard to religious ideas.

Despite differences in the form and structure of these models, two themes are constant: first, that knowledge concerning a subject need not be unitary or integrated, or even internally consistent (Rizzuto 1979); and second, that behavior and interpretations of religious beliefs are more likely to be influenced by affect-laden representations derived from perceived personal experiences of God than by theological knowledge. In other words, religious knowledge at the "heart" level based on personal experience is likely to exert stronger influence over the individual's emotions and behavior rather than "head" level, propositional knowledge. As Watts and Williams (1988) describe the importance of heart knowledge:

> *Religious insight that, like therapeutic insight, has been chiseled out of experience will have more personal consequences than merely intellectual or "notional" religious insight. Emotional and behavioural reactions are more likely to be congruent with beliefs that have been formed in this way. (74)*

Unfortunately, with the exception of those belonging to the psychoanalytic and object-relations traditions (e.g., Rizzuto 1979), psychological measures of religion do not often acknowledge this distinction between "head" and "heart" knowledge of God and knowledge of the believer's relationship and interactions with God, and instead have treated "head" and "heart" as unitary. In the next section, we discuss strengths and weaknesses of three types of methodologies that psychologists of religion have used, before presenting an overview of our own research methods and findings.

MEASUREMENT

Strictly speaking, propositional or "head" knowledge is cold, affect-free, explicit, intellectual, rational, verbal, and normative, whereas implicational or "heart" knowledge is affect-laden, experiential, emotional, and very difficult to articulate. If this is the case, the measurement of propositional knowledge should be relatively straightforward; one simply needs to ask people about the religious beliefs that they consider to be theologically true. However, the matter is not quite so simple; asking an individual what they believe to be theologically true about God may not necessarily evoke an affect-free response. For example, the individual who "knows" in his head that God loves him but doesn't feel loved by God may hold propositional knowledge of God as loving; however, this knowledge may evoke feelings of guilt or frustration because of its apparent conflict with his actual experience. Likewise, it is quite possible for individuals to profess without difficulty their belief in a God that differs significantly from theological norms (Schweitzer 2001). Thus, isolating and measuring propositional beliefs may be more difficult than initially appears.

Measurement of implicational knowledge is no more straightforward. If implicational knowledge cannot be fully articulated, then it cannot be assessed by measures that require articulated responses. In addition, the religious experiences that form people's implicational knowledge may be strongly influenced by the norms determined by their religious community, and this community may emphasize a particular aspect of doctrine (e.g., "propositional knowledge") such that it features prominently in the individual's mind (Schaap-Jonker et al. 2007).

Thus, while there is strong theoretical and anecdotal support for distinguishing between two types of religious knowledge, it appears that propositional and implicational religious knowledge in their theoretical forms may be too elusive for empirical measurement. How then can we empirically measure propositional and implicational knowledge in the religious "head" and "heart," respectively? Is it in the very least possible to assess mental representations of God that approximate these two forms of religious knowledge? We believe the answer is yes—it is indeed possible to access and measure, to some degree, people's propositional and implicational knowledge by distinguishing between their knowledge that is more doctrinally oriented and knowledge that is more experiential.[2] As Zahl and Gibson (2012) have noted, however, consideration should be given to what is meant by "doctrinal" and "experiential" representations. Doctrinal representations are presumably formed through religious and theological teaching, but these teachings are nevertheless influenced by how religious teachers themselves experience God, and transmitted through communities of faith that may emphasize particular representations of God. As such, what religious leaders and religious communities deem as appropriate "doctrinal" teachings may in fact be affected by the community's own experience of God (Aletti 2005; Shaap-Jonker et al. 2007). In addition, believers' views of what they "should believe" about God, and even what they "should experience" of God, may not necessarily be identical to the theological doctrines that are upheld by local or global believers. It is likely that the precise relationship between doctrinal and experiential representations of God is complicated by the fact that each influences the other. As we shall see, however, differentiating between the doctrinal and the experiential is a first step toward a clearer understanding of the full picture.

STRENGTHS AND WEAKNESSES OF THREE TYPES OF METHODOLOGIES: SELF-REPORT QUESTIONNAIRES, QUALITATIVE METHODS, AND COGNITIVE METHODS

The easiest way to ask a person what they think about something or someone is to straightforwardly ask. Questionnaire measures are undoubtedly the most common method of assessment in psychology; they are simple, easy to administer and score, and a relatively large amount of data that can be compared across different populations can be collected in a short period of time. That the majority of instruments in Hill and Hood's (1999b) *Measures of Religiosity*, the most extensive compilation of such measures to date, are questionnaire measures might suggest that measuring religious beliefs is an easy and exact task. However, most of these questionnaires tacitly assume that people's religious cognition is a unitary construct, and few if any of the measures in the volume explicitly distinguish between doctrinal and experiential knowledge. For example, when asked to consider the question "What is God like?" one individual may respond based on the theological doctrines they hold, while another individual may answer the same questions based on how they have personally experienced God. In addition, the meaning of items may vary from individual to individual depending on the faith tradition or belief background that respondents come from; instruments that were developed and standardized on a Christian sample may not generalize to a population of a different tradition. Questionnaire measures in general are also close-ended, subject to reading-level limitations, and respondents may be motivated to answer in a socially desirable manner. Data collected with self-report questionnaires must be interpreted with these issues in mind.

Those who criticize questionnaire data as lacking in depth and insight are often proponents of qualitative or ethnographic methodologies. Qualitative data gathered through open-ended questions are more likely to reflect the richness and nuance of religious behavior and experience and may provide greater insight into how religion is lived and experienced. Qualitative methods may be able to elicit aspects of the individual's experience that are pre- or subconscious (e.g., George, Kaplan, and Main 1985), and as such they may be best suited to probe deeper into individuals' implicational religious knowledge. However, interviews are also much more time-consuming to conduct, transcribe, and analyze when compared to questionnaire measures. In addition, there is often a lack of standardization, making it difficult to develop metrics for comparing individuals or groups, rendering this method less suitable for researchers who wish to gather and compare data from larger groups of people.

A number of psychologists (e.g., Gibson 2006; Kim 2008; Wenger 2003; Yarborough 2009) have begun to adapt and develop implicit methods drawn from cognitive psychology for studying religious beliefs and experiences. Some researchers have employed subliminal priming methodologies to activate religious representations in order to prevent biases due to socially desirable responding (e.g., Birgegard and Granqvist 2004). Others have measured judgment speeds and memory of relevant stimuli as proxy for cognitions that are automatic and of which individuals may not even be aware. These methods have the potential to provide details about the content and processes underlying individuals' internal representations of religious concepts and are less likely to be subject to social desirability and other response biases.

They are, however, less convenient: administration often requires a computer, and data needs to be manipulated before results can be interpreted. Even so, this methodology is, in theory, perhaps most parsimonious with the concept of propositional and implicational religious knowledge, since the concept originated from cognitive psychology itself. However, some may also argue that these measures lack validity, as they are so far removed from actual religious experience.

Like many other psychologists of religion, we have primarily utilized self-report questionnaire measures in our own research and have attempted to account for the difference that might exist between doctrinal and experiential religious representations. We believe that this issue can be addressed by specifying to participants whether their responses should be made in reference to their theological beliefs or in reference to their personal experience. In other words, the simple act of manipulating instructional wording in a questionnaire—asking respondents to consider and contrast their theological beliefs and personal experience, so that respondents are made aware of the potential difference between their doctrinal and experiential knowledge—may be sufficient to draw out a meaningful difference between the two. Our own research suggests that meaningful differences between doctrinal and experiential representations can indeed be found using questionnaire measures. We now turn to research and findings in three areas: representations of God's characteristics, relationship with and closeness to God, and emotions toward God.

RESEARCH AND FINDINGS

Representations of God

What *is* God like? Throughout history, theologians from Augustine to Barth have offered insight into God's attributes, in addition of course to teachings from the Old and New Testaments. God has been variously described as merciful (Deuteronomy 4:31); faithful (Exodus 34:6); a refuge (Psalm 46:1); approachable (Psalm 145:8); gracious and full of compassion (Psalm 116:5); one who sustains (Psalm 54:4) and saves (Psalm 68:20); loving (John 3:16); slow to anger (Psalm 145:8); wise (Romans 11:33); self-sufficient (John 5:26); kind, just, and righteous (Jeremiah 9:23–24); eternal, immortal, invisible, and the only God (1 Timothy 1:17); omnipresent (Psalm 139:7–10); omniscient (Psalm 139:1–4); and omnipotent (Romans 13:1). Not surprisingly, psychologists have used some of these adjectives to create scales to measure people's beliefs about the nature of God.

The most commonly used instruments to measure people's representations of God are perhaps the Loving and Controlling God Scales (Benson and Spilka 1973) and some form of an adjective checklist, such as Gorsuch's God Concept Adjective Checklist (1968). The Loving and Controlling God Scales is a semantic differential scale, in which respondents are presented with ten pairs of bipolar adjectives (e.g., loving-hating) and asked to choose where his or her position lies between the poles. As the name implies, adjective checklists are comprised of a list of adjectives that respondents are asked to rate on the basis of whether each word is descriptive of their personal view of God; Gorsuch's God Concept Adjective Checklist consists of ninety-one items. Having a positive view of God (i.e., seeing God as loving) has been found to be associated with higher self-esteem (Benson and Spilka 1973) and positive coping (Wong-McDonald and Gorsuch 2004), while psychiatric problems have been found to be linked with more negative views of God (Schaap-Jonker et al. 2002). However, neither Benson and Spilka's nor Gorsuch's original scales in their original forms specified whether respondents were to answer based on their doctrinal knowledge about God or their experiential knowledge of God.

To explore whether meaningful differences could be observed between doctrinal and experiential knowledge, we asked a sample of four hundred and fifteen Christians recruited from university-based Christian fellowships in the United States and the United Kingdom to complete the Loving and Controlling God Scales and rate thirty-two adjectives for God, but to do so in two ways: respondents were asked to provide two ratings for each item, one that is based on what they "should believe that God is like" (intended to capture doctrinal representations) and the other based on what they "personally feel that God is like" (intended to capture experiential representations; Zahl and Gibson 2008; 2012). To amplify the possible difference between the two types of responses, the scales were presented in such a way that required respondents to give each item a doctrinal rating first and an experiential rating immediately after. Our data from the Loving and Controlling God Scales showed significant differences between doctrinal and experiential ratings: respondents personally felt that God was significantly *less loving* than what they think they should believe about God (Zahl and Gibson 2008). Data collected using adjectives of God's characteristics also showed meaningful differences between doctrinal and experiential ratings. Respondents thought they *should* believe God to be more positive (i.e., more reliable, more intimate, and more accepting) than what they in fact personally felt God to be like.

We also found doctrinal and experiential ratings to be predicted by different variables. Positive doctrinal ratings were positively predicted by the degree to which individuals held orthodox Christian beliefs and negatively predicted by anxious attachment to God (the extent to which individuals were anxious about losing God's love for them). Stronger positive experiential ratings were predicted by more orthodox Christian beliefs, stronger religious commitment, greater self-esteem, less avoidant attachment to God (the extent to which individuals were avoidant of intimacy with God), and less anxious attachment to God. Additionally, doctrinal ratings of God as critical were predicted by greater anxious attachment to God, while experiential ratings of God as critical were predicted by lower self-esteem and greater anxious attachment to God. Thus, the relationship found by Benson and Spilka (1973) between self-esteem and God representations was replicated only for experiential representations of God as critical. Experiential ratings also predicted satisfaction with life, but doctrinal ratings did not (Zahl and Gibson 2012). The fact that experiential ratings were more strongly related to emotional and behavioral outcomes such as well-being and self-esteem was consistent with theory concerning propositional and implicational religious knowledge. Making people aware of the possibility of discrepancy between their head and heart knowledge of God appeared to affect religious individuals. Experiencing more discrepancy correlated with feeling fewer positive emotions toward God (Sharp 2011), but need not always produce conflict. As found by Schaap-Jonker and colleagues, religious saliency and educational level influenced whether an individual experiences conflict as arising from the discrepancy between what they term "normative" and "personal" God image (Schaap-Jonker et al. 2007). Additionally, they found that the amount of discrepancy felt was related to both mental health and denomination.

These results provide support for the effectiveness of manipulating instructions in a questionnaire to elicit doctrinal and experiential knowledge about God as proxy for propositional and implicational knowledge. A subsequent study with a community sample of two hundred and sixty-three self-identified Christians confirmed these findings. We asked respondents to provide ratings for fifty-five adjectives describing God, but altered the wording used to elicit doctrinal and experiential knowledge. Doctrinal knowledge was elicited using either "What is theologically true about God" or "What you are supposed to believe that God is like," whereas experiential knowledge was elicited using either "What you have personally experienced God to be like" or "Your personal experience of God." Meaningful differences between doctrinal and experiential ratings were again observed: where a positive view of God was concerned, respondents' experiential ratings tended to be lower than their doctrinal ratings (Zahl and Gibson 2009).

Concerning cognitive measures of God's character, three studies from unpublished dissertations have utilized cognitive methodologies, but the interpretation of some of these findings has not been straightforward. These cognitive measures use participants' reaction times when making judgments about God's character in order to make inferences about their implicit God representations. Previous research utilizing judgment speed paradigms to assess individuals' representations of themselves and others have found that self-referent material is judged more quickly than other-referent material, because information about the self is more easily accessed than information about others (Kuiper and MacDonald 1981). Judgment speeds for other-referent material decrease and become more like speeds for self-referent material when the target in the other-referent condition becomes more intimate and familiar (Bradley and Matthews 1983). Using a modified self-referent encoding task, Gibson (2006) found atheists and Christians to be equally efficient in making judgments concerning self-referent and mother-referent material, but Christians were significantly faster to make positive-schematic judgments (answering "yes" to positive adjectives and "no" to negative adjectives) for God-referent material. Atheists, in contrast, were slow to make God-referent judgments irrespective of the emotional valence of the material. These findings confirmed Gibson's hypotheses that individuals who held well-organized, intimate, and frequently used knowledge about God (i.e., committed, practicing Christians) would show facilitated processing of God-referent material compared to individuals whose knowledge about God was less developed, less intimate, and infrequently used (i.e., atheists).

Yarborough (2009) extended this paradigm to investigate the effects of depression on Christians' self- and God-referent judgment speeds. He hypothesized that depression, which in previous studies has been associated with a more negative view of the self but not of others (Kuiper and MacDonald 1981), would be associated with a more negative view of the self but not of God. Contrary to his hypothesis, Yarborough found that depressed Christians were slower to respond to positive schematic God-referent material than nondepressed Christians, which suggests that depression—the chronic experience of depressed mood and absence of positive affect—did in fact exert an effect on the individual's personal experience of God. In a similar vein, Zahl (2010) explored the relationship between anger at God and God representation in samples of self-identified Christians, agnostics, and atheists. Consistent with her hypothesis, anger toward God was associated with slower processing of positive-schematic God-referent material; contrary to hypothesis, however, anger toward God was not associated with differences in judgment speeds for God as targeted in the Christian sample. The precise reasons behind these unexpected findings warrant further research.

In sum, our research highlights two particularly promising areas of research of the religious heart. Despite the elusiveness of propositional and implicational knowledge to direct measurement, ours and others' research (Schaap-Jonker et al. 2002; 2008) find promise in using paper-and-pencil questionnaire measures to elicit doctrinal and experiential knowledge of God. Researchers for whom qualitative and cognitive measures are simply too impractical may find this method useful to draw out the difference between head and heart knowledge in their investigation of the relationship between representations of God and other variables of interest. Researchers whose primary interest is in experiential God representations may find it sufficient to instruct respondents to provide adjective ratings based on their personal experience of or feelings about what God is like. To complement self-report data, cognitive and implicit measures of God's character can be further developed and refined to elucidate the processes and knowledge of which respondents may not be conscious. Researchers are encouraged to utilize both self-report and experimental paradigms for a comprehensive study of internal representations of God's character.

Relationship with and Closeness to God

A related topic in the study of mental representations of God is how individuals mentally represent their relationship with God. Over the past two decades, attachment theory has become one of the most popular current theories in the psychology of religion (for a review, see Granqvist and Kirkpatrick 2008; Hill and Gibson 2008). Attachment theory posits that repeated interactions with primary caregivers during infancy and early childhood form mental representations about the self and others, and these representations guide subsequent interpretation and anticipation of another person's behavior during times of distress. While God representations concern individuals' view of what God is like (e.g., Gorsuch 1968), attachment to God focuses on the dynamic interaction between God and self. Beliefs about what God is like (God representations) are likely to overlap with one's attachment relationship with God.

The general consensus among psychologists is that for some people, God functions as an attachment figure, which Kirkpatrick (1999; 2005) defines as the extent to which the individual views God as a haven of safety, seeks proximity to God, sees God as a secure base for exploration, and feels distressed when experiencing separation from God (Kirkpatrick 2005). There are currently four published self-report questionnaire measures of attachment to God: the three-item measure developed by Kirkpatrick and Shaver (1992), the nine-item measure developed by Rowatt and Kirkpatrick (2002), the twenty-eight-item Attachment to God Inventory (AGI; Beck and McDonald 2004), and the sixteen-item Attachment to God Scale (Sim and Loh 2003), and they differ in the theoretical basis of their development. Kirkpatrick and Shaver's (1992) measure was patterned after Hazan and Shaver's (1987) measure of romantic attachment; in this scale, respondents are asked to select one of three descriptions (describing either secure, avoidant, and anxious-ambivalent attachment) that best characterizes their beliefs about and relationship with God. Both Rowatt and Kirkpatrick's nine-item measure and the AGI were developed to synthesize with existing adult attachment measures that assessed the attachment dimensions of Avoidance of Intimacy and Anxiety about Abandonment, and items in the AGI were based on items in the Experiences in Close Relationships Scale (ECR), which is a validated measure of adult attachment (Brennan, Clark, and Shaver 1998). The Attachment to God Scale was developed based on the four aspects of attachment to God as specified by Kirkpatrick (1999). Attachment to God has been found to be associated with a host of variables: secure attachment predicted optimism (Sim and Loh 2003), while insecure attachment correlated with neuroticism and negative effect and inversely with agreeableness and positive effect (Rowatt and Kirkpatrick 2002). Zahl and Gibson (2012) have also found experiential representations of God, to be more strongly predicted by attachment to God.

The study of human relationships contains many paradigms and methodologies for measuring the ways in which people understand and relate to each other. Self/other overlap is one of these methods, which measures the perceived relationship between a subject and a target individual. It is a measure of the perceived closeness with another person, or understood differently, a measure of the sense of including aspects of another person within the self. In effect, participants have a sense of "us," rather than "you and me" with the other person (Aron, Aron, and Smolan 1992; Myers and Hodges 2012). The more overlap that is shown, the closer the relationship is determined to be, because the self and other form an "us," and greater self-other overlap is generally associated with greater relationship satisfaction and commitment (Aron, Aron, and Smolan 1992; Aron and Aron 1997).

Self-other overlap has been measured in a variety of ways, but the assessment most applicable to studying the religious heart is the Inclusion of Other in the Self Scale (Aron, Aron, and Smollan 1992). It is a single-item graphic scale that consists of a series of seven pairs of circles (representing self and other) that vary from no overlap but almost touching, to almost complete overlap. Respondents are instructed to pick the pair that best represents their relationship. A recent analysis by Myers and Hodges argued that this form of overlap should be called "perceived closeness"—it is primarily an affective measure that is correlated with variables such as relationship quality measures (Myers and Hodges 2012). Recent studies (Hodges et al. 2012 ; Sharp, Johnson, and Gibson, unpublished manuscript) have shown that this measure is applicable to assessing believers' relationships with God, and that by using wording similar to that used to measure representations of God, we can assess these individuals' doctrinal and experiential overlap with God.

Overlap with God in itself can be envisaged as a kind of "heart" religiosity, as it addresses the quality of relationship with God. Closeness as measured in this way was related to two factors, in particular: fundamentalism and awareness of God, which each independently predicted greater self/other overlap on the overlapping circles in U.S. Christian samples (Hodges et al. 2012). However, even within this "heart"-like measure of religion, a further distinction can be made between how close people feel they are to God theologically/philosophically and how close they feel to God in their personal experience. While not all people make this distinction, a large number of people do—with most envisaging themselves as having complete (or nearly complete) overlap with God theologically, while in their personal experience feeling more distance from God. Though there was not much variation in people's doctrinal overlap with God, making analyses of variance spurious at best, the variation within people's experiential overlap with God was predicted by several composite measures of religiosity and well-being. A positive view of God (consisting of measures of positivity in the relationship with God, believing in the benefits of religious faith, positive emotions toward God, awareness of God, avoidant attachment to God [reversed], and God locus of control) and well-being (depression, self-esteem, and hypersensitive narcissism) positively predicted experiential overlap with God, while a negative view of God (consisting of negative emotions toward God, anger toward God, fear and guilt toward God, and anxious attachment to God) negatively predicted overlap (Sharp, Gibson, and Johnson 2011). Thus, these measures focusing on the relationship with and closeness to God describe real and important differences in people's experiences of God. Attachment style and self/other overlap provide us with two approaches to measuring the quality of people's relationships with God.

Emotions toward God

Our discussion of the religious heart would not be complete without mention of emotions. In his theological classic, *A Treatise Concerning Religious Affections*, Jonathan Edwards discussed two groups of sacred emotions—those that were characterized by approval (gratitude, love, joy) or disapproval (hatred, fear, sorrow)—which he saw as signs of genuine spiritual experience (Edwards 1754/2009). Psychologists have also begun to explore so-called "sacred emotions"—emotions that are frequently experienced in religious settings, through spiritual or religious activities, and by people who self-identify as religious (Emmons 2005). From a psychological perspective, emotions typically involve some kind of appraisal of a situation or event, and they influence motivation and behavior (Power and Dalgleish 1997). Religion influences both the generation of emotion (e.g., gratitude, awe and reverence, wonder, and hope) as well as the regulation of emotional responses (e.g., through forgiveness and mindfulness). Not all sacred emotions are positive, however. Just as religion can provide feelings of joy, peace, and comfort, so too can it be a source of struggle and strain (Exline and Rose 2005).

The religious emotions most relevant to the research we have described in this chapter are emotions toward God. As we have discussed, individuals' representations of God include knowledge about relating to God, and inherent in relationships with God are emotions that arise when interacting with God. Researchers have generally assessed emotions toward God by providing a list of emotions and straightforwardly asking individuals to rate the extent to which they experience (or have experienced in the past) each emotion toward God. There is considerable agreement in factor analytic studies of emotions toward God that there are three basic dimensions (Exline et al. 2011; Murken et al. 2011; Schaap-Jonker et al. 2008; Wood et al. 2011; Zahl and Gibson 2009). The first is positive emotions toward God, which includes feelings such as affection, love, thankfulness, gratitude, security, closeness, and trust. The second dimension consists of negative emotions toward God, which includes emotions such as anger, disappointment, dissatisfaction, doubt, and frustration. The third factor also consists of negative emotions, but these emotions concern the self in relation to God rather than emotions directed at God, such as guilt, fear of being punished, fear of being rejected, shame, and failure.

In theory, there is little reason to assume that emotions toward God would vastly differ from interpersonal emotions; put differently, the social cognitive appraisals underlying emotions toward God should parallel those underlying interpersonal cognition. For example, anger is an emotion that accompanies attribution of blame and negative intent to a perpetrator, directed at someone who blocks or frustrates one's own goals, and increases with the level of harm or suffering that is experienced (Power and Dalgleish 1997); we should therefore expect individuals who are angry at God to blame God for a negative event, to infer God's ill will toward them, and to be more angry if the event was more severe or negative. This was indeed observed in a study conducted by Exline and colleagues (2011): anger at God was predicted by attributions of blame to God for an incidence of suffering, attributions of God's cruel intentions (e.g., "God wanted to hurt me," "God wanted to see me suffer," "God had turned away from me"), and severity of the event. Schapp-Jonker and colleagues (2008) found that anger toward God was negatively correlated with religious saliency and seeing God's actions as supportive. Individuals to whom religious faith was a significant aspect of their lives were more likely to experience positive emotions toward God and less anger toward God; they were also more likely to see God's behavior as supportive and dominating, rather than passive. Interestingly, they also found that participants' interpretations of God's behavior varied according to their religious denomination and mental health status. In particular, psychiatric patients found the dominating aspects of God's behavior to be anxiety-provoking, while nonpatients generally did not.

In keeping with the emphasis on the interpretation of God's behavior, and drawing from previous research on petitionary prayer (Krause et al. 2000; Ladd and Spilka 2001), Zahl and Gibson (2011) investigated the relationship between prayer expectancies, which can be construed as a type of appraisal, and emotions toward God. They hypothesized that individuals who believed that God *could, but did not* answer a petitionary prayer, as well as individuals who believed that God *should, but did not* answer a petitionary prayer, were more likely to experience anger toward God, as God would be perceived as somehow *intentionally failing* to grant a prayer request that God could or ought to have answered. Their hypotheses were partially confirmed in a sample of 177 respondents who completed an online questionnaire. When three variables—respondents' perception of whether God could have answered a prayer, whether the prayer was answered, and the interaction between the two, were entered into a regression analysis, the interaction between whether God could have answered the prayer and whether the prayer was answered predicted anger toward God. That is, individuals who felt that God *could have* answered the prayer *and* experienced the prayer as unanswered were more likely to experience anger toward God. When the perception of whether God *could* have answered the prayer was replaced by the perception of whether God *should* have answered the prayer, the regression analysis found anger at God to be marginally predicted by perception of whether God *should* have answered the prayer. The authors argued that prayer expectancies—beliefs about whether prayers are answered, the timing of prayers, and beliefs about how prayers are answered (cf. Krause 2004)—are related to an individual's internal representations of God and influence individuals' emotions toward God.

Because individuals' relationships with God are closely related to their emotions toward God, Beck (2006) conducted a factor analytic study of items from various measures of emotions toward God drawn from attachment, object relations, and triangular love theories.

He found two orthogonal factors that he labeled "Communion" and "Complaint." As their names suggest, Communion reflects feelings of closeness, intimacy, and love, while Complaint reflects feelings of frustration, mistrust, anger, and disappointment. Beck argued that the existence and comingling of Communion and Complaint in individuals' relationships with God gives such relationships an emotional dynamic similar to that observed in human close relationships. His findings are consistent with the assumption that emotions toward God are not unlike those experienced in interpersonal contexts and involve the same social cognitive processes.

A relatively unexplored aspect of emotions toward God and a logical next step in this line of research is the relationship between emotion and belief. We would expect, of course, to find that individuals who *believe* in God experience emotions toward God. What of individuals who profess to be atheists but also feel negatively toward God? Exline (2006) has coined the term "emotional atheism" to describe a type of atheism—loss of belief in God and even active disbelief in God—that is a result of a negative emotional experience with God, such as severe disappointment or anger toward God. Emotional atheists are those who arrive at their atheistic beliefs through an emotional experience and may continue to harbor negative emotions toward God despite belief in God's nonexistence. In a cluster analysis of self-report nonbelievers, Gibson (2011) found a group of "emotional" nonbelievers—individuals who profess not to believe in the existence of God, but nevertheless feel anger toward God. This is not to say that emotional atheists' disbelief is somehow less legitimate or well thought through; it is simply a term to describe atheism that has an emotional component. Just as belief in God has both propositional (doctrinal) and implicational (emotional) aspects, it is quite likely that *disbelief* in God also has propositional (theoretical/rational) and implicational, affective aspects. Future research can tease out the dynamic relationship between belief, nonbelief, and emotion.

Conclusion

Psychologists of religion have taken a bottom-up approach in their study of the religious heart: rather than assuming that religious emotions ought to manifest themselves in theologically appropriate ways, psychologists of religion have attempted to examine religious hearts as they, for lack of a better word, beat. In this chapter, we have presented a brief overview of psychological theory and research relevant to three aspects of the religious heart: representations of God's character, closeness to God, and emotions toward God. It is clear from our overview that we have come far in understanding the religious heart from an empirical perspective, but many questions remain unanswered concerning the psychological processes that underlie the experience of God in these three areas.

On a methodological level, we argue that there are multiple ways of accessing the religious heart through psychological measures. For some questions, simply altering the wording of the instructions will provide us with a useful proxy for head and heart knowledge of God and of other religious beliefs—people intuitively understand the difference between head- and heart-level representations, as conceptualized through our instructions for doctrinal and experiential representations of and overlap with God, and can answer accordingly. This type of method is particularly pertinent to questions that are more ambiguous—simply asking "How descriptive of God is the word [loving]?" may prompt participants to answer according to either their religious head or heart. Asking "How descriptive of God is the word [loving] *in your personal experience of God*?" lessens that inherent ambiguity. Additionally, there are methods available that naturally tap the more "heart"-like aspects of people's experiences. Cognitive measures such as reaction time experiments allow us to access people's more automatic, "gut-level" representations of God. Additionally, measures of attachment style and emotion scales measure the *quality* and *affective* aspects of the God-relationship—once again, tapping into the experiential side of people's God representations.

If we equate the religious heart with implicational knowledge of God that cannot be communicated verbally, then direct measurement of the religious heart would be nearly impossible since even the cognitive measures, which are the most nonverbal of our existing measures, require assessment (albeit speeded judgments) of verbal (i.e., written and articulated) material. However, in this chapter we have described methods and findings from studies that have begun to triangulate just what the religious heart might encompass. We have argued that aspects of the religious heart might be illuminated by understanding how people represent God in their minds based on their experience of God, how they process information about God, how they construe their relationship with God and their feelings about this relationship, and their emotions toward God. These concepts all involve the more automatic and relational aspects of people's representations of God, and we have shown that these various approximations of the religious heart have affective and behavioral consequences. For those individuals who perceive their relationship with God as being central to their identity, these constructs may bear significant consequences to their adjustment and well-being. In our review we have also highlighted several areas of future research in empirical research of the religious heart. From a theoretical perspective, ongoing dialogue between theologians, philosophers, and psychologists may help clarify and define what exactly the religious heart is, so that it can be most effectively operationalized in empirical research in a consistent manner. Clinical research, particularly on the relationship between religiosity, spirituality, health, and well-being, would benefit by drawing from current theories on cognition and emotion as they relate to religious thought and emotion, to develop treatments that are psychologically sound and spiritually sensitive. Measures of the religious heart give us information about the ways in which people personally experience their religion, and as such, they may give information about when problems in these experiences may arise and how interventions may be developed. We are also eager to develop more accurate and sophisticated methodologies to capture the religious heart, so as to place our research in the broader field of social cognition. We believe that while it is fruitful to use and adapt existing psychological theories for the study of religious cognition and emotion, our research on religious cognition can also contribute to further development and refinement of existing theories. Although this chapter does not contain an exhaustive list of empirical measures of the religious heart—this is an area of study that calls for further exploration—it does provide a base of knowledge that is useful in determining further methods of both asking and answering questions about the religious heart.

NOTES

1. The use of the words "mental representations," "cognitive," and "human mind" might conjure up a dichotomy between the cognitions in the mind versus experiences or emotions in the heart, but this supposed dichotomy is in fact false. Theories in social cognition do not in fact see cognition and emotion as dichotomous, because the two are interrelated (Niedenthal, Krauth-Gruber, and Ric, 2006). Likewise, we do not make such a distinction between the "mind" and the "heart." When we speak of representations of God in the human mind, we are simply referring to the knowledge of God that is internal and personal to the individual. The distinction that we wish to draw attention to is between the "head" and the "heart," which we conceptualize as metaphors for the particular ways in which people understand their religious lives.

2. To avoid confusion in terminology, the terms "propositional" and "implicational" are used in the strict sense of the words—that is, they refer to knowledge that is affect-free and verbal, and knowledge that is affect-laden but inarticulable, respectively. The terms "doctrinal" and "experiential representations" refer to articulable constructs that are approximate to propositional and implicational knowledge, respectively.

References

Aletti, M. 2005. "Religion as an Illusion: Prospects for and Problems with a Psychoanalytical Model." *Archive for the Psychology of Religion* 27:1–18.

Aron, A., and E. N. Aron. 1997. "Self-expansion Motivation and Including Other in the Self." In *Handbook of Personal Relationships: Theory, Research and Interventions*, edited by S. Duck, 251–70. Hoboken, NJ: John Wiley and Sons.

Aron, A., E. N. Aron, and D. Smolan. 1992. "Inclusion of Other in the Self Scale and the Structure of Interpersonal Closeness." *Journal of Personality and Social Psychology* 63:596–612.

Barnard, P. J., and J. D. Teasdale. 1991. "Interacting Cognitive Subsystems: A Systemic Approach to Cognitive-Affective Interaction and Change. *Cognition and Emotion* 5:1–39.

Barrett, J. L. 1999. "Theological Correctness: Cognitive Constraint and the Study of Religion." *Method & Theory in the Study of Religion* 11:325–39.

Beck, R. 2006. "Communion and Complaint: Attachment, Object-Relations, and Triangular Love Perspectives on Relationship with God." *Journal of Psychology & Theology* 34:43–52.

Beck, R., and A. McDonald. 2004. "Attachment to God: The Attachment to God Inventory, Tests of Working Model Correspondence, and an Exploration of Faith Group Differences." *Journal of Psychology and Theology* 322:92–103.

Benson, P., and B. Spilka. 1973. "God Image as a Function of Self-Esteem and Locus of Control." *Journal for the Scientific Study of Religion* 123:297–310.

Birgegard, A., and P. Granqvist. 2004. "The Correspondence Between Attachment to Parents and God: Three Experiments Using Subliminal Separation Cues." *Personality and Social Psychology Bulletin* 30:1122–35.

Bradley, B. P., and A. Matthews. 1983. "Negative Self-Schemata in Clinical Depression." *British Journal of Clinical Psychology* 22:173–181.

Brennan, K. A., C. L. Clark, and P. R. Shaver. 1998. "Self-report Measurement of Adult Attachment: An Integrative Overview." In *Attachment Theory and Close Relationships*, edited by J. A. Simpson and W. S. Rholes, 46–76. New York: Guilford Press.

Bucci, W. 1997. *Psychoanalysis and Cognitive Science: A Multiple Code Theory*. New York: Guilford Press.

Edwards, J. 1754/2009. *The Works of Jonathan Edwards Volume II: Religious Affections*. New Haven, CT: Yale University Press.

Emmons, R. A. 2005. "Emotion and Religion." In *Handbook of the Psychology of*

Religion and Spirituality, edited by R. F. Paloutzian and C. L. Park, 235–52. New York: Guilford.

Epstein, S. 1994. "Integration of the Cognitive and the Psychodynamic Unconscious." *American Psychologist* 49:709–24.

Exline, J. J. 2006. "Emotional Atheism and Anger toward God." Invited address. Mid-year Research Conference of the Division 36, Baltimore, MD.

Exline, J. J., C. L. Park, J. M. Smyth, and M. P. Carey. 2011. "Anger Toward God: Social-Cognitive Predictors, Prevalence, and Links with Adjustment to Bereavement and Cancer." *Journal of Personality and Social Psychology* 100:129–48.

Exline, J. J., and E. Rose. 2005. "Religious and Spiritual Struggles." In *Handbook of the Psychology of Religion and Spirituality*, edited by R. F. Paloutzian and C. L. Park, 315–30. New York: Guilford Press.

George, C., N. Kaplan, and M. Main. 1985. "The Adult Attachment Interview." Unpublished manuscript, University of Berkeley, California.

Gibson, N. J. S. 2006. "The Experimental Investigation of Religious Cognition." Unpublished doctoral dissertation, University of Cambridge, England.

———. 2011. "Toward a Psychology of Atheism II: An Empirically Derived Typology of Non-Religiosity." Paper presented at the International Association for the Psychology of Religion Congress, Bari, Italy.

Gorsuch, R. L. 1968. "The Conceptualization of God as Seen in Adjective Ratings." *Journal for the Scientific Study of Religion* 7:56–64.

Granqvist, P., and L. A. Kirkpatrick. 2008. "Attachment and Religious Representations and Behaviour." In *Handbook of Attachment: Theory, Research, and Clinical Applications*, edited by J. Cassidy and P. R. Shaver, 906–33. New York: Guilford Press.

Hall, T. W. 2003. "Relational Spirituality: Implications of the Convergence of Attachment Theory, Interpersonal Neurobiology, and Emotional Information Processing." *Psychology of Religion Newsletter: American Psychological Association Division 36* 28:1–12.

Hazan, C., and P. R. Shaver. 1987. "Romantic Love Conceptualized as an Attachment Process." *Journal of Personality and Social Psychology* 52:511–24.

Hilgard, E. R. 1980. "The Trilogy of Mind: Cognition, Affection, and Conation. *Journal of the History of the Behavioral Sciences* 16:107–17.

Hill, P. C., and N. J. S. Gibson. 2008. "Whither the Roots? Achieving Conceptual Depth in Psychology of Religion." *Archive for the Psychology of Religion* 30:19–35.

Hill, P. C., and R. W. Hood. 1999a. "Affect, Religion, and Unconscious Processes." *Journal of Personality* 67:1015–46.

————. eds. 1999b. *Measures of Religiosity.* Birmingham, AL: Religious Education Press.

Hodges, S. D., C. A. Sharp, N. J. S. Gibson, and J. M. Tipsord. 2012. "Nearer My God to Thee: Self-God Overlap and Believers' Relationships with God." *Self and Identity,* http://dx.doi.org/10.1080/15298868.2012.674212.

Kim, S. 2008. "Attachment to Parents and God: Implicit and Explicit Investigations of the Internal Working Model Correspondence." Unpublished master's thesis, Rosemead School of Psychology, Biola University, La Mirada, CA.

Kirkpatrick, L. A. 1999. "Attachment and Religious Representations and Behaviour." In *Handbook of Attachment: Theory, Research, and Clinical Applications,* edited by J. Cassidy and P. R. Shaver, 803–22. New York: Guilford Press.

————. 2005. *Attachment, Evolution, and the Psychology of Religion.* New York: Guilford Press.

Kirkpatrick, L. A., and P. R. Shaver. 1992. "An Attachment-Theoretical Approach to Romantic Love and Religious Belief." *Personality and Social Psychology Bulletin* 18:266–75.

Krause, N. 2004. "Assessing the Relationships among Prayer Expectancies, Race, and Self-Esteem in Later Life." *Journal for the Scientific Study of Religion* 43:395–408.

Krause, N., L. M. Chatters, T. Meltzer, and D. L. Morgan. 2000. "Using Focus Groups to Explore the Nature of Prayer in Late Life." *Journal of Aging Studies* 14:191–212.

Kuiper, N. A., and M. R. MacDonald. 1981. "Self and Other Perception in Mild Depressives." *Social Cognition* 1:223–39.

Ladd, K., and B. Spilka, B. 2001. "Inward, Outward, and Upward: Cognitive Aspects of Prayer." *Journal for the Scientific Study of Religion* 41:475–84.

Murken, S., K. Möschl, C. Müller, and C. Appel. 2011. "Entwicklung und Validierung der Skalen zur Gottesbeziehung und zum religiösen Coping (SGrC)." In *Spiritualität Transdisziplinär: Wissenschaftliche Grundlagen im Zusammenhang mit Gesundheit und Krankheit,* edited by A. Büssung and N. Kohls, 75–91. Heidelberg, Germany: Springer Medizin.

Myers, M. W., and S. D. Hodges. 2012. "The Structure of Self-Other Overlap and Its Relationship to Perspective Taking." *Personal Relationships* 19:663–79.

Niedenthal, P. M., S. Krauth-Gruber, and F. Ric. 2006. *Psychology of Emotion: Interpersonal, Experiential, and Cognitive Approaches.* New York: Psychology Press.

Packer, J. I. 1973/1993. *Knowing God.* Westmont, IL: Inter-Varsity Press.

Power, M., and T. Dalgleish. 1997. *Cognition and Emotion: From Order to Disorder*. Hove, England: Psychology Press.

Rizzuto, A. M. 1979. *The Birth of the Living God: A Psychoanalytic Study*. Chicago: University of Chicago Press.

Rowatt, W. C., and L. A. Kirkpatrick. 2002. "Two Dimensions of Attachment to God and Their Relation to Affect, Religiosity, and Personality Constructs." *Journal for the Scientific Study of Religion* 41:637–51.

Schaap-Jonker, H., E. Eurelings-Bontekoe, P. Verhagen, and H. Zock. 2002. "Image of God and Personality Pathology: An Exploratory Study among Psychiatric Patients." *Mental Health, Religion & Culture* 5:55–71.

Schaap-Jonker, H., E. H. M. Eurelings-Bontekoe, H. Zock, and E. Jonker. 2007. "The Personal and Normative Image of God: The Role of Religious Culture and Mental Health." *Archive for the Psychology of Religion* 29:305–18.

———. 2008. "Development and Validation of the Dutch Questionnaire God Image: Effects of Mental Health and Religious Culture." *Mental Health, Religion & Culture* 11:501–15.

Schweitzer, F. 2001. "Distorted, Oppressive, or Fading Away?: The Dialogical Task of Practical Theology and the Human Image of God." In *The Human Image of God*, edited by H.-G. Ziebertz, F. Schweitzer, H. Haring, and D. Browning, 177–91. Leiden: Brill.

Sharp, C. A. 2011. "Discrepancies Between Doctrinal and Experiential God Representations." Unpublished raw data.

Sharp, C. A., N. J. S. Gibson, and K. A. Johnson. 2011. "Measuring Self/Other Overlap with God." Poster presented at the Society for Personality and Social Psychology, San Antonio, TX.

Sharp, C. A., K. A. Johnson, and N. J. S. Gibson. "Measuring Self/Other Overlap with God." Unpublished manuscript.

Sim, T. N., and S. M. Loh. 2003. "Attachment to God: Measurement and Dynamics." *Journal of Social and Personal Relationships* 20:373–89.

Trope, Y., and N. Liberman. 2010. "Construal-Level Theory of Psychological Distance." *Psychological Review* 117:440–63.

Watts, F. N., and M. Williams. 1988. *The Psychology of Religious Knowing*. Cambridge: Cambridge University Press.

Wenger, J. L. 2003. "Implicit Components of Religious Beliefs." *Journal of Psychology and Christianity* 22:223–29.

Wong-McDonald, A., and R. Gorsuch. 2004. "A Multivariate Theory of God Concept, Religious Motivation, Locus of Control, Coping, and Spiritual Well-Being." *Journal of Psychology and Theology* 32:318–34.

Wood, B. T., E. L. Worthington, J. J. Exline, A. M. Yali, J. D. Aten, and M. R. McMinn. 2011. "Development, Refinement, and Psychometric Properties of the Attitudes toward God Scale (ATGS-9)." *Psychology of Religion and Spirituality* 2:148–67.

Yarborough, C. A. 2009. "Depression and the Emotional Experience of God." Unpublished doctoral dissertation, Regent University, Virginia Beach, VA.

Zahl, B. P. 2010. "The Effect of Anger Toward God on God-referent Judgement Speeds." Unpublished raw data.

Zahl, B. P., and N. J. S. Gibson. 2008. "God Concepts? Depends on How You Ask: Exploring Measurement Differences in God Concept Research." Paper presented at the annual Conference of the Christian Association of Psychological Studies, Phoenix, AZ.

———. 2009. "Improving Paper and Pencil Measures of God Representations." Paper presented at the International Association for Psychology of Religion Congress, Vienna, Austria.

———. 2011. "Exploring the Relationship between Petitionary Prayer and Mental Representations of God." Paper presented at the International Association for the Psychology of Religion Congress, Bari, Italy.

———. 2012. "God Representations, Attachment to God, and Satisfaction with Life: A Comparison of Doctrinal and Experiential Representations of God in Christian Young Adults." *International Journal for the Psychology of Religion* 22:216–30.

Dual-System Theories of Religious Cognition

5

FRASER WATTS

This chapter will advocate a dual system theory of religious cognition and show how that can advance traditional understandings of "head" and "heart" in religion. The objective is to use modern cognitive theory to formulate the traditional head-heart distinction in a more rigorous and precisely specified way. The approach to head and heart from the perspective of psychological theory in this chapter complements that from empirical psychological research in the previous chapter by Bonnie Zahl and colleagues.

First, it will be helpful to clarify what is meant by a "cognitive" theory of religion, as it might be thought that a cognitive theory of religion would focus specifically on "head" aspects. In contrast, I will argue that a cognitive theoretical approach can clarify the respective contributions of both head and heart. Proposing a "cognitive" theory of religion does not imply a narrowly intellectualist or head-level view of the nature of religion. In contemporary psychology, cognition is assumed to proceed largely at a nonconscious level, and a cognitive theory of religion certainly includes both implicit and explicit aspects of religious cognition. In fact, as I will argue, it is very important *not* to assume that religion proceeds entirely at the level of conscious thought processes; it is equally important not to assume that it is entirely a matter of unconscious cognition. Cognitive science is "the study of how knowledge is acquired, represented, used, and communicated in intelligent beings" (Oatley 1992, 3). A core assumption of this chapter is that religion involves a distinctive way of performing those functions, a way of engaging with reality, making sense of it, and acting on that distinctive interpretation of it. In that sense, religion involves a kind of knowledge of reality; it engages with reality in a way that is analogous to how science engages with it (McGrath 2004). A cognitive theory of religion sets out how the various aspects of that engagement with reality proceed, using both head and heart.

The analogy between religions and emotion is instructive here. To formulate a cognitive theory of emotion (e.g., Oatley 1992) does not assume that emotion is primarily a matter of conscious thought processes; similarly with a cognitive theory of religion. My colleagues and I have argued elsewhere that an adequate cognitive theory of emotion must be a multilevel one (Williams et al. 1997). At the level of phenomenology, there are often striking discrepancies between different aspects of emotional cognition. For example, someone who is afraid of spiders may at one level (a head level) "know" that spiders are harmless, but nevertheless find themselves terrified by them at the "heart" level. Such discrepancies can only be handled by a theory that postulates at least two levels or systems. The same applies to religion.

Religion is multifaceted and includes such elements as beliefs, experience, practices (public and private), and behavioral consequences (moral and social). The primary focus of a cognitive theory of religion is on experience and belief, though there are indirect implications for behavior and practice. There are often important discrepancies between different facets of religion. For example, Davie (1994) has argued that nowadays there is often religious "believing" without "belonging." However, more relevant here is the potential dissociation of religious experience from belief and practice (Hay 1990). Hay's question to assess whether people have had a religious experience was "Have you ever been aware of, or influenced by, a presence or power, whether you call it God or not, which is different from your everyday self?" The proportion of churchgoers who have had a powerful religious experience (56 percent) was indeed higher than nonchurchgoers (26 percent). However, many believers/churchgoers had not had such an experience (though they may have had religious experiences of a more everyday kind). On the other hand, a surprising number of atheists and agnostics (24 percent) had had such an experience. Such dissociations, like the dissociation between intellectual knowledge and instinctive reactions in spider phobics, point to the need for a dual-system cognitive theory.

I will argue here that the psychological processes involved in religion can also only be understood in terms of the interplay between different levels of "cognition," which can be characterized in folk psychology as head and heart. No cognitive theory of religion that posits only one level of cognition can possibly be adequate; at the very least, a dual-system theory is needed. The religious tradition knows these two levels of cognition in terms of "head" and "heart." I will argue that the more precise understanding of religious understanding made possible by modern cognitive theory requires a similar distinction between two different cognition systems.

DUAL-SYSTEM THEORIES

There is now widespread support in cognitive psychology for some kind of two-system theory: one system that is fast and automatic, and another that is slow and conscious (e.g., Evans and Frankish 2009; Evans 2010). Most versions of two-system theory do not consider the role of affect, though some do. Where affect has been considered, the consensus is that the automatic system is involved in affect in a way that is not the case for the conscious system. I suggest that it is those versions of two-system theory that consider affect or feeling that are most relevant to religion, and especially to the distinction between head and heart in religion. These theories have been less concerned with speed of cognitive processing and more concerned with different ways in which things are encoded. So it is to such versions of two-system theory that consider affect that I now turn.

Some of these two-system theories are partially derived from Freudian cognitive theory; others have a different origin in cognitive theory. The two-system theory that stays closest to psychoanalysis is that of Wilma Bucci (1997). Her work can be seen as part of a general project of formulating psychoanalytic theory in cognitive terms, of which Erdelyi's *Psychoanalysis: Freud's Cognitive Psychology*, was one of the first (Erdelyi 1985). Bucci distinguishes between symbolic and subsymbolic cognitive systems, which are roughly equivalent to what is normally meant by "head" and "heart." Bucci's two-system theory has been applied to religion by Todd Hall (2004).

A more influential two-system theory, which takes account of Freudian theory but has broader roots and has had wider impact, is Seymour Epstein's Self Theory (Epstein 1991; 1994). Epstein's theory makes a distinction between rational and experiential systems, which again roughly correspond to "head" and "heart." Epstein's theory has played a significant role in the general development of two-system theories (see Evans and Frankish 2009). It has been applied to religion by Hill and Hood (1999), though they consider the relevance to religion of various aspects of Epstein's complex theory and not only the distinction between two different cognitive systems.

Epstein himself postulates a close link between religion and the experiential system:

> *Religion provides perhaps the most impressive evidence of all that there are two fundamentally different modes of processing information. There are few societies, if any, throughout recorded history, that have not developed some form of religion. For many individuals, rational, analytical thinking fails to provide as satisfactory a way of understanding the world and of directing their behaviour in it as does religious teaching.*

Why is this so? The answer, I believe, is that religion is better suited than analytical thinking for communicating with the experiential system. (Epstein 1994, 712)

Hill and Hood agree that a central aspect of religious experience is "an affective-based experiential component that is largely unavailable to consciousness" (Hill and Hood 1999, 1040). Following this up with empirical work, Watson et al. (1999) have used Epstein's questionnaire measure of healthy functioning of the experiential system and explored how it correlates with different modes of religion, such as intrinsic and extrinsic forms of religiousness.

There are also two-system cognitive theories that have their origin in cognitive theories of emotion or in mainstream cognitive psychology. Several cognitive theories of emotion have included some kind of distinction between fast/automatic and slow/conscious cognition. For example, Howard Leventhal (1984) has proposed a three-system theory of emotional processing that distinguishes between conceptual and schematic levels (which again roughly correspond to head and heart), as well as a sensorimotor system. A range of multisystem theories of emotional processing are reviewed by Williams et al. (1997), though they have, for the most part, not been explicitly applied to religion.

There are also neurological factors that point toward a cognitive theory that postulates two distinct cognitive systems. One approach is in terms of brain lateralization, recently reviewed in a masterly way by McGilchrist (2009). The exceptional linguistic capacities of humans are linked to greater differences between the two hemispheres than in any other species. Also, intriguingly, the two hemispheres are less interconnected in humans than in other related species. The two hemispheres thus provide alternative modes of cognitive processing, with the left brain corresponding roughly to head, and the right brain corresponding to heart. Interestingly, the right brain is more interconnected with the rest of the body, including the physical heart, than the left brain. The religious implications of McGilchrist's lateralization theory are developed by Sara Savage in chapter 6 of this book. The distinction between the different modes of cognition of the left brain and right brain provides another way of formulating a two-system cognitive theory of religion. In my own final chapter, I use McGilchrist's lateralization theory to put issues about head and heart in religion in broad historical and cultural context.

Philip Barnard has developed a general model of the cognitive architecture, known as Interacting Cognitive Subsystems (ICS; e.g., Teasdale and Barnard 1993), which has two central subsystems: a "propositional" system that is more linguistic and an "implicational" subsystem that is more intuitive and schematic. ICS thus provides a two-systems theory of central cognition, placing that in the context of a comprehensive model of the cognitive architecture. ICS brings a welcome precision to two-system cognitive theories. In my view, that makes it, at least for now, the two-system cognitive theory of choice for psychological theorizing about what is informally known as "head" and "heart." The remainder of this chapter will largely be devoted to exploring the role of head and heart in religion, taking advantage of the theoretical rigor of ICS. However, the general point of this chapter is to use ICS to illustrate what two-level cognitive theories can contribute to the elucidation of the religious head and heart, rather than to claim that ICS alone is capable of doing that.

ICS: Implicational and Propositional Meanings

Initially, Barnard's model was derived from psycholinguistic data (Barnard 1985), but revised by Teasdale and Barnard (1993), adding an extra body-state subsystem, and considering affect explicitly. In this revised version, ICS incorporated elements of two-system cognitive theories of emotion and applied the ICS model to depression. ICS has developed a broad range of other applications, including human computer interaction (Barnard et al. 1988). Watts has applied ICS to religion generally (Watts 2002a; 2002b), and Teasdale has applied it to mindfulness specifically (Teasdale 1999; Teasdale and Chaskalson 2011a; 2011b).

Mark Wynn (2005) has located the ICS way of formulating what is in effect the distinction between head and heart in broader philosophical context.

ICS sets out a general cognitive architecture consisting of nine distinct subsystems. Each subsystem has its own code, representing a different kind of meaning. Information can be transferred from one system to another, though that involves a change of code. Much of the work of the cognitive system as a whole is done through transfer from one subsystem to another. Two of the subsystems constitute the "central engine" of cognition—the "propositional" and "implicational" subsystems—and they will be the main focus of this paper. The other subsystems include two intermediate subsystems: the morphonolexical subsystem (primarily concerned with speech forms) and the object subsystem (concerned with visual space). Each of these is linked to more peripheral subsystems: two sensory subsystems (the acoustic and visual subsystems respectively) and two effector subsystems (the articulatory and limb subsystems respectively). In addition, in the revised version of ICS, there is also a body-state subsystem that is linked directly to the implicational system.

Of the two central subsystems, propositional meanings are easier to understand, largely because such meanings are more readily articulated. Propositional meanings can feed directly into the morphonolexical subsystem, and from there to the articulatory subsystem, whereas there is no comparable route from the implicational system to articulation, except via propositional meanings. Propositional meanings are therefore the kind of meanings that can readily be articulated; in contrast, the meanings of the implicational system are latent. In fact, if alternative names were being chosen for the two systems, it might not be misleading to call them the articulate or explicit (propositional) and latent or tacit (implicational) meaning systems.

Whereas propositional meanings are formulated in an essentially linguistic code, the latent meanings of the implicational system defy adequate linguistic formulation. The code of these latent meanings is more compressed and dense and does not lay everything out explicitly and sequentially in the way that language does. It is also a more schematic code in that it represents what is essentially similar about a variety of specific instances. This leads Teasdale and Barnard (1993) to talk about the latent meanings of the implicational system as representing a "very high level of abstraction." These latent meanings synthesize different components into an integrated whole, components drawn from external sensory input, from internally internal cognitive schemata, and from somatic states. It is thus characteristic of implicit meanings that they are integrative and holistic and draw together components from a variety of sources. The propositional system encodes meanings of a more narrowly cognitive kind, whereas implicational meanings are more likely to be conveyed in narrative form, for example in parables.

Religion and Implicational Meanings

Enough has probably been said already to suggest how important the latent meanings of the implicational system are likely to be in religion. Religion may be one of the domains of human activity where such implicit meanings come into their own. Indeed an important part of the human appeal of religion may be that it provides a context in which the implicational system can operate relatively freely, untrammeled by the linguistic constraints of the propositional system.

Fundamental to the thought patterns of any religious tradition are certain very general schemata. For example, in Christianity, from the New Testament onward, there has been an emphasis on what the sacrament of baptism has in common with the death and resurrection of Christ. They both involve a surrender—that is, some kind of death—in order that some kind of new life may arise. The death and resurrection schema can also be integrated with a variety of painful and difficult personal experiences to indicate how a positive outcome may arise from them. For example, it was the obvious schema with which religious leaders reflected on the significance of the bombing of the medieval cathedral in Coventry in the Second World War, leading to the building of a new cathedral that was seen as a kind of resurrection. Clearly, a schema that is operating over such diverse instances is a very general one, and in that sense is characteristically implicational.

It is another important and distinctive feature of implicational cognition that it is directly affected by bodily states, in a way that propositional cognition is not. In that sense, propositional cognition is merely intellectual, whereas implicational cognition integrates across somatic and sensory sources. The suggestion that religious meanings are essentially implicational is consistent with religious understanding being an embodied kind of cognition, and with the widespread assumption that religious understanding is a knowledge of the "heart," not just of the "head." It is also consistent with careful attention to bodily states and activity in religious practice, from the postures adopted for meditation, to the forms of physical expression that are characteristic of charismatic worship. What kind of bodily state is deemed most helpful will vary from one religious tradition to another, but the body is not something about which religious practices are indifferent.

Religious meanings also seem to be characteristically implicational in the way they draw together elements of different kinds. Teasdale and Barnard emphasize that they integrate internal and external aspects. That is comparable to the way in which the "transitional" domain, postulated by Winnicott (1971) in psychoanalytic theory, spans the divide between internal and external and has been applied fruitfully in the psychology of religion (Pruyser 1974). "Modernity," of which science is the paradigmatic example, has developed an objectifying approach to reality in which internal and external are divided from one another. Religious meanings seem to be more participatory and to assume a mutual indwelling between God and particular people (and, comparably, of individual people with others and indeed with the created world). Such participatory thinking is consistent with the cross-domain features of the code of the implicational system.

There are also differences in the way in which propositional and implicational meanings are evaluated. Intuition plays a much more

133

important role in the evaluation of implication meanings than propositional ones. They are assessed partly in terms of whether they "feel" right or true. That intuitive sense of rightness doesn't come from nowhere, but arises in an educated way out of how meanings cohere with everything else a person knows. An intuitive·sense of what is likely to be true can be quite important even in science. However, it is probably particularly important in religion. What is known as "faith," though far from completely nonrational, seems to operate largely at the intuitive level associated with the implicational system. Conscience also illustrates the sense of rightness that is a feature of the implicational system.

Implicational Meanings: High-Level or Deep?

My main misgiving about the way in which Teasdale and Barnard formulate the schematic meanings of the implicational system is their claim that they show a high level of abstraction. That seems to involve an implicit claim about how such meanings arise, that is, that meanings always start particular, and that more general meanings arise from distilling common features by a process of abstraction. Teasdale and Barnard's talk about the general meanings of the implicational system being "high-level" flows naturally from their assumption about abstraction. However, on different assumptions, these general meanings could be construed as being "deep" rather than "high-level," and the general schematic meanings could be regarded as primary rather than secondary. The heart, I suggest, is deep rather than abstract.

The issue here is rather like that of how metaphors arise. The prevailing assumption is that meanings start particular and literal and are then generalized across diverse different domains to produce metaphors. However, as I have discussed elsewhere (Watts and Williams 1988) following Owen Barfield, there are reasons for thinking that double-aspect terms that span different domains may have preceded more specific, literal meanings. Similarly, it is possible that the very general meanings of the implicational system could precede more particular, specific meanings. In some ways they may be comparable to the kind of archetypes of the collective unconscious that Jung postulates.

However, it may be unhelpful to claim that *either* implicational or propositional meanings are primary, as Barnard emphasizes that the two meaning systems have coevolved. Similarly, it may be misleading to talk about the implicational system as *either* "high-level" *or* "deep." Perhaps the two subsystems are too closely intertwined for either claim to be wholly appropriate. For those interested in parallels between psychological and theological thought, there is a similar ambiguity in Augustine about whether the soul is deep or high.

EVOLUTION AND DEVELOPMENT OF RELIGION

The task now is to show how this ICS theoretical framework, which I suggest captures the essence of the distinction between head and heart with greater theoretical precision, can be applied to illuminate a variety of topics in the psychology of religion. First I will consider the evolution and development of religion. The ICS approach to religion is one that lends itself to the interpretation of religious development, both evolutionary and personal, and elucidates the roles of head and heart in the evolution and development of religion.

Evolution

There have recently been a number of theoretical suggestions about what cognitive capacities are associated with the evolution of religion (e.g., Pyysiäinen and Anttonen 2002). For example, religion is often held to depend on the development of social intelligence and the capacity to "theorize" about other minds, or the application of personal, animistic modes of cognition to provide a causal explanation of events in the natural world. ICS provides another approach to the question of what evolutionary developments in cognition made religion possible, that is, that it arose from the evolution of a separate propositional subsystem and the interplay between it and the implicational system that then became possible (see Watts, forthcoming). To put that in everyday language, humans are unique in having both head and heart, and I suggest that it is having both that makes religion possible. The claim is that, without the separation within central cognition into distinct propositional and implicational subsystems, religious cognition would not have been possible.

The differentiation between implicational and propositional cognition appears to be a distinctively human one; there is probably no other species that has the highly developed linguistic ability that arises from a separate propositional system. Barnard has proposed, in some detail, an evolutionary development of the cognitive architecture, with the progressive addition of subsystems, from four to the full nine-system architecture (Barnard et al. 2007), in which the last stage in that development is the division of central cognition into two separate subsystems. It is proposed that this is what is distinctive about the cognitive architecture of humans, and that it made possible the various cultural developments associated with the Upper Paleolithic period, including religion (see Watts, forthcoming). Of the two central subsystems, the propositional subsystem is the more distinctively human and introduced a unique capacity for framing meanings that are capable of articulation. However, having a separate propositional subsystem would also have affected the implicational subsystem, setting it free to focus on the kind of condensed, schematic meanings described above. In other words, humans not only had a new kind of "head," but having a separate "head" enabled them to have a pure "heart" in a way that was also novel.

Perhaps the most important feature of the human cognitive architecture is not either system on its own, but having *two* meaning systems, providing an opportunity for interaction between them. For example, there is a widespread view that one of the most distinctive features of human cognition is reflective self-consciousness; that can plausibly be seen as arising out of the interaction between two discrete subsystems, rather than out of either alone. Having two meaning systems allows one system to take perspective on what is known in the other. So both head and heart were enormously enriched by the interchange between them that became possible through having both.

This is a radically different cognitive theory of the evolution of religion from that usually accepted in the so-called cognitive science of religion (CSR). However, the CSR approach is unnecessarily constricted by arbitrary assumptions (Smith 2009). For example, it assumes an unnecessarily strong position on the modularity of mind that constrains proposals about how religion might have evolved (Watts, forthcoming). Another weakness is that it advances a theory that is solely about the evolution of religion, whereas it is more parsimonious to consider, as ICS does, what developments in the cognitive architecture underpinned the whole raft of cultural developments that took place in the Upper Paleolithic period. ICS assumes a movement to a more differentiated architecture, which contrasts with Mithen's (1998) proposal that religion arises from the development of more general processing capacities from the integration of previously discrete, specialized cognitive ones. Barrett and others in the CSR school (e.g., Barrett 2004) seem to assume that religious thinking arose from a "hyper-sensitive agency detection device," which resulted in patterns of cognition that belonged to the animate world being misapplied to the inanimate world. In contrast, Watts (forthcoming) suggests that it is more plausible that emerging humanity initially lacked any clear distinction between the animate and inanimate worlds, but gradually acquired one.

Religion in Children

Similar issues arise concerning the development of religion in children, though with the advantage that theorizing can be guided by detailed empirical data. It will be helpful to pursue developmental applications of ICS in that context. So far, ICS has not been much applied to developmental psychology (though see Williams et al. 1997, 303–4). However, it would be in line with what is known about cognitive development in children from Piaget onward to postulate that the implicational system, in at least a rudimentary form, comes into operation first. In contrast, the propositional system would be seen as developing more slowly, and perhaps not becoming fully operational until Piagetian formal operations are evident. That would parallel the assumption stated previously that the propositional system is a late evolutionary development. One might say that, in young children, there is no clear distinction between head and heart, and that the cognition of young children is more heart than head. Gradually, a separate system of head-level cognition develops, which in turn also makes a separate heart possible.

In relating Piaget and ICS in this way, the assumption is that the code of the propositional system is more characteristic of formal operations than of concrete operations, and that the development of the capacity for formal operations is linked to the full development of the propositional system. There is much evidence (e.g., Goldman 1964; Hyde 1990) that children's religious understanding, like their intellectual understanding of almost everything else, follows a developmental path from the concrete to the formal. The ICS distinction between propositional and implicational highlights an important caveat about the interpretation of this developmental sequence. It emphasizes that what develops is primarily the capacity to think about religious matters in a way that is capable of articulation. It remains possible that children who cannot articulate their religious understanding nevertheless have a much richer, albeit largely inarticulate, religious understanding than is often supposed.

Similarly, I have emphasized elsewhere (Watts and Williams 1988) that there is an important difference between being able to use metaphors, including religious metaphors, and being able to explain them. The capacity to explain metaphors depends on the head. In ICS terms it depends on the propositional system and, in Piagetian terms, is probably linked to the development of formal operations. However, the capacity to understand and respond to metaphors in a largely inarticulate way may come on stream much earlier and be more a matter of the heart; in ICS terms, it arises from the implicational system. Religious understanding may thus develop at a latent and intuitive level much earlier than the capacity to explain such understanding, though there are obvious methodological problems in testing that hypothesis rigorously.

This would have educational implications. There have been widespread reservations about the educational conclusions that Goldman drew from his research, essentially that religious ideas should not be taught until the age at which children can demonstrate the capacity to understand them. However, if the capacity to understand antedates the capacity to explain and articulate, there might be much to be gained educationally from providing exposure to religious meanings at an earlier age, even though they will only be understood intuitively. Educational approaches such as Godly Play (Berryman 1991) are designed to make provision for that.

The proposal that the capacity to understand religious meanings intuitively antedates the capacity to explain them is also consistent with research that demonstrates spiritual experience in young children. Converging research from Tamminen (1991) and Hay and Nye (1998) has shown that spiritual experience in young children is common and powerful, if "spiritual" experience is broadly conceived, and such experience is explored using sensitive methodologies. Such rich spiritual experience in young children would hardly be credible if they had only the very limited capacity for religious understanding that appeared to be demonstrated by Goldman. The present proposal is thus that the spiritual experience of young children arises from their capacity to grasp religious meanings at the intuitive level of the implication or system.

What is also intriguing is Tamminen's finding that the spiritual experiences of young children decline as they grow up. There are various explanations for this. For example, spiritual experience may be pushed into the background by increasingly diverse activity, or there may be a growing feeling that such experiences are not "grown up." However, there may also be a cognitive explanation, in that the capacity for spiritual experience may be impaired by the increasing capacity for the articulate intellectual understanding of religion demonstrated by Goldman and others. As the capacity for propositional religion develops in children, so there may be a loss of the more purely implicational aspects of religion. In other words, the development of a religious head may overlay and obscure the religious heart that preceded it.

Of course, one would not expect all children to have equally rich religious meanings. The present theory claims only that there is a cognitive capacity for latent religious meanings in children. Depending on background circumstances, some children will have rich religious meanings, while others will have relatively thin ones. Even where religious meanings are rich, the lack of fully fledged interaction between two distinct meanings systems would impose a significant constraint on religious understanding. The ICS perspective highlights the limitations of a Piagetian approach to intellectual development of religion taken by Goldman and others, which overemphasizes the articulation of meaning.

Conversion and Life-Span Development

The ICS approach can also be extended to life-span development. From the earliest days the psychology of religion has been much occupied with conversion, though there has also been widespread recognition of the diversity of conversion experiences. Some conversions appear to be primarily intellectual, while others are primarily social or moral (e.g., Thouless 1971). There have also been a number of intriguing examples, such as that of C. E. M. Joad, referred to by Thouless, of people who had long adhered intellectually to atheism, but who nevertheless had a powerful religious experience late in life. That seems to set up a striking disjunction between an articulate atheism (which has the hallmarks of the propositional system) and a latent religious understanding that cannot be articulated (which has the hallmarks of implicational cognition). In other words, an atheist head comes into conflict with a religious heart. This disjunction is as striking as that of a spider phobic who intellectually knows that spiders are harmless but who nevertheless has a strong instinctive fear of them.

It seems to be relatively rare for conversion to arise from intellectual argument alone. Though there are many philosophical arguments for and against religious beliefs, it would be widely recognized that these are seldom the decisive factor in leading people either to embrace or to abandon religious faith. People seldom come to religion through their heads. In as far as intellectual arguments weigh at all, it may be by way of removing intellectual objections to a faith that, for intuitive reasons, people are already predisposed to hold. From an ICS perspective it would be assumed that cognitive conversions usually arise at the implicational (heart) rather than the propositional (head) level. That is consistent with the proposal that religion is quintessentially implicational in nature. Once a cognitive conversion has been made, at the implicational level, there is much further work to be done to develop a cognitive elaboration of religious beliefs in a form that is capable of articulation. That would be largely carried out at the propositional level.

It is also interesting to consider Fowler's model of Faith Development (Fowler 1981) in relation to ICS. Stages 1–3 (intuitive-literal, mythic-literal, and synthetic) seem to present a transition from concrete to more abstract religious thought similar to that set out in Piagetian approaches such as that of Goldman. Stage 4 is not primarily a cognitive stage at all, but is more concerned with growing independence from religious authority. However, interestingly, stage 5 seems to be a cognitive stage of a new kind. Its focus on paradox, and on deeper aspects of self, suggests a reemphasis on the dense, highly general code of the implicational system. The status of Fowler's theory has been much debated (see the fuller discussion by Sally Myers in chapter 8), and it is questionable how far it has empirical support, or whether it simply reflects a set of values about the nature of religious maturity. Whatever position one takes about that, it is interesting that Fowler seems to be postulating a kind of religious maturity that comes full circle back to the heart and, like the religion of young children, focuses again on the distinctive approach to religious meaning of the implicational system.

It is very interesting that there can sometimes be a mature recapitulation of a cognitive form of religion that has the hallmarks of the dense, latent, schematic meanings of the implicational system. Though it is probably a relatively small proportion of people who recover a distinctively implicational form of religious cognition in late adulthood, the fact that it happens at all is significant. It raises interesting issues about how the difference between mature implicational religion, in cross talk with a fully fledged propositional system, differs from the implicational religion of children that antedates the full development of propositional cognition. Mature implicational religion will be self-aware and deliberately chosen to a degree that is not possible for children who have not yet achieved the full development of formal operations.

HEAD AND HEART IN RELIGIOUS PRACTICE

We will now turn to religious practices that seem designed to allow people to use their hearts in a way that is relatively unaffected by their heads. All religion probably does that to some extent, but there are some religious practices that essentially seem designed to facilitate the religious heart. Interestingly, such practices can be found in very different traditions. Using the rigorous theoretical framework of ICS, I will focus first on two rather contrasting examples: meditation (and the associated phenomenon of ineffability) and speaking in tongues (or glossolalia). Both seem designed to give the religious heart as free a rein as possible. It will also be helpful to contrast the modes of cognition involved in sacrament-based Catholicism and word-based Protestantism. I will suggest that each of these forms of religion has its own ways of giving greater priority than normal to the religious heart, that is, to implicational cognition, but that each of them also makes provision for a close interchange between head and heart, that is, between implicational and propositional religion. ICS thus provides a helpful way of formulating the distinctive features of different forms of Christianity.

Meditation and Mindfulness

Meditation, and the mystical state of consciousness associated with it, provides another fruitful application of ICS. There are, of course, many different approaches to meditation, spanning different religious traditions. However, most work on ICS and meditation has come from a Buddhist perspective and explored how the mind is configured to produce a state of "mindfulness." Teasdale et al. (1995), Teasdale (1999), and Williams (2008) have focused especially on why mindfulness enhances the efficacy of Cognitive-Behavioral Therapy (CBT) in the treatment of depression, and Teasdale and Chaskalson (2011a; 2011b) have related an ICS understanding of mindfulness to the Buddhist concept of Dukkha. The basic claim is that meditational practices that induce mindfulness allow the implicational system to operate without being overshadowed by propositional cognition or, in everyday language, to allow the heart to operate without the head.

Multiple cognitive subsystems normally permit a variety of different operations to be performed simultaneously; "multitasking" is the norm. However, Teasdale and colleagues suggest that mindfulness involves practices that suspend this normal multitasking in favor of a more coordinated use of our multiple cognitive subsystems so that only one thing is happening at the time (Teasdale et al. 1995). It is consistent with this formulation, though they perhaps don't emphasize it as clearly as they might, that some of the peripheral subsystems are virtually shut down. Perhaps it is not so much that the whole set of central and peripheral subsystems are actively working, in a fully coordinated way. Rather, it may be that the level of activity in peripheral subsystems is minimized, so that the central engine of cognition is not occupied with interfacing with them, but can set its own agenda. Either way the normal multitasking of the network of subsystems seems to be reduced by meditation.

A feature of ICS that is helpful in formulating what happens in meditation is that of "buffering." Much of the time, the cognitive subsystems operate in "direct processing" mode, in which each subsystem is predominantly occupied with responding to streams of information coming from other subsystems. However, it is possible for one system to become "buffered." When that happens, the buffered subsystem is occupied with processing accumulated input within itself, rather than with responding to input from other subsystems. There is a distinctive certain kind of intellectual concentration that reflects buffering in the propositional (head) system. In contrast, in mindfulness, Teasdale (1999) suggests that the implicational subsystem is buffered, enabling people to focus on the understanding of the heart.

Meditation thus changes the balance between head and heart, that is, between the propositional and implicational systems within the "central engine" of cognition. Propositional cognition is closed down as far as possible, creating space for implicational cognition. Different methods of meditation use a variety of techniques to achieve this, and the effect is achieved more radically in experienced than novice meditators. At an introductory level, words and symbols may merely be used sparingly in meditation, and used in relative isolation rather than being embedded in propositions. The intention is to dwell on particular words and symbols in order to probe the depths of their meaning. However, at a more advanced stage of meditation, meanings that are capable of articulation are dispensed with altogether in favor of the more condensed meanings that, from the standpoint of ICS, are recognizable as those of the implicational system.

Though the practice of meditation often seems to bias cognition toward the implicational level and away from the propositional, there is again an alternative explanation. Just as Teasdale et al. (1995) proposed that the whole network of cognitive subsystems is employed in a coordinated way in meditation (as opposed to the usual multitasking), so it is possible that the propositional system is not so much shut down as used in a way that is coordinated with the implicational system. In religious practice, the two systems become "enmeshed" and used in an integrated way. In other contexts, as in depression, the propositional and implicational systems can get "interlocked" (Teasdale and Barnard 1993) in a way that is pathological. Religious practice may provide an interesting example of where the two systems become enmeshed in a closely integrated but adaptive way.

One way in which these ideas about meditation need refining, as Barnard (personal communication) has suggested, is in terms of the changing sequence of states over time. A dynamic model of the effects of meditation is needed, not a merely static one. In almost all meditators there are changes of state from one moment to another, especially in inexperienced meditators. As people become more experienced in meditation, they probably stay in a single state for longer, and they have more control over movement between different states.

Ineffability

This ICS view of meditation yields an explanation of the sense of ineffability that is often associated with mystical experience, as William James (1902) noted. Ineffability is open to various kinds of explanations that are not mutually exclusive. First, there is a sense in which God is uniquely indescribable amongst all sources of human experience. Thus, in as far as mystical experience leads to experience of God, it is likely to be "ineffable" for that reason. Second, from a social constructionist point of view, there is a claim (e.g., Proudfoot 1985) that ineffability arises from a social learning process. On this view, there may be no validity at all to the claim that there is ineffable knowledge; it may just be a learned habit of speaking.

The approach to religious cognition being developed here provides yet another approach to the explanation of the claim that religious experiences are ineffable. From an ICS point of view, the way in which the cognitive apparatus is used during meditation suggests a reliance on the general, condensed, latent meanings of the implicational system that are not open to direct articulation. In other words, things are said to be "ineffable" because they have been experienced by the heart rather than by the head, and heart meanings are not open to articulation in that form.

It is relevant here to note that despite the claims to ineffability made by mystics, they often write at some length about their experiences. This is consistent with the ICS assumption that implicational meanings can be translated into propositional meanings, though at the cost of being recast in a different kind of code. It does not seem to be impossible to write about mystical experience, but there is a strong sense that, in doing so, the nature of the original experience has been changed. There is both loss and gain here. A propositional articulation of mystical experience gains in explicitness over the original implicational experience. On the other hand, it loses some of the dense, affective "gleam in the eye" quality of the original implicational meaning.

This ICS approach is also consistent with the questionnaire research on mystical experience of Ralph Hood and his colleagues (see Hood et al. 1996). Their mysticism scale, consisting of thirty-two items, has been subjected to factor analysis in a series of studies, with broadly consistent results. In two-factor solutions, a distinction emerges between a factor emphasizing the phenomenal experience of unity and a more interpretive factor reflecting religious beliefs and claims. In three factor solutions, the former factor separates into introvertive and extrovertive factors, but the interpretive factor remains intact. In terms of ICS, the interpretive factor seems to reflect the propositional interpretation of mystical experience whereas the unitive factors seem to reflect the more implicit meanings of the implicational system.

Speaking in Tongues

Issues similar to those that arise in connection with meditation also arise with the apparently very different religious practices of charismatic religion. In particular, the practice of glossolalia invites an explanation in terms of how the network of cognitive subsystems is used; fortunately, it is a religious phenomenon on which there is a good deal of relevant research (e.g., Malony and Lovekin 1985). Though speaking in tongues involves speech, which is normally an expression of the ideas of the head, in glossolalia there seems to be an unusual form of speech that may be an expression of the heart, with minimal involvement of the head.

It is clear from psycholinguistic studies of glossolalic speech that it is not normally language (Samarin 1972). The pattern of speech sounds is too repetitive and rhythmic. Indeed, it seems that no exact propositions are normally being expressed in glossolalia, and that neither listener nor speaker knows exactly what is being said. Nevertheless, the speech sounds of glossolalia are not devoid of content. Clearly, the general import of glossolalia is normally the praise of God and a prophetic vision of his unfolding purposes. These highly general meanings associated with glossolalia are characteristic of the implicational system, rather than the propositional.

In glossolalia, in a way that is very unusual, speech sounds seem to arise largely from the latent meanings of the implicational system. In terms of ICS, it must be assumed that implicational meanings are routed through the propositional system, through the morphonolexical system, to the articulatory system. However, it seems that the propositional system is quite unusually passive in glossolalia. Though glossolalia is distinctive in the way in which it gives a rather passive role to the propositional system within the framework of speech production, it may not be unique in this. The way in which people talk to babies is interestingly similar in the way it articulates a general mood in speech sounds, with minimal propositional involvement. It seems to be a kind of speech that comes from the heart rather than the head.

Sacramental Religion

Surprisingly, sacramental religion has been much less investigated in the psychology of religion than, say, fundamentalist or charismatic religion. Ritual can be used in different ways, just as the use of words in religion can be either dry or evocative. Sometimes, as Freud (1907) pointed out, it can be an obsessional defense against anxiety. However, alternatively, as neo-Freudians have pointed out (Pruyser 1974; Erikson 1978), it can be evocative and provide a space in which mystery is sensed and important cognitive processing is done, albeit in an inarticulate way. Also, as Whitehouse (2000) has recently pointed out in his theory of "modes" of religiosity, some rituals are novel while others are very familiar, involving different kinds of processing. Familiar rituals can be performed in different ways; sometimes they are performed in a way that is merely mechanical; alternatively, despite familiarity, they can be invested with much meaning and significance.

From an ICS perspective, sacramental Christianity provides rich scope for an implicational approach. It clearly emphasizes visual and other sensory experiences, as well as bodily action and participation. The visual impact of liturgy is probably the most striking of all, but sacramental religion makes use of a broad range of sensory experience (the "smells and bells" traditionally associated with ritualistic worship) in order to heighten the sensory impact. In addition, ritual actions such as genuflecting and crossing involve the limb system. Sensory input from the visual system and motor output from the limb system are both linked more closely with the implicational system than with the propositional system. In terms of ICS, the implications for different forms of religion are clear; the sacramental approach seems to prioritize the implicational system.

However, it would probably be a mistake to see sacramental religion as abandoning the propositional system completely in favor of the implicational. It is noteworthy that the Catholic tradition has always insisted on the integration of word and sacrament within the framework of the Eucharist or Mass. Nonpropositional meanings are preceded by, and embedded within, a more propositional context. So, once again, it seems that sacramental religion, in its own way, is facilitating a close linkage between these two subsystems, despite the apparent bias toward nonpropositional meanings.

Word-Based Protestantism

The listening and speaking that are prominent in forms of religion that emphasize preaching and the Word of God are most directly linked to the propositional system (via the morphonolexical system). Thus, on the face of things, the word-based religion associated with Reformed Christianity seems to prioritize the propositional system. However, things may not be as clear-cut as that suggests, because the way in which language is used in religion is often distinctive and unusual. Language can be used in religious contexts in a way that is less dry and rationalistic than normal; in contrast, it is used in a more evocative and poetic way that speaks more directly to the "heart."

In ICS terms, it seems as though even word-based forms of religion use language in a way that is unusually closely tied into the richer code of the implicational subsystem. That can lead to a kind of "enmeshment" between the systems. Thus, the condensed, latent meanings of the implicational system can give rise to a stream of words or symbols, capable of articulation, that express those condensed meanings. That stream of words and symbols can, in turn, feed into the more condensed religious meanings that are not themselves open to direct articulation.

Similar issues arise about how words are used in prayer, a religious practice on which there is an increasingly rich psychology (e.g., Brown 1994; Watts 2001). Whereas meditation often aspires to be wordless, prayer characteristically makes use of language. However, language can be used in different ways in prayer. Some prayer can be largely a matter of mechanical recitation, which would make little contact with the implicational system. Other forms of prayer can involve rich cross-traffic between the propositional and implicational systems, in a way that sets up a similar kind of enmeshment. For example, aspects of prayer such as confession and thanksgiving that involve reflection on recent experience can provide the opportunity for a significant reconfiguration of personal meanings. In ICS terms, the distinction is between prayer that is merely propositional and prayer that involves a rich cross talk between propositional and implicational systems.

Conclusion

The central claim of this chapter is that current theories of cognition in psychology, which mostly emphasize that humans have two cognitive systems, can be used to elucidate the traditional distinction between head and heart with a new rigor and precision. That has been developed here largely with reference to one particular model of the human cognitive architecture: ICS. However, ICS has been used only illustratively. It would be consistent with the general thrust of this chapter for the distinction between head and heart to be elucidated using other versions of two-system cognitive theory. ICS provides a theoretical framework for formulating the roles of head and heart in religion, but that can likewise be done using alternative two-system cognitive theories.

It has been suggested that religion is possible because of an evolutionary development that gave humans two different modes of cognition: a "head" mode that is intellectual and linguistic and a "heart" mode that is more tacit and intuitive. The "head" allows humans to reflect in a new and distinctive way, but having a separate "head" system that can do that liberates the "heart" to develop the distinctive, intuitive mode of understanding that is at the core of religion. Moreover, having both head and heart makes it possible to have a fruitful interplay between them, in a way that is simply not possible with only one mode of central cognition. Some of that process of evolutionary development is recapitulated as people develop through childhood and the life span. Children gradually develop a religious head as well as a religious heart but, later in life, people can rediscover, in a new way, the value of the religious heart.

Many religious practices seem designed to allow space for the heart to operate without too much head. In meditative religion, the heart is allowed free rein, and the head is either largely switched off or enmeshed with the heart. In the charismatic phenomenon of glossolalia, heart-level meanings are articulated, but in a way that gives the head an unusually limited and passive role. In sacramental religion, there is an emphasis on the intuitive experience of the religious heart, but that is linked to religious teaching that engages the head. In the word-based religion of the Protestant tradition, there is an emphasis on language, but it is used in a distinctive way that keeps it closely linked to the heart.

This view of the interplay between head and heart in religion has implications for theology and religious education. Theology has an unavoidable commitment to articulation, which keeps it tied to head rather than heart, that is, to propositional rather than implicational levels of religious meaning. It is a challenge for theology to develop a way of theorizing about religion that, while articulate, nevertheless take proper account of the inescapably inarticulate nature of much religious cognition. The approach to head and heart developed here in terms of two different cognitive systems also has practical implications, some of which are explored in the next section of this book.

REFERENCES

Barnard, P. J. 1985. "Interacting Cognitive Subsystems: A Psycholinguistic Approach to Short-Term Memory." *Progress in the Psychology of Language* 2:197–258.

Barnard, P. J., D. J. Duke, R. W. Byrne, and I. Davidson. 2007. "Differentiation in Cognitive and Emotional Meanings: An Evolutionary Analysis." *Cognition and Emotion* 21:1155–83.

Barnard, P. J., M. Wilson, and A. MacLean. 1988. "Approximate Modelling of Cognitive Activity with an Expert System: A Theory-Based Strategy for Developing an Interactive Design Tool." *The Computer Journal* 31:445–56.

Barrett, Justin L. 2004. *Why Would Anyone Believe in God?* Lanham, MD: AltaMira Press.

Berryman, J. W. 1991. *Godly Play: A Way of Religious Education.* San Francisco: Harper.

Brown, L. B. 1994. *The Human Side of Prayer: The Psychology of Praying.* Birmingham, AL: Religious Education Press.

Bucci, Wilma. 1997. *Psychoanalysis and Cognitive Science: A Multiple Code Theory.* New York: Guilford Press.

Davie, G. 1994. *Religion in Britain since 1945: Believing without Belonging.* Oxford: Blackwell.

Epstein, S. 1991. "Cognitive-Experiential Self-Theory: An Integrative Theory of Personality." In *The Relational Self: Convergences in Psychoanalysis and Social Psychology,* edited by R. Curtis, 111–37. New York: Guilford Press.

———. 1994. "Integration of the Cognitive and the Psychodynamic Unconscious." *American Psychologist* 49:709–24.

Erdelyi, M. H. 1985. *Psychoanalysis: Freud's Cognitive Psychology.* New York: W. H. Freeman.

Erikson, E. H. 1978. *Toys and Reasons: Stages in the Ritualization of Experience.* London: Boyars.

Evans, Jonathan. 2010. *Thinking Twice: Two Minds in One Brain.* Oxford: Oxford University Press.

Evans, Jonathan, and Keith Frankish, eds. 2009. *In Two Minds: Dual Processes and Beyond.* Oxford: Oxford University Press.

Fowler, J. W. 1981. *Stages of Faith: The Psychology of Human Development and the Quest for Meaning.* San Francisco: Harper & Row.

Freud, S. 1907. "Obsessive Actions and Religious Practices." In *The Standard Edition of the Complete Psychological Works of Sigmund Freud,* vol. 9, edited by J. Strachey, 116–29. London: Hogarth Press.

Goldman, R. 1964. *Religious Thinking from Childhood to Adolescence.* London: Routledge & Kegan Paul.

Hall, T. W. 2004. "Christian Spirituality and Mental Health: A Relational Spirituality Paradigm for Empirical Research." *Journal of Psychology & Christianity* 23:66–81.

Hay, D. 1990. *Religious Experience Today: Studying the Facts.* London: Mowbray.

Hay, D., and R. Nye. 1998. *The Spirit of the Child.* London: Fount.

Hill, P. C., and R. W. Hood. 1999. "Affect, Religion and Unconscious Process." *Journal of Personality* 67:1015–46.

Hood, R. W., B. Spilka, B. Hunsberger, and R. Gorsuch. 1996. *Psychology of Religion: An Empirical Approach.* New York: Guilford Press.

Hyde, K. E. 1990. *Religion in Childhood and Adolescence: A Comprehensive Review of the Research.* Birmingham, AL: Religious Education Press.

James, W. 1960 (1902). *The Varieties of Religious Experience: A Study in Human Nature.* London: Collins.

Leventhal, H. 1984. "A Perceptual Motor Theory of Emotion." In *Approaches to*

Emotion, edited by K. R. Scherer and P. Ekman, 271–91. Hillsdale, NJ: Lawrence Erlbaum.

Malony, H. N., and A. A. Lovekin. 1985. *Glossolalia: Behavioural Science Perspectives on Speaking in Tongues*. New York: Oxford University Press.

McGilchrist, Iain. 2009. *The Master and His Emissary: The Divided Brain and the Making of the Western World*. New Haven, CT: Yale University Press.

McGrath, A. E. 2004. *The Science of God: An Introduction to Scientific Theology*. Grand Rapids, MI: William B. Eerdmans Pub.

Mithen, S. J. 1998. *The Prehistory of the Mind*. London: Phoenix.

Oatley, K. 1992. *Best Laid Schemes: The Psychology of Emotions*. Cambridge, England: Cambridge University Press.

Proudfoot, W. 1985. *Religious Experience*. Berkeley: University of California Press.

Pruyser, P. W. 1974. *Between Belief and Unbelief*. New York: Harper & Row.

Pyysiäinen, I., and V. Anttonen, eds. 2002. *Current Approaches in the Cognitive Science of Religion*. New York: Continuum.

Samarin, W. J. 1972. *Tongues of Men and Angels: The Religious Language of Pentecostalism*. New York: Macmillan.

Smith, Barbara Herrnstein. 2009. *Natural Reflections: Human Cognition at the Nexus of Science and Religion*. New Haven, CT: Yale University Press.

Tamminen, K. 1991. *Religious Development in Childhood and Youth: An Empirical Study*. Helsinki: Suomalainen Tiedeakatemia.

Teasdale, J. D. 1999. "Emotional Processing, Three Modes of Mind and the Prevention of Relapse in Depression." *Behaviour Research and Therapy* 37:S53–S77.

Teasdale, J. D., and P. J. Barnard. 1993. *Affect, Cognition and Change*. Hove: Lawrence Erlbaum.

Teasdale, J. D., and M. Chaskalson. 2011a. "How Does Mindfulness Transform Suffering? I: The Nature and Origins of Dukkha." *Contemporary Buddhism* 12:89–102.

Teasdale, J. D., and M. Chaskalson. 2011b. "How Does Mindfulness Transform Suffering? II: The Transformation of Dukkha." *Contemporary Buddhism* 12:103–24.

Teasdale, J. D., Z. V. Segal, and J. M. G. Williams. 1995. "How Does Cognitive Therapy Prevent Depressive Relapse and Why Should Attentional Control (Mindfulness) Training Help?" *Behaviour Research and Therapy* 33:25–39.

Thouless, R. 1971. *An Introduction to the Psychology of Religion*. 3rd ed. Cambridge: Cambridge University Press.

Watson, P. J., R. J. Morris, R. W. Hood Jr., L. Miller, and M. G. Waddell. 1999. "Religion and the Experiential System: Relationships of Constructive Thinking with Religious Orientation." *International Journal for the Psychology of Religion* 9:195–207.

Watts, F. N. 2001. "Prayer and Psychology." In *Perspectives on Prayer*, edited by F. N. Watts, 39–52. London: SPCK.

———. 2002a. *Theology and Psychology*. Baskingstoke: Ashgate.

———. 2002b. "Interacting Cognitive Subsystems and Religious Meanings." In *Neurotheology: Brain, Science, Spirituality, Religious Experience*, edited by R. Joseph, 183–88. San Jose: California University Press.

———. Forthcoming. "Religion and the Emergence of Differentiated Cognition." In *Evolution, Religion and Cognitive Science: Critical Enquiries*, edited by F. Watts and L. Turner. Oxford: Oxford University Press.

Watts, F. N., R. Nye, and S. B. Savage. 2002. *Psychology for the Christian Ministry*. London: Routledge.

Watts, F. N., and J. M. G. Williams. 1988. *The Psychology of Religious Knowing*. Cambridge: Cambridge University Press.

Whitehouse, H. 2000. *Arguments and Icons: Divergent Modes of Religiosity*. Oxford: Oxford University Press.

Williams, J. M. G. 2008. "Mindfulness, Depression and Modes of Mind." *Cognitive Therapy and Research* 32:721–33.

Williams, J. M. G., F. N. Watts, C. Macleod, and A. Matthews. 1997. *Cognitive Psychology and Emotional Disorders*. Chichester: John Wiley.

Winnicott, D. W. 1971. *Playing and Reality*. London: Tavistock Publications.

Wynn, Mark. 2005. *Emotional Experience and Religious Understanding*. Cambridge: Cambridge University Press.

PART 3

Application

Head and Heart in Preventing Religious Radicalization

6

Sara Savage

This is the first of a group of chapters that will look at practical applications of the psychology of head and heart, building on the theoretical framework set out in the previous chapter. The focus of this chapter will be religious radicalization. Emotive topics such as the twin towers, sectarian violence, Islamist militancy, and Christian fundamentalism seem to suggest that religious radicalization emerges when the heart takes over from the head. However, I will propose the more subtle hypothesis that it arises from a separation of "head" from "heart." The extremes of religion represent an intensification of broader trends in which we all play a part—a bias toward the "head" in religion and Western globalized culture more generally. Ironically, when the head is split off from the reasons of the heart, it leans toward greater aggression in order to defend sacred values.

Precise distinctions between fundamentalism, radicalization, terrorism, and extremist violence are subjects of endless debate and reflect the standpoint of the definer. Each definition is valid for some contexts, but not others. Given how interminable debates about these terms are, I am content that these distinctions are beyond the remit of this chapter. I hope I will be forgiven for considering radicalization in religion as a broad contemporary trend—while acknowledging that it takes many different forms and can pertain to any belief system. The approach to radicalization that I elaborate in this chapter was developed with my colleagues in the Psychology and Religion Research Group at Cambridge (Savage, Liht, and Williams 2011; Savage and Liht 2010), and from this work we developed an empirically assessed prevention method (Savage and Liht 2010; Boyd-MacMillan and Savage 2013). To this model I bring the lens of recent neuroscience, taking a new look at what the prevention of radicalization reveals concerning reasons of the heart.

Our approach to radicalization is based on the idea of complexity in thinking, a psychological construct developed by Peter Suedfeld and colleagues (Suedfeld et al. 2003; 2006) termed integrative complexity (IC). Integrative complexity concerns how complexly we perceive the social world, whether we see the world in black-and-white dichotomous categories (low IC), or whether we are able to see some validity in competing viewpoints (the differentiation aspect found at moderate IC levels), or whether we are able to perceive linkages between different views or dimensions within a higher order framework (the integration aspect of higher levels of IC). Decades of research in IC show that when levels of complexity in thinking drop from the thinkers' normal baseline, violent conflict between the parties is predicted (e.g., Suedfeld and Tetlock 1977; Tetlock 1984; Guttieri, Wallace, and Suedfeld 1995; Suedfeld and Leighton 2002). According to one model, what motivates people to raise the complexity of their thinking is their desire to maximize more than one human value when both these values are in tension, and when they are deemed comparable and important (Tetlock 1986). Complexity in values underpins the ability to think in complex ways, and this is key to our approach.

We argue that extremist ideology *of any kind* avoids complexity. When human values are in tension, extremist discourse tends to focus upon a single value (such as justice for the oppressed) with regard to the issue at hand. This one value acts like a magnet, drawing *what can be thought* about the issue, like metal shavings, tightly around this one value. Other human values, such as freedom or achievement values, are left out of the picture, and a more simplified version of social reality results. Toward the end of this chapter I will describe how our approach to enhancing integrative complexity (Savage and Liht 2010) works to build resilience against religious radicalization, and how both head and heart are involved. But first, a foray into what recent neuroscience reveals in regard to these matters.

A Perspective from Neuroscience

In the previous chapter, Fraser Watts indicated that "head" and "heart" can be formulated theoretically in terms of dual-process models of cognitive architecture (such as Interacting Cognitive Subsystems), or through models based on the structure of the physical brain such as the brain lateralization theory proposed by McGilchrist (2009). Here I will pursue the latter, relating neuroscience studies to radicalization and its prevention.

Studies from cognitive neuroscience go a long way to answer a question that has increasingly perplexed me: given the social, cognitive, and employment costs of even the early stages of radicalization, why is it so easy for well-meaning people to become radicalized? A partial answer, I propose, lies in the dynamic tensions that underpin *normal* brain processes. Conversely, it is also possible for people to deradicalize, and neuroscience provides fascinating insight to that as well.

In bringing the lens of cognitive neuroscience to bear on this topic, my intention is not to shift our focus from the thinking, valuing, and meaning-making of human beings in favor of a reductionist, biologically based account. Any cognitive processing is unavoidably dependent upon the neurological substratum that supports it, and it is enlightening to understand how this works and to bring this alongside psychological accounts. The question of whether ultimate causation is due either to "disembodied" cognition, or to the biology of neurons, is moot. The plasticity of the brain means that the exercise of our thinking will, over time, lead to the development of the neuronal networks to support it, and this becomes self-perpetuating once these particular pathways are ready and waiting to process this particular kind of cognition. Well-carved pathways mean that thinking "more of the same" becomes easy. Likewise, any changes in our thinking will diminish some neuronal pathways while promoting others—even over relatively short periods of time (Pascual-Leone 2001). The brain is not unlike a muscle in operating a "use it or lose it" policy. Causality here should be imagined as a spiral that can move in both directions: spiraling upward with increasing neuronal power following copious practice of relevant cognitions, or spiraling backward if those pathways attenuate through lack of use.

With any complex cognitive processing, the human brain can be imagined as a symphony in which all parts of the brain are dynamically involved. Yet within this complex symphony there are three fundamental oppositional forces, including the opposition referred to in everyday language as between "head" and "heart." Some processes in the brain inhibit processes arising in other parts of the brain, so that the activity of relevant regions of the brain can come to the fore in order to meet the demands of the current task. Hundreds of studies in neuroscience support a view of the functioning human brain as a system of **three opponent processes:**

1. *Top-down*—pertaining to the oppositional tension between the higher-order thinking of the more recently evolved neocortex and the deeper limbic region that is the home of emotion and more basic, primitive thinking categories.

2. *Right-left*—pertaining to the oppositional tension between the right hemisphere and the left hemisphere with their different ways of paying attention to reality.

3. *Front-back*—pertaining to the tension between the frontal lobes (where personal identity, deliberate choice, and our sense of self in relation to others arises) and the hind brain (including the cerebellum where automatic processing occurs so quickly, unconsciously, and powerfully).

In the next three sections I explore how these three opponent processes deepen our understanding of radicalization and its prevention. In my view, they help to explain *why* it is so easy for highly moral people (Ginges et al. 2011) to become radicalized, despite the costs. Stating the obvious, these normal brain processes make radicalized cognition possible. There are wider implications from this, too, for our "everyday thinking," given that these opponent processes are normal features arising from brain architecture; they are not just features of the radicalized.

It will be convenient to begin with the second of these opponent processes, that between the left and right hemispheres. Simply put, the left brain tends for many people to correspond to "head" and the right brain to "heart." Neuroscience helps us to understand more precisely what is involved in the contrast between head and heart, and how the relationship between these two hemispheres can polarize, as I argue is the case in radicalization. I will then indicate how this is complexified by the other oppositional tensions between top-down and front-back. That will lead into a summary of our approach to radicalization, and the intervention that illustrates this theoretical perspective. Finally, I will conclude this chapter with a thumbnail sketch of the radicalized mind in our contemporary context—a cultural context that is slanting all three opponent processes (if we are to believe the hundreds of studies coming from neuroscience) in directions that favor certain kinds of separation of "head" from "heart." These emphases provide fertile conditions not just for religious radicalization, but also for extremes in "everyday" thinking.

Right-Left Opponent Processes

These opponent processes arise from the specialization and bifurcation of the human brain's left and right hemispheres.

The widely acknowledged popular distinction between "head" and "heart" ways of knowing accords with a number of dual process cognitive models that distinguish between "head" rational, linear, word-based knowing and "heart" emotional, implicit, embodied,

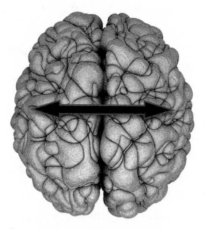

RIGHT-LEFT OPPONENT PROCESSES

interpersonal knowing. There is now huge empirical evidence from neuroscience that these two different ways of processing information arise from the right and left hemispheres' different specialisms, and this makes good sense of this popular and psychological distinction. As stated in the beginning of this chapter, radicalization does not emerge simply from an overflow of emotion, as one might presume when face-to-face with the vehemence of extremism. Rather, I argue that radicalization is fostered (along with the top-down shift sparked by threat) by a culture-wide separation of head knowing from heart knowing. This does not involve just a simple dichotomy of thinking versus emotion, but rather a distinction between the kinds of emotion and kinds of thinking that pertain respectively to the right and left hemispheres.

Iain McGilchrist (2009), in his highly regarded review of hundreds of neuroscience studies, argues that among primates it is only in humans that the right and left hemispheres of the brain operate quite independently. Humans have, as it were, two "brains" with distinct ways of paying attention to reality, producing two different worldviews and two different "agendas," from which one consciousness emerges. McGilchrist argues that the two hemispheres, whose relationship is marked by the need for separation and mutual inhibition as well as a degree of intercommunication, are in humans operating more independently now than in previous human history, with an increasing shift toward left hemisphere dominance.

The initial seeds of this shift in human history are glimpsed in the post-Socratic philosophers with their search for reliable foundations for knowledge. The Reformation of the sixteenth century, the first great search for certainty in modern times, is a noticeable turning point away from symbolic and implicational processing toward more word-based, conceptually abstract, "left brain" processing. McGilchrist goes on to argue that since the Industrial Revolution, we have created a left brain world through architecture, art, science, and technology. That "left brain" environment then shapes how we think and what we see—inescapably so for a large part of the world's population living in urban areas. The imprint of this left brain world unsurprisingly shapes how we "do" religion. Not that the left hemisphere should be personified as an "agent" somehow taking over the human brain; there are swings back and forth between right and left hemisphere dominance over the course of human cultural evolution when the dominance of one hemisphere ceases to be adequate for the challenges of the day, prompting a swing back to the other hemisphere's specialisms (McGilchrist notes the swing to the romantic movement at the height of the social dislocations of the Industrial Revolution). This back-and-forth movement between hemispheres becomes salient in the next sections.

Though much more thoroughly detailed by McGilchrist, we may present some durable generalizations arising from neuroscience studies concerning left-right distinctives. The left hemisphere deals with pieces of information in isolation, whereas the right deals with the information as a gestalt—as a whole. The left hemisphere specializes in linear, analytic processing; the right hemisphere proceeds with parallel processing from sense perception, bodily states, emotion and thought. The left "brain" is focused on what it already knows, filtering new information through its preformed schemas, categories, and scripts, in accordance with research in cognitive psychology supporting the ideas that humans are cognitive misers who seek to protect existing knowledge systems against dissonance (for example, Janis 1982; Herek, Janis, and Huth 1987; Greenwald 1980). In short, the left hemisphere is somewhat closed to new information as it seeks to maintain its conceptual system based on clear-cut categories and logical rules. Existing abstract ideas are prioritized over new information coming from the senses. This is not to disparage the crystal clear thinking in which the left hemisphere excels; the advances of science and technology are thanks to it.

In contrast, the larger, heavier, more powerful right brain seeks what it does not know. It is interested in the "other" and is highly connected with the rest of the nervous system, with bodily states and emotions. The right brain deals with real-life particulars, not abstractions. The right brain is interested in faces and individuals; it is the seat of empathy, moral sense, and self-awareness conceived in relation to others. The right brain takes a broad, contextualized view and puts things into a wider perspective. The right brain is crucial to living in the real world; for example, stroke patients can continue to function with an impaired left brain, but they cannot function at all with an impaired right brain. It is able to accommodate opposite views, give them perspective, and weave them into a wider gestalt.

The most crucial difference is the way the two hemispheres pay different kinds of attention to the world: the right pays a broad, contextualized, particularistic yet networked attention; the left pays a narrow, focused, categorized, instrumental attention (McGilchrist 2009). The kind of attention we pay to the world alters the world we live in. Inevitably, we bring something to the act of perceiving, then we behave in accordance to how we "see" the world. Within limits, that world gradually takes shape around us.

Both right and left hemispheres can "do" religion, but as Fraser Watts suggests in the previous chapters, they do religion in a different manner, just as the hemispheres "do" language and mathematics, but in different ways and to differing extents. The more complex a task is, the more this will involve a symphony of processing using many regions of the brain, including both hemispheres. Even so, there is a "winner takes all" tendency in the brain, whereby the hemisphere that is "best" at doing something at a particular time will take upon itself the whole of that task, even though there are costs to that strategy. Tremendous cognitive advances have resulted from greater left hemispheric independence and dominance, but the downside is a greater tension between brain hemispheres, and thus greater instability (with attendant costs such as an apparently growing prevalence of various schizoid conditions in which emotion tends to be flattened out or misaligned with thinking). Individuals differ in terms of which hemisphere is dominant, but in most people, the left hemisphere, dealing with language, abstract reasoning, categorization, and focused attention, is the dominant hemisphere. The analytical left hemisphere drives modern culture with all its phenomenal technological achievements, and right brain specialisms are now marginalized in education and culture. Many of these right-left distinctives are pertinent to our focus here on religious radicalization.

What does intensified left hemisphere dominance look like in religion? How does this relate to radicalization in religion? The next section reviews studies of fundamentalism and radicalization in this light.

Left brain Religion

Since the upsurge of fundamentalisms from around 1979 onward, sociologists have noted the instrumental use of modern technology (radio, TV, cassette tapes, video tapes, and Internet) to spread the message of so-called "backward-looking" fundamentalisms around the globe. Deeper analysis reveals that, far from being a throw-back to earlier mythical and symbolic ways of religious understanding (as often portrayed in the media), the footprint of modernity is evident in the kind of thinking in which fundamentalisms excel.

Shepherd (1987) noted that an "engineering," "black and white" mentality exists among Christian fundamentalists. Barr (1981) observed how Christian fundamentalism stresses the material-physical accuracy of the Bible, and how it takes its method from a Newtonian model of science. Whereas many Christian fundamentalists are antievolutionist, they display a preference for hard facts and proper rational techniques. Biblical authority will always supersede scientific authority, and if that entails denying evolution, so be it. But objective truth is preferred, and this is what the Bible is considered to be. Fundamentalists' epistemological strategy is to find an irrefutable starting position and then proceed from there with clear logical rules. This is achieved through structuring the fundamentalist belief system around a central authority belief—the plenary version of belief in scriptural inerrancy (it is the words, not just the meaning that are deemed true). This foundational inerrancy belief is deemed sacred and beyond refute; it serves to legitimate all other fundamentalist beliefs in a one-way direction, with no "back talk" returning to modify the authority belief (which an open system of thinking would allow, Rokeach 1960). Once this, admittedly, circular premise is accepted by adherents, fundamentalist thinking then proceeds logically and systematically (Hood, Hill, and Williamson 2005).

A similar picture emerges from a study I carried out into the moral reasoning of fundamentalists and nonfundamentalists (Savage 1998; 2008). This research showed that the fundamentalist participants emphasized the person, action, or issue in isolation, apart from the social context (arguably a left hemisphere preference), while nonfundamentalists emphasized the person, action, or issue in relationship with others or embedded within a wider social context (arguably, a more holistic, right hemisphere specialism). It seemed to me that the perspective or "lens" applied to the moral problem preferred by fundamentalists (seeing persons, actions, or issues in isolation) is in line with the philosophic stance that we can know things in and of themselves (following empiricists such as Locke and Scottish Common Sense Realists), and that language, perception, and thinking all work to economically and veridically relate this word to that reality (a one-to-one correspondence theory of language). Harris (1998) also argues that this epistemology informs Christian fundamentalism in a diffuse, background way and represents the substratum upon which a theory of literal scriptural inerrancy could most easily be built: the words *equal* truth. In contrast, the selective "lens" used by nonfundamentalists accords with postmodern, contextual theories of language. Both fundamentalist and nonfundamentalist perspectives on the moral problem are an example of the way "hot" commitments can drive supposedly "cold" cognitions (Haidt 2006). We see the world according to the way our intuited philosophic commitments predispose us, and fundamentalists perceive the world in a way that manages to conjoin a commitment to scriptural inerrancy with a sciencelike, left hemisphere approach.

A preference for science-like arguments also colors recent radical discourse. Ironically, Islam (which unlike Christianity, suffered no historical conflict between science and religion) now seems to be adopting a similar creationist stance with its own version of creationism promoted worldwide from a base in Turkey.[1] This new Islamic creationism borrows heavily from the "sciencelike" arguments in contemporary Christian creationism concerning Intelligent Design. Islamic tracts handed out on university campuses typically stress the rationality of Islam, and radical versions of Islam deploy their most scathing attacks against traditional Muslim symbolic ritual practices. Sufi brotherhoods, once the dominant means of the spread and practice of Islam, are considered "bida" (reprehensible innovation) by radical Islamists. More recently, Gambetta and Hertog's (2009) research demonstrates that engineers, graduates from a discipline that proceeds on clear mathematical answers to well-defined problems, are vastly overrepresented among violent extremists.

In short, there is a modernist trend to elevate word-based, abstract, rational knowing over more implicit, symbolic knowing in both fundamentalisms and radical discourses. Monotheistic religion has always had a doctrinal (word-based) element, but prior to the Enlightenment religious knowing involved a greater balance between word-based propositions and more symbolic, implicit forms of knowing that comprised the bedrock of traditional ritual practice (Armstrong 2000; Sløk 1996). As science has become the main model to which other sources of knowledge aspire, Western and now Islamic societies have been losing the capacity to read their texts in a metaphorical-symbolic sense. Instead, they have become preoccupied with the empirical veracity of their content. Symbolic, implicational processing is somewhat despised among radicals, and this seems to make religious knowing more inflexible.

It is fair to say that our contemporary cultural context underresources people in how they think about their religious beliefs. In studies on terrorism, lack of religious background is one of the few consistent features that pertain to those who have carried out acts of terror. Young people without a rich religious background are more vulnerable to word-based, left brain, modernist versions of religion that radicalizers use to promote violent mobilization. Radical religion appears to be more seamless with our left brain dominant culture than it would be with a culture that balances the two hemispheres more gracefully.

TOP-DOWN OPPONENT PROCESSES

I now turn to top-down opponent processes in the brain and outline how these are relevant to radicalization. These tensions occur between the higher cognitive functions arising from the neocortex and the activity of deeper brain structures, sometimes called the "primitive" or "old brain," comprising the limbic system and brain stem. These latter two systems act in concert with one primary goal: survival.

The brain stem promotes our survival by regulating breathing, heartbeat, and other tasks governed by the autonomic nervous system—both in response to threats to our survival and in recovery when the threat disappears. The limbic system (or midbrain) is the region where emotions and some basic mental categories are processed. The up-down tension results from the needful inhibiting processes of the neocor-

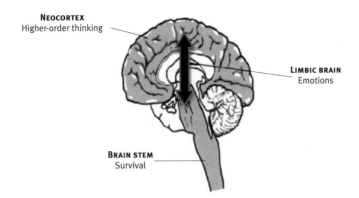

NEOCORTEX
Higher-order thinking

LIMBIC BRAIN
Emotions

BRAIN STEM
Survival

TOP-DOWN OPPONENT PROCESSES

tex acting upon the more rapid, powerful responses of the subcortical regions. Without the inhibition of the neocortex, the fast, powerful but less complex responses of the limbic region tend to overwhelm higher thinking, which is slower, requiring more conscious deliberation.

A critical part of the emotional, limbic brain is the small almond-shaped amygdala. The amygdala is the home of anxiety and fear. Fear is saying that something is wrong. Its job is to save our lives; not to provide nuanced accuracy. Research by neuroscientist Joseph Le Doux (1996) shows that the neocortex's neuronal messages are weaker and slower than the fast, powerful fear messages of the amygdala. So, fear and anger (often a response to fear) can easily overrule thinking; they really do shout louder when we feel threatened. Other studies show that under conditions of stress, the blood flow in the brain is sent preferentially away from the frontal cortex (the site of conscious reasoning and sense of individual selfhood) and toward the deeper parts of the brain, thus enabling faster, more automatic processing in response to threat, while our higher-order thinking goes somewhat "blank" (McGilchrist 2009).

In psychological studies, a recurring finding is that stress or fear states produce cognitive constriction; people are less able to think complexly. Peter Suedfeld and colleagues' empirical work in integrative complexity (2003; 2006) shows a clear relationship: when people undergo

169

long-term stress or perceive a threat to their important values, significant drops in integratively complex thinking (IC) follow. Low IC is hardly unusual: around 50 to 60 percent people measured in dozens of studies receive an IC score of around 1 (black-and-white thinking), suggesting floor effects to the coding system. Stress is not the only precursor for low IC (as measured by IC coding in the Baker-Brown et al. 1992 coding framework). Contexts where comparable and important values are not in tension simply don't require higher IC (Tetlock 1986). Nevertheless, threat or stress does make IC drop from the thinker's usual baseline, and this feature seems to link with the top-down opponent process.

It must be said that integrative complexity researchers themselves refrain from explaining *why* this drop occurs; they simply observe that IC does drop in response to stress or threat. They then observe the behaviors and real-world events that ensue (such as intergroup violence following a drop in IC). But it is not far-fetched to link the findings of integrative complexity research to the stress literature and recent imaging studies. These studies show that the brain stem and limbic (emotional) brain are particularly active in fear or stress states. The "emotional" limbic brain evolved to respond quickly and powerfully to perceived threats (Haidt 2006)—the fight/flight/freeze response that both mammals and modern humans exhibit. The limbic system works on very basic mental categories such as predator, mate, offspring, food, ingroup, and outgroup—categories pertinent to bonding, safety, and survival. The limbic region is not directly linked to the outside world through the five senses, nor is it able to distinguish past from present. The limbic brain cannot make qualified or complex distinctions the way our highly evolved thinking neocortex can; the real world "out there" is available only in a limited way. If the opponent tension is tipped away from the neocortex toward these deeper subcortical limbic regions, complex thinking is diminished.

A large body of research over four decades by Inglehart and Welzel

(2005; 2007) indicate that threat to traditional values is a widespread experience for people living in the globalized condition. Under the changes brought about by modernization and globalization, different cultures, traditional and postmodern, are rubbing shoulders in new and invasive ways. This research shows there are significant changes to value priorities brought about by modernization and globalization: traditional religious values change to secular rational values and survival values change to self-enhancement values (Inglehart and Welzel 2005). In response to this shift, people who feel their traditional worldview and values are under threat tend to retrench to a value monist position that conserves tradition and promotes the self-transcendence values of traditional cultures (the setting aside of personal enhancement in order to conform to social duties). This shift to a single value pole is evident in radical discourse. It has many adherents because of the way it protects people from the uncertainty states brought about by the competing value priorities between, for example, Western host (postmodern) and immigrant (traditional) cultures.

Intergroup conflict and misunderstanding can spiral upward in a series of mutually threatened perceptions and reactions; low IC afflicts both sides of most conflicts. Hormones and other long-acting chemicals released into the body during fear or anger can then return to the brain and lock it into that state. In this state, the radicalized binary message of "ingroup versus outgroup," "they are attacking us; we must attack them" makes sense to the hearer. Past and present are not distinguished by the limbic system; the Crusades are very much alive and present-day in the radical imagination, much to the surprise of Westerners who think it is "all in the past."

Further, radicalizers seek to cause stress in their hearers by presenting traumatizing images on the Internet: harrowing accounts of persecution of the ingroup or examples where the purity of values is threatened. Radicalizers seek out young people who are experiencing the stress of exclusion, bullying, or some other kind of "cognitive crack," which provides an entrée for their low IC radical message (Wik-torowicz 2005). It is unfortunate that negative stimuli has such power. Research in the Prospect Theory paradigm (Tversky and Kahneman 1981) shows that this bias is quite universal: increases in the domain of loss are evaluated as more costly and emotionally salient than equiv-alent increases in the domain of gain. Christopher Peterson and Mar-tin Seligman (2004) consider that the negative biases of the human brain arise from the pressures of evolution during the Pleistocene ice age. Natural selection favored human brains that were hyperalert and reactive to negative stimuli such as danger or loss under the hostile environmental conditions. This helps to explain the ease with which radicalizers find ready listeners among those undergoing some kind of stress, threat to values, or experience of injustice.

Given these arguments, we envision that a shift from neocortex to some degree of limbic dominance occurs within the process of radi-calization. Further, there is at least one known interaction that links top-down opponent processes to left hemisphere dominance. Imaging studies show that stress inhibits the spread of neuronal activity *exactly in the manner that favors the very tightly focused kind of attention that the left hemisphere specializes in*. So rather than activating the broad, holistic attention of the right hemisphere to the complexities of lived reality, stress and threat to values (with its impact on subcortical amyg-dala and limbic activity) predisposes people to the left brain's style of paying attention to the world. The shift to limbic functioning prompted by stress can intensify an already pervasive cultural preference for the left hemisphere's "take" on reality. However, the left hemisphere is also vital for protection from stress. In neuroimaging studies on the effects of meditation, amongst meditation "adepts" there is heightened activ-ity in the left pre-frontal cortex, which is linked to resilience to stress (Begley 2009). Interestingly, meditation is among the kinds of religious practices that radicalizers eschew. Stress, not its alleviation, is useful to radicalizers.

Front-Back Opponent Processes

The third major category of opponent processes in the brain seems to play a role in the more advanced stages of violent radicalization. Front-back opponent processes involve the inhibiting effects of the frontal lobes (that enable a sense of self) on the posterior cortex.

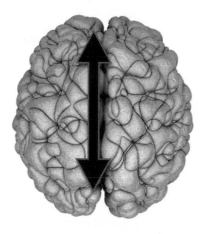

FRONT-BACK OPPONENT PROCESSES

Our sense of individual selfhood arose in evolution as both frontal lobes expanded and provided the necessary cognitive distance to observe the self as distinct, enabling humans to move beyond being fused with the social context or wider natural world. While both right and left frontal lobes confer the necessary distance to observe and perceive the self as distinct (and morally aware), it is the right frontal lobe that perceives the self in relation to others and perceives another's point of view. The right prefrontal cortex is the most highly evolved and most extensive of the two frontal lobes and concerns holistic thinking and awareness of self in relation to others. Part of the posterior cortex is the cerebellum, the most densely neuronally networked region of the human brain, with approximately one million times more processing power than the neocortex (Begley and Schwartz 2002). Here our automatic processing occurs, liberating conscious cognition from an otherwise huge overload so that it can be focused and deliberate. We are able to manage walking over uneven terrain while deep in conversation because walking is an automatic skill. Habitual behaviors are rapid and bypass consciousness. Addictive behaviors are similar, with a cocktail of processes pulling the individual away from conscious choice. The front-back opponent processes mean that, when slanted frontally, we have a modicum of moral "free will," identity, and empathy. If slanted toward the back, these diminish in favor of the vastly more powerful automatic processing of the hind brain, at least temporarily. The frontal lobes confer the ability for the self to be understood in relation to others and to know that others are real people—like ourselves. This can be thought of as another version of "heart knowing," which can be dulled by the pull of automatic behaviors and the powerful drive for release and pleasure.

Research and commentary linking cultural trends with front-back imaging studies seem to be at a more preliminary stage, so making links between the field of radicalization and the front-back tension is even more exploratory than what I have offered in the previous sections. Later stages of violent radicalization involve, according to terrorism studies, engagement with a totalist group (Crenshaw 2000)—a group that gains an almost "total" influence upon its members. Separation from wider society and deep personal ties (Ginges et al. 2011) is pivotal in violent radicalization. These sequestered conditions foster polarization toward the most extreme ingroup view (Fraser et al. 1971). In totalist groups, the group leader (usually male) earns the role of being leader *because* he exemplifies the most extreme position. The pressures to conform to group norms lead to more extreme views being adopted by its members, while separation from family and wider society means that sources of disconfirming evidence are cut off. It is not hard to adopt inflated views about the rightness of the ingroup (Janis 1982), followed by dehumanizing views toward the outgroup (Crenshaw 2000). From that point, normal moral barriers to killing can be overcome because those who are deemed enemies are "not really human anyway."

Immersion in a totalist group brings about de-individuation of its members, according to in-depth interviews carried out on failed terrorists (Crenshaw 2000). The individual's personal sense of identity and their usual sense of moral responsibility are eroded as the individual fuses with the group, becoming "one" with the group, while handing over moral responsibility to the leader. It must be said that an individual within an extremist group is likely to be immersed in a left hemisphere dominant milieu: ideologies are by nature word-based and geared to instrumental action. They are likely also to be tipped toward limbic, threat-driven overload: "the purity of our values are under threat!" In sum, the front-back shift described here in the context of extremisms probably occurs alongside shifts in the other two opponent processes (left-right and top-down) in an unanticipated but malign concatenation.

Admittedly, connecting the front-back axis of opponent processes with these latter stages of violent radicalization is a bit of a leap, although a great deal of initial radicalization happens over the Internet. There is growing concern about the de-individuating impact of communication technologies and IT on young people. Neuroscientist Susan Greenfield argues that young people's brains may be altered by their immersion in modern technology (2003), slanting front-back opponent processes toward the automatic hindbrain. The average young person spends 7.5 hours per day in front of a computer screen, while face-to-face social relationships are being replaced with "virtual" relationships. Increasingly violent and realistic video games are empirically linked to shorter attention spans, decreased communication skills, and a possible decrease in the sense of self. Video games are all about the task, and winning or achieving the goal releases a rewarding pleasure-burst of the neurochemical dopamine. Dopamine makes you feel good, but too much dopamine damages the prefrontal cortex, resulting in a limited ability to understand much beyond the immediate moment, along with a diminished sense of self and other. Seeking short-term rewards drives the brain to seek ever-stronger sensations; studies on Internet porn addiction indicate this tendency, along with shrinkage in the frontal cortex. In the virtual world of young people today, seeing life as a series of logical tasks that merely demand immediate action may be the result of extensive time spent on video games and on the Internet.

Though initial radicalization is known to often happen over the Internet, it is real people who are the entrée into violent extremism, as shown by Marc Sageman's (2004) study in which every known violent activist supporting or carrying out acts of terrorism in the United Kingdom was linked by social networks of friends, family, and acquaintances—networks that fostered and abetted their extremism. Ordinary young people today immersed in video games and social networking sites seem to take a less extreme pathway toward de-individuation in comparison with totalist groups, but both may be engendering a similar loss of a sense of self and relatedness to other people.

A surprising finding begins to make sense in the light of the front-back opponent processes. Prior to carrying out an attack, it is not unusual for terrorists to engage, not so much in prayer, but with Internet pornography sites. Researchers have been surprised to find these imbedded within or linked to radical sites. It is doubtful that this practice is explicitly encouraged within strict puritanical radical discourse itself. However, the emotional and social detachment, sensation blunting, and reward seeking that immersion in pornography sites produce are probably not at all deleterious to terrorists achieving their specified goals.

A connection to the top-down opponent process is also salient here. Social isolation is linked to strong amygdala responses to perceived threat. Whether from living in a virtual world, or through immersion in totalist groups entailing separation from wider society, research shows that social isolation leads toward exaggerated responses to perceived threats.

Even with the recent advances in neuroscience, the human brain remains a mystery. We must assume that along with the opponent processes mentioned here there are other processes yet unknown that may complexify the picture painted here. In the absence of greater knowledge, a full-blown pernicious cycle seems to be possible: social isolation and de-individuation (the front-back tension) links to the top-down tension via an increased response to threat. This top-down shift toward limbic functioning, away from complex neocortex functioning, restricts the spread of neuronal activity exactly in the manner of the left hemisphere's tight attentional focus. The shift to the defended left hemisphere means that the potential for the right hemisphere to offer up wider understanding, empathy, connection, larger perspective, and the ability to hold in tension opposing human values is lost.

Preventing Radicalization through Enhancing Integrative Complexity

While young people usually mature over time toward greater cognitive complexity, we think that most radical groups run contrary to this natural developmental pathway toward complexity and actively block the ability to find trade-offs to maximize more than one human value at a time. The binary, black and white structure of the radical narrative (whether Islamist, Christian fundamentalist, or sectarian) is maintained by the compelling draw of a potent moral value (such as justice for the oppressed community or purity in religion) to the exclusion of all other values that could be in tension with it (such as liberty or free speech). The structure of simplified thinking heightens "us versus them" hostilities, and this is maintained by excluding dissenters from the ingroup.

Research in persuasion shows that people who have a more complex view of the social world are not attracted to low IC, black-and-white messages. Having a more complex view of the world, we argue, protects against radicalizers' single-value, low IC message—as it is perceived as less convincing and less attractive. High IC helps people to resolve conflict and to see other people's viewpoints, while not sacrificing their own. Other options to solve problems become possible, and people do not need to resort to violence as the only way.

Based on these principles, we have developed a way of fostering complexity in values and thinking through our IC courses. We assess these interventions by measuring participants' integrative complexity, along with their spread of values, evidenced in their verbalizations, before and after the course. One such course is entitled *Being Muslim Being British* (Savage and Liht 2010), an eight-session prevention course designed to expose young participants (ages fifteen and older) to a range of different value priorities that influential Muslims embody, and to structure group activities that allow participants to experiment with taking different positions along value continuums, thus enabling them to explore all value positions on an issue, free from criticism or social pressure. After participating in the course, the statistically significant benchmarks observed in the group discussions before and after seven pilot courses are as follows. IC is raised from IC level 1 (seeing the world in black-and-white, "us versus them" as in extremist ideology) to IC level 3 (being able to perceive that other people's values and worldview have some validity, without having to sacrifice one's own important values). A greater range of values is evident: the extremist single value structure is overcome. People are able to balance values that are in tension rather than succumbing to the single-value structure of extremism. Conflict resolution style shifts significantly to win/win strategies (collaboration and compromise) and away from compete, accommodate, or avoid conflict styles (which can store up problems for the future and feed ongoing conflicts), evident in written moral dilemmas. Religious values increase, but they do so in a way that is "universalizing," that is, respecting the value of *all* human beings.

Given the arguments put forth so far, we think our IC model of prevention can be applied to a range of extremisms, as many will share the structural features described in this chapter. An *IC for Churches* course has been created and successfully assessed to address theological worldview clash, and other courses are under way: an adaptation of *Being Muslim Being British* for use in Pakistan, a new course to address sectarianism in Scotland, and an all-extremisms course (including right-wing and gangs) for schools in the United Kingdom is in the planning stage. IC courses such as these are designed for primary prevention—in other words, they are designed to reach the broadest population to protect from radicalization or worldview clash, before extreme "symptoms" are evident or advanced.

In our approach (Savage and Liht 2010), we assuage threat to values through using both "head" (rational, linear, word-based) and "heart" processing (a more holistic, implicit processing linked with emotions and bodily states). I stumbled upon the secret of using both head and heart ways of processing information several years ago when first piloting the raising of IC, working with bishops and senior clergy of differing theological orientations (Boyd-MacMillan, Savage, and Liht 2008). The bishops and clergy participating in our IC workshop showed complex thinking in regard to their own worldview, yet they remained "stuck" in their black-and-white thinking in regard to the "theological other." Every "head-centered" teaching strategy I tried in the workshop failed to get beyond this "stuckness." At that time I was ignorant of the insights coming from neuroscience that might have been relevant to this task, but I acted upon an intuition and invited the participants to get out of their seats and move slowly around the room "like monks in the cloister," hoping that changing participants' bodily states might spark a change in their cognition. A glimmer of improvement ensued, and this led to our eventual inclusion of activities that engage the right hemisphere, using Theater of the Oppressed–inspired pedagogy (using mime, movement, visual symbols, narrative, role-play, and drama, Boal 1998), as I explain next.

The first step in our method involves enabling people to perceive multiple perspectives on social, moral, and religious issues (the beginning of differentiation). We resource this step by showing filmed interviews of well-known speakers who present an array of competing viewpoints on "hot" topics often used by radicalizers to increase cleavage between, for example, Muslim and Western worldviews. In our *IC in Scotland* program (Boyd-MacMillan and Savage 2013), we enable differentiation on topics relevant to Protestant-Catholic conflict in a similar way. Each viewpoint is labeled in a neutral way and presented as a valid response to an important underlying question. To motivate the extra cognitive work, IC requires we create the conditions that encourage value pluralism. We abstract the viewpoints and plot these along a pertinent spectrum of values—such as economic justice versus economic freedom—each value pole having importance for human life (Tetlock et al. 1984).

This "laddering" down to explore the deep values underlying the viewpoints leads to the second step: the ability to embrace a wider array of values in one's moral reasoning (the second part of differentiation). While extremist ideologies concentrate, for example, on the magnetic pull of one value, such as "economic justice," to the exclusion of "economic freedom," we aim to enable young people in our courses to explore the "magnetic pull" of both ends of a value spectrum (e.g., justice *and* freedom), to discover where they feel most at home. Exploring a value spectrum involves understanding the dynamic, real-world tensions that are incurred in the outworking of both ends of the values spectrum. We have found that to enable greater specificity in thinking (to avoid black-and-white categorization) we encourage participants to "think with their bodies and emotions" (Williams et al. 2000). We do this by inviting them to physically explore all points along a value spectrum, laid out across the floor, and by standing in different positions, to imagine the pushes and pulls of the opposing values, in order to discover where they as individuals want to stand, and make their own value trade-offs. In this way, young people avoid threats to their own important values on the issues exploited by radicalizers, and thus avoid the cognitive constriction that results.

From here, the next step of IC becomes possible: the finding of linkages and higher-order syntheses of apparently opposing perspectives (the integration aspect of IC). Participants explore various integrations on an issue using role-play or mime. All this happens with the help of an IC-trained facilitator who protects participants from undue stress through leadership that protects boundaries and is free from criticism or judgment. As the learning experience moves back and forth between both "head" and "heart" processing, limbic overload leading to cognitive constriction and "stuckness" in the left brain are avoided. The right hemisphere is enabled to take in new information via the senses, felt values, and embodied knowing, and this feeds into the higher-order thinking of the neocortex, now resourced to expand beyond the left hemisphere's fixed "take" on social reality.

FACILITATING LEFT-RIGHT HEMISPHERE COMMUNICATION IN THE PREVENTION OF RADICALIZATION

Our experience of running IC courses suggests that integratively complex thought involves a back-and-forth interweaving of "head" and "heart" knowing. Communication between left and right hemispheres is also suggested by the robust and reliable coding frame developed to measure IC (Baker-Brown et al. 1992). Using this coding frame, IC coders measure changes in the two aspects of IC (the ability to differentiate and the ability to integrate). Most people start out with low IC: the social world is viewed through simple, black and white, clear-cut categories, seen from only one evaluative viewpoint (verbal data showing these features is coded as IC code 1). Black and white thinking indicates a left hemisphere concern with keeping categories clear-cut. An initial gain in IC is apparent through *implicit* references to more than one viewpoint (the beginning of differentiation, IC code 2). These hinted, intuited perceptions suggest a right hemisphere approach, with its broader, implicational focus. When these implicit perceptions become explicit, with a clear articulation of differentiation applied in a rulelike manner, a gain in IC is evident (code 3), suggesting a left hemisphere, clear-cut focus. Further gains in IC are seen in verbally implied linkages between the differentiated array (IC code 4), suggesting a broad right hemisphere focus. When those glimpses of linkages or integrating frameworks are made verbally explicit in a rulelike way (IC code 5), knowing seems now to have passed once again to the left hemisphere for organization and clear articulation. All this suggests a weaving back and forth between implicit and explicit ways of knowing as IC progresses toward greater complexity (with a maximum IC score of 7, Baker-Brown et al. 1992). McGilchrist (2009) similarly argues that with any cognitive processing there is a requisite passing back and forth of information from right to left hemispheres.

In all this, right hemisphere knowing is primary. In order to know anything at all, argues McGilchrist, the right brain has priority, as the right hemisphere first experiences and *presents* lived reality in all its particularities, ambiguity, emotions, relationships, and embodiment. The right hemisphere offers its way of paying attention to reality to the left hemisphere, which then *re-presents*, abstracts, and categorizes the right brain's implicit, gestaltlike knowing into a clear-cut conceptual system, which can be articulated and held in focused awareness for instrumental purposes (such as using an abacus, or landing on the moon). Far from requiring the silencing of the right hemisphere's implicit "heart" style of knowing in favor of the left hemisphere's explicit rational "head" knowing, McGilchrist (2009) argues that thinking requires both right and left hemispheres. IC would be no exception. The right hemisphere "gifts" the left hemisphere with its rich, networked, embodied presentation of reality. Without the left hemisphere's instrumental "grasp" of what the right hemisphere offers, we would not be able to make clear, reliable use of our knowing. The problem we face in modern culture is that the increased dominance and separation of the left hemisphere means that once the information is organized in the left hemisphere, we easily can get *stuck* in that hemisphere's defended, fixed conceptual system, and the optimal continued back and forth, right-left-right-left communication is curtailed. In Western contemporary culture, the left hemisphere tends to silence the foundational role the right hemisphere plays: after all, it is the left hemisphere (the more language-oriented of the two) that is the mouthpiece!

In our prevention model based on IC and values complexity, once differentiation is achieved (for example, in the value spectrum activities described above), we use embodied group activities such as role-play and mime to further explore various integrations of the differentiated viewpoints. The role-plays are designed to enable participants to try out different integrations until the participants are satisfied that their solution to a social problem is true to their own values, as well as "true to life." In doing this, all viewpoints are given consideration, even the extreme ones, but without having to sacrifice other competing values—which is required when people are expected to adopt *every aspect* of a radical position. For example, one activity involves participants evaluating two different modes of political decision making: one democratic (involving the value of self-direction) and the other religious, for example, under a Caliphate (involving the value of religious tradition and conformity to social roles). When first describing these two decisional methods verbally, no commonalities or ways of relating them was found by participants; they were seen as black-and-white oppositional contrasts. But when the participants created nonverbal mimes to exhibit both modes of decision making (and performed them for "a visiting Martian"), the mimes enabled participants to see with greater detail the areas of commonality between democratic and religious modes of decision making: more information became available through acting it out. From this kind of experiential learning, participants are able to reflect upon the tension between consensus and leadership present in both systems and to articulate what they have learned, freed from value monism and the social pressure arising from radical discourse that presents democracy and theocracy as completely alien to each other.

Another role-play explores the impact of the tension between communitarian versus individualist pressures, acted out in role-play in which different male suitors try to "sell" themselves to "Aisha," a potential bride, while other group members play Aisha's parents, family, and community/religious leaders who seek to influence her. The different roles allow the enacting of communitarian influences, pitted against Aisha and her friends who are arguing for individualism in regard to marriage choice. This activity is geared to enable participants to explore new ways to find integrations, middle-ground value trade-offs, in order to maximize, as the participants see fit, something of both communitarian and individualist values.

It seems that as participants engage in multiple level processing using movement, symbol, emotion, and social interaction, they move intuitively toward a sense of "gestalt" underlying the viewpoints in tension. Through the group activities, we draw on the body's implicit way of knowing. The mind needs the body for successful engagement with the world (Damasio 1999; Hohmann 1966), and body sensations help us to know what is important to us—our own and other's values. Bringing awareness to bodily sensations through group tasks that naturally use some "everyday" movement is effective at switching off the conceptual mode of mind with its tendency to categorize, rather than perceive the particulars (Watkins and Teasdale 2004). This helps with precision in thinking as it enables people to get beyond blunt black-and-white categorizations (a left hemisphere specialism) and to attend, in a more right brain way, with greater specificity to the complexity of the present (Williams et al. 2000). Thus the embodied activities provide a bridge to enable people to translate these intuitive glimpses into words (McMullin 2000) as they speak out their viewpoints in the role-plays.

Integrations between opposing viewpoints are achieved, according to studies in neuroscience, not primarily by arduous deliberate effort in the left hemisphere, but by a _discovery of the gestalt_ linking opposing ideas that already exists in the lower subcortical regions, even deeper than the limbic system, nearer to the brain stem. Neuronally linked to these deep regions, the right hemisphere does not experience opposing viewpoints as antithetical. The right hemisphere is able to tolerate multiple viewpoints, multiple causality, and multiple interpretations, and hence is an ally in the goal of developing IC.

The fact that this sensed "gestalt" is available to us only in an intuited way, via the right hemisphere, accords with research on creativity in both arts and sciences (Koestler 1989). This body of research suggests that the new insights needed to resolve incompatible paradigms are often *discovered*—aha!—after a long incubating struggle, rather than being achieved analytically, in a left brain way.

What I am suggesting occurs through our prevention model is a back-and-forth communication process between the hemispheres. I am not implying that a one-way reactionary swing to right brain processing alone would be helpful, as if tree-hugging or group encounter sessions alone could resolve our contemporary dilemmas. What is needed to resolve current value tensions in our globalized context is the back-and-forth movement between hemispheres—so that more integrated insights can be offered up to the left brain for clear articulation and testing against the constraints of reality. At the same time, the neocortex needs to be applying inhibition to the less complex categorizations of the limbic system. Together, these processes complement the activity of the right frontal lobe in maintaining a sense of self in relation to others.

As I have been arguing, it seems that integrative complexity (IC) requires this kind of synthesis between both head and heart ways of knowing. True, the right hemisphere is more densely neuronally linked with the emotional limbic system than the left hemisphere, but much of its work is to inhibit limbic arousal. What is salient for radicalization is the *kind* of emotional processing that is done. The emotions that the right hemisphere specializes in are sadness, empathy, and pity (which encourage perceiving another's perspective), whereas the left hemisphere specializes in anger and mood-inflation, along with competition to achieve instrumental goals. The capacity for the left pre-frontal cortex to promote resilience to stress may be excluded if meditational religious practices are eschewed, as they often are among extremist groups. Thinking and feeling are not mutually exclusive in either hemisphere. Thinking cannot proceed rationally without emotions, for emotions provide the *meaning* in regard to what is thought. From this, it seems that to foster integrative complexity it is important to avoid left hemisphere emotions (anger, inflation) while allowing right brain emotions, for example through activities in which participants need to identify with others as well as connect to their own deep values.

Conclusion

The brain is shaped by what we think and do (within the constraints of brain architecture). It is highly plastic: "use it or lose it" is its rule of thumb. I have been depicting the consequences of opponent processes slanting toward lack of complexity under stress, toward left brain defensiveness and toward de-individuation and moral disinhibition. The good news is that this potentially pernicious confluence, which I argue underpins extremism, can also move in directions that favor complex thinking, openness to the "other" and moral responsibility. If a long view of evolution is taken, complexity seems to be the direction of life. But, given current cultural trends, this may not be fulfilled unless we put much more energy into embedding complexity into our neural networks via a cultural evolution that enables balanced dialogue between various kinds of "head" and "heart" knowing that arises, I suggest, from a combination of these three opponent processes.

The rather sparse findings coming out of the flurry of radicalization and terrorism studies begins to make sense in the light of the opponent processes described in this chapter. Socioeconomic status does not distinguish who will turn to extremist violence nor does individual pathology. Far from terrorists being imported external enemies, most have had significant immersion in Western culture. Engineers are overrepresented in terrorist ranks, and most have had minimal if any religious background. Internet sites carry the message and provide images to blunt the sensibilities and promote a cognitive crack. Totalist groups complete the task of de-individuation and dehumanization of the outgroup. The neuronal substratum for violent radicalization is catered for, it seems, through small shifts in these three normal opponent processes.

In this light, I now draw a thumbnail sketch of the radicalized brain:

Top-Down

The journey starts with radical discourse with one moral value drawing thinking tightly around it—a means of protecting against threat to important values provoked by the context of globalization. Low complexity thinking with black and white contrasts and the limbic system's basic, primitive ingroup/outgroup categories provide ready confirmation of radical discourse. The limbic system's tendency to not distinguish past offences from present realities intensifies threat, and a drop to lower IC inhibits the spread of attention in the manner of left hemisphere specialism.

Right-Left

The radicalized brain prefers logical, linear, and abstract thinking within focused attention for instrumental purposes. It is adept at defending its self-contained system of thinking, perceiving only what it expects to perceive, and following its system's rules and its desires for certainty. It operates quite independently of the right brain's connection with emotions of sadness and pity and empathy with others. It eschews the wider context, sees things in isolation, apart from the embodied particularities of lived life. It is cut off from the right hemisphere's ability to discover a gestalt to weave together opposing views. It despises implicit, metaphoric, and multidimensional aspects of lived religion and seeks to replace those with precise meanings cast in words.

Front-Back

In the later stages of radicalization involving sequestration from wider society within a totalist extremist group or network, the radicalized brain is becoming fused with the group, de-individuated, losing a sense of self, and particularly a sense of self in relation to others (outside the ingroup). Detached from wider society, the ingroup is glorious and the hated outgroup is subhuman. In this small isolated world, a sense of threat increases; it is "them against us." The radicalized brain may find support for its socially and emotionally detached state through heavy Internet use, and to seek, not for patterns of meaning in life, but rather to achieve the next logical task in order to gain a dopamine blast of ultimate reward.

Can we test these ideas through brain imaging studies? It won't be easy. The more complex cognition is, the more likely it is that many regions of the brain will be involved. It is unlikely there will be an "IC" spot that conveniently lights up like a lightbulb. Even so, it is possible that carefully constructed studies could make some inch-by-inch progress to support some of the connections I have suggested.

To conclude, I have argued that the IC and values complexity framework outworked within group experiential learning helps to assuage threat to important values resulting in value monism, thus avoiding limbic dominance. Thinking complexly is further enabled when communication between right and left hemispheres is resourced, and when experienced in a group context where real people matter.

The implications of this foray into neuroscience leads me to think that the radicalized brain is perhaps different in degree from everyday thinking, but not in kind. Given the current cultural conditions, our everyday thinking probably undergoes the shifts described here pertaining to top-down, right-left, front-back opponent processes on a fairly regular basis. Most of us are quite stressed in work and in finances, if not in our relationships and worldview as well. We may calm our limbic responses with numbing or addictive behaviors, living habitually rather than deliberately and interpersonally. Isolated, we live and move in a left hemisphere–designed world, and in order to succeed, we develop the left hemisphere's style of defended, focused, instrumental thinking. All of us are pretty damn sure that *our* take on reality is correct. Competing viewpoints are screened out. What distinguishes our ordinary thinking from radicalized thinking is perhaps greater flexibility; we move in and out of these opponent shifts without getting stuck. Will that flexibility attenuate if it does not get regular exercise?

There is a need for new kinds of education to balance the left hemisphere style of knowing that Western education predominantly rewards and to return people to the domain of embodied, rather than virtual, human experience. Far from opportunistically pitting one particular way of knowing against the other, through our IC values interventions (admittedly a drop in a cultural ocean), we recognize the good in both Western secular and traditional religious worldviews and maintain that, in the absence of fear, an integration of head and heart ways of knowing holds the possibility of renewal and cross-fertilization for our globalized context.

Notes

1. http://www2.truman.edu/~edis/writings/articles/islamic

References

Armstrong, K. 2000. *The Battle for God*. New York: Alfred A. Knopf.

Baker-Brown, Gloria, Elizabeth J. Ballard, Susan Bluck, Brian De Vries, Peter Suedfeld, and Philip E. Tetlock. 1992. "The Conceptual/Integrative Complexity Scoring Manual." In *Motivation and Personality: Handbook of Thematic Content Analysis*, edited by C. P. Smith, J. W. Atkinson, D. C. McClelland, and J. Veroff, 401–18. Cambridge: Cambridge University Press.

Barr, J. 1981. *Fundamentalism*. 2nd ed. London: SCM Press.

Begley, S. 2009. *The Plastic Mind*. London: Constable.

Begley, S., and J. Schwartz. 2002. *The Mind and the Brain*. New York: HarperCollins.

Boal, A. 1998. *Legislative Theatre: Using Performance to Make Politics*. London: Routledge.

Boyd-MacMillan, E., and S. Savage. 2013. *I SEE! Life Skills for a Changing Scotland*. Multimedia course materials. Cambridge: IC Thinking, Cambridge Enterprise, University of Cambridge.

Boyd-Macmillan, E., S. Savage, and J. Liht. 2008. *Conflict Transformation among Senior Church Leaders with Differing Theological Stances*. London: Foundation for Church Leadership.

Crenshaw, M. 2000. "The Psychology of Terrorism: An Agenda for the 21st Century." *Political Psychology* 21:405–20.

Damasio, A. 1999. *The Feeling of What Happens: Body and Emotion in the Making of Consciousness*. London: Heinemann.

Eidelson, R. J., and J. I. Eidelson. 2003. "Dangerous Ideas: Five Beliefs That Propel Groups toward Conflict." *American Psychologist* 58:182–92.

Erickson, K. A., and H. A. Simon. 1984. *Protocol Analysis: Verbal Reports as Data*. Cambridge, MA: MIT Press.

Fraser, C., C. Gouge, and M. Billig. 1971. "Risky Shifts, Cautious Shifts and Group Polarization." *European Journal of Social Psychology* 1:7–30.

Gambetta, Diego, and Steffen Hertog. 2009. "Why Are There So Many Engineers Among Islamic Radicals?" *European Journal of Sociology* 50:201–30.

Ginges, J., S. Atran, S. Sachdeva, and D. Medin. 2011. "Psychology Out of the Laboratory: The Challenge of Violent Extremism." *American Psychologist* 66:507–19.

Greenfield, Susan. 2003. *Tomorrow's People: How 21st Century Technology Is Changing the Way We Think and Feel*. London: Allen Lane.

Greenwald, A. G. 1980. "The Totalitarian Ego: Fabrication and Revision in Personal History." *American Psychologist* 35:603–18.

Guttieri, K., M. D. Wallace, and P. Suedfeld. 1995. "The Integrative Complexity of American Decision Makers in the Cuban Missile Crisis." *The Journal of Conflict Resolution* 39:595–621.

Haidt, J. 2006. *The Happiness Hypothesis*. London: Arrow Books.

Harris, H. A. 1998. *Fundamentalism and Evangelicals*. New York: Clarendon Press.

Herek, G. M., I. L. Janis, and P. Huth. 1987. "Decision Making During International Crises: Is Quality of Process Related to Outcome?" *Journal of Conflict Resolution* 31:203–26.

Hohmann, G. W. 1966. "Some Effects of Spinal Cord Lesions on Experienced Emotional Feelings." *Psychophysiology* 3:143–56.

Hood, R. W., P. C. Hill, and W. P. Williamson. 2005. *The Psychology of Religious Fundamentalism*. New York: Guilford Press.

Inglehart, R., and C. Welzel. 2005. *Modernization, Cultural Change, and Democracy: The Human Development Sequence*. New York: Cambridge University Press.

———. 2007. "Modernization, Cultural Change, and Democracy: The Human Development Sequence." *American Journal of Sociology* 112:1248–50.

Janis, I. L. 1982. *Groupthink: Psychological Studies of Policy Decisions and Fiascos.* Boston: Houghton Mifflin.

Kirkpatrick, Lee A., Ralph W. Hood, and Gary Hartz. 1991. "Fundamentalist Religion Conceptualized in Terms of Rokeach's Theory of the Open and Closed Mind: New Perspectives on Some Old Ideas." *Research in the Social Scientific Study of Religion* 3:157–59.

Koestler, Arthur. 1989. *The Act of Creation*, London: Penguin.

Le Doux, J. E. 1996. *The Emotional Brain: The Mysterious Underpinnings of Emotional Life.* New York: Simon and Schuster.

Liht, J., S. Savage, and R. Williamson. 2012. "Being Muslim Being British: A Multimedia Educational Resource for Young Muslims." In *Islamist Radicalisation in Europe and the Middle East: Reassessing the Causes of Terrorism,* edited by G. Joffe, 34–57. London: IB Tauris.

Liht, J., and S. Savage. Forthcoming. "Preventing Violent Extremism Through Value Complexity: Empirical Assessment of 'Being Muslim Being British.'" *Journal of Strategic Security.*

Lipton, B. 2005. *The Biology of Belief.* London: Hay House.

Marty, M. E., and R. S. Appleby. 1995. *Fundamentalisms Comprehended.* Chicago: University of Chicago Press.

McGilchrist, I. 2009. *The Master and His Emissary: The Divided Brain and the Making of Western Culture.* London: Yale University Press.

McMullin, R. E. 2000. *The New Handbook of Cognitive Therapy Techniques.* New York: Norton and Company.

Norris, P., and R. Inglehart. 2004. *Sacred and Secular: Religion and Politics Worldwide.* New York: Cambridge University Press.

Pascual-Leone, Alvaro. 2001. "The Brain That Plays Music and Is Changed by It." *Annals New York Academy of Sciences* 930:315–29.

Peterson, C., and M. E. P. Seligman. 2004. *Character Strengths and Virtues: A Handbook and Classification.* Oxford: Oxford University Press.

Rokeach, Milton. 1960. *The Open and Closed Mind: Investigations into the Nature of Belief Systems and Personality Systems.* New York: Basic Books.

Sageman, Marc. 2004. *Understanding Terror Networks.* Philadelphia, PA: University of Pennsylvania Press.

Savage, S. 2008. "Towards Integrative Solutions to Moral Disputes between Conservative and Liberal Christians." *The Journal of Psychology and Christianity* 27:320–28.

Savage, S., and J. Liht. 2008. "Radical Religious Speech: How to Assemble the Ingredients of a Binary World View." In *Extreme Speech and Democracy*, edited by I. Hare and J. Weinstein, 488–507. Oxford: Oxford University Press.

Savage, S., and J. Liht. 2010. *Being Muslim Being British: A Multimedia Course for Young Muslims*. Cambridge: University of Cambridge.

Savage, S., J. Liht, and R. Williams. 2011. "Being Muslim Being British: Preventing Extremist Violence through Raising Integrative Complexity." In *Global Security: A Vision for the Future*, edited by M. Sharpe and F. Gere, 80–94. Amsterdam: IOS Press.

Shepherd, W. 1987. "Fundamentalism: Christian and Islamic." *Religion* 17:355–78.

Sløk, J. 1996. *Devotional Language*. Berlin: W. de Gruyter.

Suedfeld, Peter, K. Guttieri, and Philip E. Tetlock. 2003. "Assessing Integrative Complexity at a Distance: Archival Analyses of Thinking and Decision Making." In *The Psychological Assessment of Political Leaders: With Profiles of Saddam Hussein and Bill Clinton*, edited by J. M. Post, 246–72. Ann Arbor: University of Michigan Press.

Suedfeld, Peter, and Dana C. Leighton. 2002. "Early Communications in the War against Terrorism: An Integrative Complexity Analysis." *Political Psychology* 23:585–99.

Suedfeld, Peter, Dana C. Leighton, and Lucian G. Conway. 2006. "Integrative Complexity and Cognitive Management in International Confrontations: Research and Potential Applications." In *The Psychology of Resolving Global Conflicts: From War to Peace, Vol. 1*, edited by M. Fitzduff and C. E. Stout, 211-37. New York: Praeger.

Suedfeld, Peter, and Philip Tetlock. 1977. "Integrative Complexity of Communications in International Crises." *The Journal of Conflict Resolution* 21:169–84.

Suedfeld, Peter, and Alistair B. C. Wallbaum. 1992. "Modifying Integrative Complexity in Political Thought: Value Conflict and Audience Disagreement." *Interamerican Journal of Psychology* 26:19–36.

Tetlock, Philip. 1984. "Cognitive Style and Political Belief Systems in the British House of Commons." *Journal of Personality and Social Psychology* 46:365–75.

———. 1986. "A Value Pluralism Model of Ideological Reasoning." *Journal of Personality and Social Psychology* 50:819–27.

———. 2003. "Thinking the Unthinkable: Sacred Values and Taboo Cognitions." *Trends in Cognitive Sciences* 7:320–24.

Tetlock, Philip, Orie Kristel, S. Beth Elson, and Jennifer S. Lerner. 2000. "The Psychology of the Unthinkable: Taboo Trade-offs, Forbidden Base Rates, and Heretical Counterfactuals." *Journal of Personality and Social Psychology* 78:853–79.

Tetlock, Philip, Jennifer S. Lerner, and R. Peterson. 1996. "Revising the Value Pluralism Model: Incorporating Social Context." In *The Psychology of Values*, edited by C. Seligman, J. M. Olson and M. P. Zanna, 25–51. Mahwah, NJ: Lawrence Erlbaum.

Tetlock, Philip E., and Anthony Tyler. 1996. "Churchill's Cognitive and Rhetorical Style: The Debates over Nazi Intentions and Self-Government for India." *Political Psychology* 17:149–70.

Tversky, A., and D. Kahneman. 1981. "The Framing of Decisions and the Psychology of Choice." *Science* 211:453–58.

Watkins, E., and J. D. Teasdale. 2004. "Adaptive and Maladaptive Self-focus in Depression. *Journal of Affective Disorders* 82:1–8.

Wiktorowicz, Q. 2005. *Radical Islam Rising: Muslim Extremism in the West.* Oxford: Rowman and Littlefield.

Williams, J. M. G., J. D. Teasdale, Z. V. Segal, and J. Soulsby. 2000. "Mindfulness-Based Cognitive Therapy Reduces Overgeneral Autobiographical Memory in Formerly Depressed Patients." *Journal of Abnormal Psychology* 109:150–55.

O

Head God and Heart God   7

Pastoral Work to Help Clients Overcome Harmful God Images

GLENDON L. MORIARTY

Clergy, pastoral counselors, and mental health professionals often hear clients discuss differences between their head understanding of God and their heart understanding of God. These clients report discrepancies between what they intellectually believe about God and how they emotionally experience God. In the Christian faith, for example, clients commonly report believing in a God that is close and forgiving. However, it is not uncommon for these same clients to report experiencing God as distant and unforgiving. They may believe in the concept of grace, yet still feel like they have to earn God's approval. Broadly, these differences between head and heart understandings of God are known as God images and God concepts. God images are the personal, emotional, and relational understandings of God, whereas God concepts are the abstract, intellectual, and theological understandings of God. Psychodynamic, object relations, and attachment theories have provided rich descriptions of how these differences develop. Research has also highlighted factors that contribute to God image development, including self-esteem, primary caregivers, religious doctrine, and culture. Additionally, several studies have shown that God images can shift through the therapeutic process. This chapter will begin by reviewing theory and research on God image development and change. Next, easy-to-use pastoral assessment tools will be shared to help counselors differentiate between head and heart understandings of God. Finally, a number of practical techniques and exercises will be discussed to help the reader shift away harmful God images.

HEAD GOD AND HEART GOD: PASTORAL WORK TO HELP CLIENTS OVERCOME HARMFUL GOD IMAGES

Martin Avery is a forty-two-year-old Caucasian male. He graduated with a master of divinity from Princeton Theological Seminary when he was twenty-five years old. He has been pastoring for over seventeen years—first as an assistant and now as a senior clergyperson. He conducts careful word studies and works deliberately on his sermons on a weekly basis. Martin has been teaching on the central tenets of the Christian faith for years and thoroughly understands the key concepts of forgiveness and grace. Martin has a very deep, comprehensive, and systematic understanding of the Christian God. There is one big problem, however: Martin does not believe that God *likes* him.

Martin is Presbyterian and identifies as evangelical. He has always believed in having a personal relationship with God. He feels that God is a fundamentally relational being as illustrated in the Trinity. Martin, however, does not feel like God is particularly interested in having a relationship with him. This sense has nagged Martin since he first came to the faith. Despite years of careful study and prayer, his emotional experience of God has only shifted slightly. Martin *knows* that God is gracious, but Martin *feels* like he has to earn God's approval. He *knows* God has forgiven him, but he *feels* like God is upset with him for falling short.

- Why does Martin have these two experiences of God?
- Why hasn't Martin's theological work significantly impacted his emotional experience of God?
- Can Martin learn to emotionally experience God's grace and forgiveness?

This chapter aims to answer these questions. We will begin by first defining the cognitive and the emotional, or the head and the heart, ways of understanding God. Next, we will discuss the history and research behind these ways of experiencing God. Third, we will turn our attention to psychological research that highlights some of the main ingredients that go into impacting our relational, emotional, and personal understandings of God. Finally, we will discuss how the heart understanding of God can be shifted to more accurately reflect a person's faith. We will review a practical assessment tool and psychological techniques that can help the reader learn how to shift harmful emotional understandings of God.[2]

Understanding Head and Heart Experiences of God

Martin's experience is not all that uncommon. Many people who believe in a personal God experience a gap between what they cognitively believe about God and what they emotionally experience in their relationship with God. Nicholas Gibson tells a story about a pastor asking his congregation to raise their hand if they feel like God loves them. Every hand in the church shot up. Next, the pastor asked his congregation to raise a hand if they felt like God *liked* them. Only two or three hands were raised. Like Martin, some people believe in God and attribute many wonderful characteristics to God, but experience God in a manner that is contrary to what they theologically believe about God. Why does this occur?

Broadly, this difference between cognitive and emotional understandings of God exists because people have two main ways of understanding God, which we may characterize here as head understanding and heart understanding. For the purposes of this chapter, I take these two understandings to broadly parallel the differences between the rational/explicit cognitive system and the affective/implicit emotional system outlined in detail throughout this text. With that said, the differences between heart and head understandings of God should not be overstated. We are still in the beginning stages of comprehending these differences and there is some overlap between the two.

Let us first begin by defining God concepts. God concepts are the intellectual, theological, abstract understandings of God (Richards and Bergin 1997; Rizzuto, 1979). One can think of God concepts as primarily consisting of the content, or the "what," of a person's understanding of God. God concepts are informed by religious instruction, books, devotionals, sermons, Sunday school, or catechism. They are mostly comprised of doctrinal content. Davis, Moriarty, and Mauch (2013) further suggest that God concepts are processed by the rational-information system that Epstein (1994) calls the cold cognitive system. This rational system is very slow, conscious, language-based, deliberate, and left-hemispheric (Garzon 2007; Gibson 2006; Metcalfe and Jacobs 1998; Siegel 2010; 2012). When thinking about God concepts, think about listening to a lecture or sermon on God's characteristics. Think about the slow and reflective—oftentimes arduous process—of better understanding a theological construct. In short, God concepts are the head understandings of God.

God images, on the other hand, are the personal, emotional, immediate understandings of God (Hall 2004; Richards and Bergin 1997; Rizzuto 1979). They activate the relational system, or attachment system, that the person utilizes in their relationships with significant others, like parents, spouses, and good friends. These relational patterns are learned through early relationships with parents and help the person learn to predict how other people will respond to them. This relational "software" or program becomes automatic and unconscious. God images activate these earlier learned patterns (Badenoch 2008; Davis 2010; Noffke and Hall 2007).

An illustrative example highlighting the differences between God concepts and God images can be found in the ways that some evangelical Christians report experiencing God after sinning or behaving in a manner they regret (Moriarty 2009). They often report feeling like God is angry, distant, or mad at them (God images), even though their theology suggests that God remains close and loving (God concepts). They can report feeling like God is distant and like they have to earn God's approval again. This seems to echo how they experienced their parents in that they report having had to win back their parents' love and acceptance after behaving in a manner that they regret.

Davis, Moriarty, and Mauch (2013) further contrast God images with God concepts. Whereas God concepts are slow, conscious, explicit, and left hemisphere based, God images are quick, largely unconscious, implicit, and right hemisphere based (cf. Bargh and Williams 2006; Chartrand and Bargh 1996; Davis 2010; Gibson 2006; Hall et al. 2005; Horowitz 1991; cf. Kihlstrom 2008). They utilize the emotional-experiential information-processing or what Epstein (1994) calls the hot emotional system. Gibson (2007) has suggested that people have a number of different God images. The particular God image that is activated at any one time will differ based on the internal and external characteristics of the situation. In short, God images are a person's heart understandings of God.

History and Research

Freud was the first person within psychology to conceptualize what would later be known as God images. Freud's work is well known. He put forth the projection hypothesis, which suggested that God is a type of psychological crutch to help people cope. In his words:

> A personal God is, psychologically, nothing other than an exalted father. Biologically speaking, religiousness is to be traced to the small human child's long-drawn-out helplessness and need of help; and when at a later date he perceives how truly forlorn and weak he is when confronted with the great forces of life, he feels his condition as he did in childhood, and attempts to deny his own despondency by a regressive revival of the forces which protected his infancy. (Freud 1910)

Freud made many other observations about religious individuals that are now seen as less relevant. The core idea, however, that the emotional idea of God is a religious projection that shifts along with the person's self remains very relevant.

Several object relations theorists expanded upon Freud's work. Object relations therapists focus on a person's early childhood relationships with their parents. The gist is that early parent relationships are brought inside and people learn to treat themselves as their parents first treated them. For example, if your parents were highly critical, then you will tend to be highly critical of yourself. Contemporary cognitive behavioral therapists call this self-talk. Essentially, everyone has an internal intercom system that is continuously commenting on their experiences and relationships. Object relations therapists agree with this, but trace these internal—and unconscious voices—to a person's early experience of their parents.

Whereas Freud saw religion as primarily unhelpful and neurotic, these theorists saw religion as helpful and healing. Ian Suttie (1935) saw religion as psychotherapeutic. Harold Guntrip (1956) viewed religion as a cure for harmful early relationships and poor object relations: "Religion has always stood for the saving power of the good object relationship [by providing] a God, a Saviour, and a Church . . . to whom the anxious soul can fly for refuge and salvation" (as cited in Wulff 1997). Perhaps the greatest contribution, however, came from D. W. Winnicott.

Winnicott (1971; 1975) introduced the idea of transitional space, which is the space between the inside world and the outside world. Transitional objects exist in the external world and can be verified by other people; however, they have internal meaning that the person imbues upon them. We might look at a piece of art together. The piece of art exists in the outside world; however, the internal meaning of that piece of art will be different for you and me. Similarly, God is a type of transitional object (Jones 1991; Rizzuto 1979). The idea of God exists in the external world, but individuals experience God in different ways.

Rizzuto (1979) leveraged Winnicott's work and reconceptualized Freud's classic psychoanalytic way of looking at God through object relations theory. She also drew from Erik Erikson and outlined how God images shift through life transitions. Like Freud, Rizzuto focused primarily on early childhood relationships with caregivers. Parents primarily inform the material that the child uses to construct their God images. Parents are, after all, godlike in that they are idealized by young children. In the very early years, children determine whether the world is safe. This helps them develop a sense of trust. If their needs are met and they are loved, then they conclude that the world is a safe place. This basic process gets mapped over onto God. God is safe. Next, children begin to differentiate from their parents. If parents are secure, then the child can become their own person. If the parents are insecure, then the child will limit impulses to explore and differentiate and instead invest energy in taking care of the parent. Similarly, God will later be experienced as secure and affirming or as insecure and needy. The individual's relationship with God continues to evolve with their emerging personality. Puberty, early adulthood, and middle age all impact the person's emotional experience of God; however, the early years are much more impactful than the later years. The above summary does not do justice to her work and the interested reader should review *The Birth of the Living God* (1979) for additional details.

Early theory building was primarily based on case study material. Research on God images then gradually began to shift to more sophisticated methods. Initial studies focused on which parent was the most influential in informing God image characteristics. Freud suggested that the father was the only model and that the mother had no influence. The current consensus is that God images are informed by both the mother and the father (Birky and Ball 1988; Dickie et al. 1997). Another interesting finding is that God images are related to self-esteem (Buri and Mueller 1993). Benson and Spilka (1973) used cognitive consistency theory to highlight their findings. Basically, if a person feels positive about themselves, then they will likely feel that

God feels positive about them as well. If a person has low self-esteem, then it is more likely that they will experience God as less positive. Stated another way, positive self-esteem is related to experiencing God as loving and nurturing, whereas low self-esteem is related to experiencing God as more controlling and punishing. Individuals with more mature object relations tend to have healthier God images and those with less mature object relations tend to have unhealthier God images (Brokaw and Edwards 1994).

This brief review of the theoretical history and main findings in the early research converge with more recent efforts in understanding God images through attachment theory. Attachment theory was created by John Bowlby (1969/1982; 1973; 1980). He drew from ethology, evolutionary biology, and control systems theory to better understand how human infants attach or bond to their caregivers. Bowlby observed that infants have a hardwired attachment system that helps the infant maintain a close proximity to the parent. He hypothesized that this system is ultimately adaptive because it helps the infant survive internal and external dangers. Strangers, predators, and loud noises are all external triggers that send the infant to the parent. Internal dangers include exhaustion, sickness, and anxiety. These internal and external dangers trigger the attachment system, which causes the infant to cry, lift hands, or cling to the parent. Once a feeling of security is reestablished, the infant can then move out and explore their environment again. Adults also have an attachment system. It is not triggered by the same dangers that trigger an infant's attachment system, but it is triggered. When a person is going through a challenging time, they do not lift their hands up and ask to be held. Instead, they share what is happening with another person and the other person soothes them with their words—much like a parent would soothe an infant with a hug.

Mary Ainsworth and others also observed different attachment styles or patterns (Bretherton 1992). There are four primary types, but they can most easily be understood in terms of either secure attachment or insecure attachment. Securely attached people feel like they can trust and rely upon others. Insecurely attached people do not feel like they can trust and rely upon others.

Kirkpatrick (2005) was one of the first people to observe that God is an attachment figure. Individuals with a personal relationship with God tend to maintain proximity to God much like an infant maintains proximity to a parent. God is omnipresent and always available just as a parent is to a young child. Additionally, God can be a haven of safety in which people turn to God during challenging times. Finally, God can be a secure base. Just as an infant gets "fueled up" by being held by a caregiver, believers can get fueled up by spending time in prayer or communion with God.

There has been a significant amount of research conducted on God images and attachment. Four different ways of conceptualizing attachment to God have emerged from the research (Davis 2010; Moriarty and Davis 2012). Here we will discuss the most relevant models. The first is the internal-working-model correspondence hypothesis (Kirkpatrick 1992; Kirkpatrick and Shaver 1992), which suggests that the attachment style the person learned with their caregivers parallels the attachment style they have with God. Insecure attachment to parents corresponds to insecure attachment style with God. The next is the emotional compensation hypothesis, which states that the person has an insecure attachment with their caregivers, but compensates for this lack of care with a secure attachment to God. Through this lens, God is a type of parent surrogate. A third is the implicit-relational-knowledge correspondence hypothesis (Hall 2004; Hall et al. 2005). This latter hypothesis helps to address some of the seeming inconsistencies between the internal-working-model correspondence and the emotional compensation hypothesis. How can an insecure attachment pattern with caregivers result in both an insecure attachment with God (correspondence) and a secure relationship with God (compensation)? This model suggests that insecurely attached individuals that report a secure relationship with God are actually insecurely attached. They report feeling close and connected to God and engage in a number of religious practices; however, under the surface, these practices are motivated out of an insecure attachment. For example, they participate in regular prayer, but do so out of fear that God would abandon them if they were not consistent in their prayer times. Explicitly they look securely attached, but when you dig a bit deeper you see that they are actually insecurely attached.

SHIFTING GOD IMAGES

Now that we have outlined the history, theory, and research support-ing God images, let us turn our attention to ways to shift God images from being harmful to being helpful. This section will briefly high-light some of the research that has illustrated how God images can be shifted through psychotherapy. Next, we will discuss practical assess-ment exercises that can be used to better understand a client's God images. Third, we will explore pragmatic techniques that can be used to change God images.

There are three primary studies that outline ways that God images can shift. Tisdale and colleagues (1997) worked with depressed patients in an evangelical inpatient setting. The patients regularly participated in religiously oriented dynamic group psychotherapy over the course of time in treatment. On a number of instruments, patients reported experiencing significant shifts in God images so that their experience of God was more loving, close, present, and accepting. Thomas, Moriarty, Davis, and Anderson (2011) facilitated a group psychotherapy program utilizing a variety of interventions with an outpatient sample of twenty-six patients. Group participants reported significantly less insecure attachment to God and reported experiencing God as more accept-ing, intimate, and supportive and less distant, harsh, and disapproving. A third study by Cheston et al. (2003) assessed God image change via individual outpatient therapy. They found that patients reported experiencing God in a more positive and agreeable fashion. An inter-esting note about this study is that the content of the therapy was not necessarily religiously oriented. This suggests that common healing factors employed in psychotherapy can shift God images whether God is explicitly mentioned or not (Moriarty and Davis 2012).

Assessing God images can be a complex process that utilizes a variety of interviews and different tests. For our purposes, the goal is to keep things practical and easy to implement. When working with a client, it is important to keep in mind that, almost by default, clients will answer questions about their emotional experience of God in a way that taps their God concepts or intellectual understandings of God. Clients often do this because there are "right" ways of talking about how you experience God. Despite many people having problematic God images, it is not something that many people have language for and it is not a common topic, so people can sometimes feel ashamed admitting that they experience God in ways that are inconsistent with the nature of their faith. One way to overcome this cognitive bias is to start the assessment process off with the Draw God assessment exercise (Moriarty 2006). This tool requires a pencil or pen and three pieces of paper. Moriarty and Davis (2012) outline the administrative steps:

1. Give the client the first piece of paper and instruct him or her: "Please draw a picture of you and God." Once this first drawing is completed, move on to step 2.

2. Give the client the second piece of paper and instruct him or her: "On this piece of paper, draw a picture of how you FEEL that you and God look when you do something wrong. Draw what you feel, not what you think."

3. When the client is done with the second drawing, ask him or her: (a) "How do you feel?" (b) How does God feel?" (c) "How close or distant do you feel from God, on a scale of 1 to 10, with 1 being very close and 10 being very distant?" and (d) "If you feel distant from God, what usually happens or has to happen for you to feel close to God again?"

4. After you have processed the second picture with the client, present the third piece of paper and instruct him or her:

"Draw a picture of how you WOULD LIKE TO FEEL you and God look when you do something wrong. Again, draw how you would honestly like to feel, not necessarily how you think you should feel." Then process this drawing.

The first picture typically taps God concepts, whereas the second picture usually taps God images. The second picture can be used to help clients specifically process how their caregivers or parents might have treated them. The question of how you *feel* when you have done something wrong can be particularly helpful in triggering emotional schemas around discipline and parenting issues. This can help clients gain insight into how their parents may have impacted their emotional experience of God.

Another easy-to-use tool simply provides a number of adjectives (loving, kind, distant, harsh) and asks clients to rate how frequently they experienced their mother and father or their caregivers in this way (Moriarty 2006). Once they have their mother and father rated, they are then asked how often they experience God on those same characteristics. A final step overlaps the rating for the mother with the God rating, and does the same with the father rating, so that the client can see what specific attributes were mapped onto God from their parents.

There are a variety of interviews, qualitative tests, and quantitative instruments that can be utilized to comprehensively address God images. The interested reader is referred to Gibson (2007) and Moriarty and Davis (2012) for a thorough review and criticism of these different ways of assessing God images.

Once you have interviewed the client and conducted a basic assessment of God images, you are in a better position to assess whether their emotional experience of God is a salient piece of their overall presentation. Some religious clients will present for spiritual direction, pastoral counseling, or traditional therapy with specific God image struggles. They will report feeling like God is distant, out to get them, or absent. They will not use God concepts/God images language, but they will highlight the gap between their professed or explicit theology and their operational or implicit theology (Jordan 1986). Other clients will report psychological symptoms that are impacting or influencing their emotional experience of God. For example, people who are depressed often report feeling negative about themselves, others, and the future. Their depression colors how they experience the world around them. Some people who are religious and depressed will similarly report experiencing God in less positive ways (Yarborough, Gibson, and Moriarty 2009). That is, their psychological issues may result in clinically significant religious impairment, which Hathaway defines as "a reduced ability to perform religious activities, achieve religious goals, or to experience religious states, due to a psychological disorder" (2003, 114). Just as a clinician would address occupational issues to help a person overcome depression, that same clinician might address God image issues to help a client overcome depression.

If you determine that God images are a salient issue to address in your work with the client, then there are several ethical issues that you should also keep in mind. Tan (2003) has outlined these in detail. First, you do not want to focus on God image issues when there are other more pressing matters. That is, it would be unethical to focus on God image issues in the middle of a crisis. Second, you want to be careful to respect where clients are coming from and not impose your own beliefs on the client. Theological debates are not terribly helpful in a counseling context. Third, you want to be sure to practice within the boundaries of your competence. Competence is broadly understood as an area where you have received both coursework and supervision. With the assessment conducted and these ethical issues in mind, you are now ready to begin to work with clients to therapeutically address harmful God images.

There have been a number of theoretical orientations and techniques used to shift God images (Moriarty and Davis 2012; Moriarty and Hoffman 2007). Psychodynamic, cognitive-behavioral, narrative, and experiential techniques have all been researched and shown to be helpful in shifting God images (Cheston et al. 2003; Thomas and Moriarty 2009;

Tisdale et al. 1997). This broad support is consistent with the trend toward psychotherapy integration (Norcross 2002). What the research on integration suggests is that there are common factors shared across orientations that are helpful in addressing issues. Additionally, there are discrete disorders that are best addressed with a specific orientation or a subset of techniques. For example, I might primarily conceptualize the world through a psychodynamic lens, but choose to use cognitive-behavioral therapy (CBT) to help a client struggling with generalized anxiety or panic disorder. I would choose CBT in this instance because it has been shown to be more helpful with these disorders. We are still at the very early stages of understanding how to shift God images, so we do not know exactly what orientations are the most helpful for shifting specific God image problems (Moriarty, Thomas, and Allmond 2008). However, we can look to the broader trends in the literature to inform which God image techniques might be the most helpful. In general, if the client presents with long-term relational issues, then dynamic or interpersonal interventions might be more helpful. If a client reports less ingrained issues that seem more episodic or situational, then cognitive-behavioral interventions might be more prominent. As with all forms of therapy, the heart of the work comes down to the therapeutic alliance with the client, which allows you to ask for feedback and tailor the interventions to best help the client. With this understanding in mind, we will now highlight several interventions that have been found to be helpful.

Psychodynamic or interpersonal interventions primarily focus on the therapeutic relationship with the client (Greenberg and Mitchell 1983). In general, this approach is best for people with long-standing relational challenges (Levenson 1995; Strupp and Binder 1984). For example, imagine a person who has dependent characteristics. These people are sometimes popularly referred to as "people pleasers." They are very astute at making other people feel comfortable by conforming themselves to others' expectations. The focus in therapy is on helping the client learn to experience themselves and the therapist in a new and healthier manner. The therapy relationship is seen as a microcosm of their normal life. The client unwittingly recreates their problems with the therapist. The person who struggles with long-term dependency experiences themselves as weak and unable to make decisions. Other people tend to respond to them by treating them like they are weak, telling them what to do, and making decisions for them. They unconsciously set up a relational pattern or cyclical maladaptive pattern where they present as weak and pull on others to tell them what to do (Levenson 1995). This person will come to therapy and act out this same pattern with the therapist. The therapist will experience them as vulnerable and clingy. The therapist will be pulled into treating them like they are weak and respond by being overly assertive toward the client. The therapist, unconsciously, has been *hooked* into acting out the same relational pattern with the client that the client acts out with others outside of therapy (Levenson 1995). The goal of therapy is to get "unhooked" and provide the client with a new experience and understanding. Toward this end, the therapist must become aware of the hook and then act in ways that counter the cyclical maladaptive pattern. For example, in this instance, using a variety of dynamic interventions, the therapist would help the client see that this pattern occurs and that a new pattern can be developed. The client can learn to express their real needs to other people and other people will respond in a respectful and validating manner.

One key psychodynamic intervention utilized to create awareness and change is interpretation. Strength (1998) built upon Davanloo's triangle of person to illustrate how a person's relationship with God can follow the same patterns found in past, present, and therapeutic relationships. The goal of the interpretation is to connect the four corners of the square to help the client see how the same pattern manifests across relationships. A therapist might say to the person struggling with dependency issues:

When I hear about your experience of your mother (past relationship), it seems you had to be perfect in order to win her love. Similarly, when you talk about your wife (present relationship), it sometimes seems that you have to work very hard to make her happy. You don't seem comfortable being authentic with her about your real needs. What I see happening in here (therapy relationship) is that you seem afraid that I might also become unhappy with you if you are not the perfect client. I sometimes wish you could be more forthright about what you are thinking and feeling. I'm also reminded of your relationship with God (God images relationship). I hear echoes of your experience of your mother when you talk about God. I get the sense that you feel like God might also withdraw if you are honest about your struggles; like God also expects you to always be happy and perfect, even in the midst of very trying circumstances.

Interpretation is just one dynamic intervention among many. The common theme amongst all interpersonal interventions is the therapeutic relationship. The therapist uses the relationship in the here and now to give the client a different experience of themselves and the therapist that can then generalize to other relationships, including the person's relationship with God.

Cognitive-behavioral interventions focus on changing thoughts in order to change feelings and behavior. For example, a person struggling with depression might interpret a neutral interaction with their supervisor in a negative manner. They might feel like their supervisor is mad at them for some reason. A nondepressed person might have this same encounter and interpret the situation quite differently. They might conclude that the boss is simply busy, distracted, or having a bad day. The nondepressed person likely sees the situation in a less emotional and more rational manner. Interventions focus on the automatic thoughts a person experiences in order to challenge and change them so that they more accurately reflect reality. In the above example, the person struggling with depression had automatic thoughts like "I am no good," "I've done something wrong," "My boss should be mad at me. I'm not performing." These thoughts come unbidden, are outside of awareness, and result in the person feeling—often unsure why—depressed.

God image interventions focus on the automatic thoughts and cognitive errors that a person experiences in their relationship with God (Moriarty 2006). A depressed person, for example, may have automatic thoughts about God that are colored by their depression. They might feel like God is distant or mad at them. They might feel like God is particularly upset with them when they sin or make a mistake. They will likely believe in the ideas of God's grace or forgiveness, but these negative automatic thoughts will be a stronger reality for them. One technique utilizes the God image automatic thought record to counter these negative beliefs (Moriarty 2006). Moriarty and Davis outline the steps in the process.

1. Briefly describe an actual event that made you feel like God was probably having negative thoughts about you and/or negative feelings toward you.

2. List any negative feelings that you felt as a result (for example, sadness, shame, abandonment, rejection, anxiety, fear, anger). Then rate the strength of each feeling, on a scale from 0 to 100, with 0 indicating *total absence of the emotion* and 100 indicating *overwhelming presence of the emotion*.

3. Now list any negative thoughts and/or feelings that you felt like God was probably having about you or toward you in that moment. Then rate the degree to which you believed God was thinking/feeling that way toward you at that time, on a scale from 0 to 100 percent, with 0 indicating "I was *not at all confident* that God was thinking/feeling that way toward me" and 100 indicating "I was *100 percent confident* that God was thinking/feeling that way toward me."

4. Next, knowing what you know about the Real God (as

described by your scriptures, teachings, or leaders), what do you think God was perhaps more realistically thinking and feeling toward you in that moment? Write out the more plausible Real God response. Then rate the degree to which you believe that the Real God response is probably how God *really* thought and felt toward you at that time, on a scale from 0 to 100 percent, with 0 indicating "I am *not at all confident* that the Real God was thinking/feeling that way toward me" and 100 indicating "I am *100 percent confident* that the Real God was thinking/feeling that way toward me."

5. Now close your eyes and get a mental picture of the Real God—whatever God may look like to you, whether a person such as Papa from *The Shack*, the father in the Prodigal Son parable, or perhaps even a mythological figure such as Aslan from The Chronicles of Narnia. Look into the eyes of the Real God. Allow yourself to experience whatever emotions and bodily sensations arise as you gaze into each other's eyes. Then allow yourself to experience the Real God responding to you in the way you described. Let that response fully sink in—let it spread throughout your mind, fill your heart, and soak into your body. Stay in this experience for a minute or two and then slowly open your eyes.

6. Finally, relist the negative emotions that you initially felt, as a result of the original situation. Then rate the strength of each feeling, after imagining the Real God's thoughts/feelings toward you, on a scale from 0 to 100, with 0 indicating *total absence of the emotion* and 100 indicating *overwhelming presence of the emotion* (2012, 151).

There are a number of other helpful techniques that pastoral counselors and therapists can use to shift God images around issues of suffering. It is not uncommon for people who have experienced trauma or deep pain in life to feel like God let them down. These individuals can sometimes harbor anger toward God. Again, this is heart-level affect and often inconsistent with their head knowledge of God. Many Christians are actually afraid to express anger toward God (Strength 1998). They often unconsciously feel like God will become mad at them— like a parent might have—if they were to express anger or frustration toward God. Julie Exline (2002; 2004; 2011) has published widely in this area and recommends a number of interventions that can be helpful.

Writing a letter to God can be a useful tool to get at painful, unresolved issues. The empty chair technique is another option where the client imagines God in an empty chair. They can then say things to God to help them talk through and resolve their challenges. A third tool is bibliotherapy, which occurs when a client reads a book and reflects on the content. In one of the God image group therapy programs we facilitated, we utilized the *Horse and His Boy* from C. S. Lewis's Chronicles of Narnia. This book focuses on the role that God plays in suffering. The main client, Shasta, has a number of painful experiences in his life. Toward the end of the book, he confronts Aslan (the God character and also a lion) and asks why he let those things happen to him. The Aslan character puts the painful experiences in context and shows how his behaviors were actually interventions that ultimately helped Shasta. For example, in one instance Shasta asks why Aslan scratched his back when he was riding a horse. The scratch hurt Shasta and caused him to ride faster. If he hadn't ridden faster, then a much more painful experience would have occurred. Interestingly, we have not found that the famous "Footprints" poem is helpful in shifting clients' experience of God and suffering. Fictional literature is effective because the reader identifies and vicariously experiences what the character experiences. This narrative process occurs automatically; the person does not have to try to feel what the character feels—it just naturally happens.

Imagery techniques also have a rich history in spiritual direction and psychotherapy (Boyd 2004). These techniques, like reading fiction, take the readers from their current place and surround them in a new place. Like a good book, the clients almost feel themselves in a new environment. Imagery is the most helpful when it taps the senses, so that the person can vividly see, hear, and touch what is happening around him. For Christians, meditating on scripture passages can help them feel these narratives at a heart level (Propst 1997).

A final technique that is gaining more and more support is God image narrative therapy (Brokaw et al. 2009; Davis 2010). Narrative therapy helps clients break their life down into different chapters (McAdams 2008). Oftentimes a person's life story just kind of jumps from chapter to chapter. That is, the transitions are not clear; the story is not emotionally integrated. Narrative therapy helps to build bridges across chapters/experiences that ultimately help the person achieve emotional integration. God image narrative therapy does the same thing by helping the client break down their story with God into chapters. Various techniques are used throughout the process to facilitate integration. Preliminary results (Olson et al. 2012) from a God image narrative group with thirty-one outpatient clients suggests that the program increases a person's emotional experience of God as supportive, reliable, and helps close the gap between head and heart understandings of God.

In sum, the primary tool to shift God images is the relationship with the client. The client needs to feel like the therapist is on his or her team. Common factors like unconditional positive regard, authenticity, and empathy are essential to helping clients internalize the relationship with the therapist, which can, in turn, impact attachment to God images. Specific relational, cognitive, experiential, and narrative techniques take place against this therapeutic backdrop.

CONCLUSION

Head and heart understandings of God can broadly be understood through God concepts and God images. God concepts are the intellectual, abstract, explicit understandings of God, whereas God images are the personal, emotional, implicit understandings of God. Heart understandings of God, or God images, have a rich history that started with Freud's conceptualization of God as an immature projection. His work has been reformulated through object relations theory and more recently through attachment theory. Research has shown that God images are informed by self-esteem, parental characteristics, and attachment patterns. Initial research also suggests that harmful God images can be shifted to be more healing through practical techniques in the context of a therapeutic relationship.

In closing, let's revisit the case of Martin that we discussed at the beginning of the chapter. Martin was a forty-two-year-old, Caucasian, evangelical clergyperson with a comprehensive theological understanding of God. He believed in a personal God that loved and forgave him, but he experienced a God that seemed distant and unforgiving. Stated another way, Martin believed that God loved him, but did not feel God liked him. Martin's gap in his head and heart understandings of God can be best understood through God concepts and God images. Despite his intensive theological work, this discrepancy between his head and heart understanding persisted because his intellectual work did not address the personal and relational aspects of his relationship with God. The last, and perhaps the most important, question we asked was: Can Martin learn to emotionally experience God's grace and forgiveness? The answer is a tentative yes. Martin's God images can likely be shifted by utilizing techniques in the context of a caring therapeutic relationship. There are many people like Martin. They struggle with the language to capture this discrepancy between their head and heart understandings of God. I believe that clergy, pastoral counselors, and therapists are in a key place to help people close this gap so that they can learn to experience the God they believe in.

Notes

1. Correspondence concerning this chapter should be addressed to Glendon L. Moriarty, Doctoral Program in Clinical Psychology (PsyD), Regent University, 1000 Regent University Dr., CRB 161, Virginia Beach, VA 23464. E-mail: glenmor@regent.edu.
2. For a more clinical perspective on these issues, see Moriarty and Davis 2012.

References

Badenoch, B. 2008. *Being a Brain-wise Therapist: A Practical Guide to Interpersonal Neurobiology.* New York: Norton.

Bargh, J. A., and L. E. Williams. 2006. "The Automaticity of Social Life." *Current Directions in Psychological Science* 15:1–4.

Beck, R., and A. McDonald. 2004. "Attachment to God: The Attachment to God Inventory, Tests of Working Model Correspondence, and an Exploration of Faith Group Differences." *Journal of Psychology and Theology* 32:92–103.

Benson, P., and B. Spilka. 1973. "God Image as a Function of Self-Esteem and Locus of Control." *Journal for the Scientific Study of Religion* 12:297–310.

Birky, I. T., and S. Ball. 1988. "Parental Trait Influence on God as an Object Representation." *The Journal of Psychology* 122:133–37.

Bowlby, J. 1969/1982. *Attachment and Loss: Vol. 1. Attachment.* New York: Basic Books.

———. 1973. *Attachment and Loss: Vol. 2. Separation.* New York: Basic Books.

———. 1980. *Attachment and Loss: Vol. 3. Loss, Sadness and Depression.* New York: Basic Books.

Boyd, G. A. 2004. *Seeing Is Believing: Experience Jesus through Imaginative Prayer.* Grand Rapids, MI: Baker Books.

Bretherton, I. 1992. "The Origins of Attachment Theory: John Bowlby and Mary Ainsworth." *Developmental Psychology* 28:759–75.

Brokaw, B., E. B. Davis, M. Carafa, and P. Hudson. April 2009. "Storying God Images: Narratives and Neurobiology." Presentation at the Annual CAPS International Conference, Orlando, FL.

Brokaw, B. F., and K. J. Edwards. 1994. "The Relationship of God Image to Level of Object Relations Development." *Journal of Psychology and Theology* 22:352–71.

Buri, J. R., and R. A. Mueller. 1993. "Psychoanalytic Theory and Loving God Concepts: Parent Referencing Versus Self-referencing." *The Journal of Psychology* 127:17–27.

Chartrand, T. L., and J. A. Bargh. 1996. "Automaticity of Impression Formation and Memorization Goals." *Journal of Personality and Social Psychology* 71:464–78.

Cheston, S. E., R. L. Piedmont, B. Eanes, and L. Patrice. 2003. "Changes in Clients' Images of God over the Course of Outpatient Psychotherapy." *Counseling and Values* 47:96–108.

Davis, E. B. 2010. "Authenticity, Inauthenticity, Attachment, and God-image Tendencies among Adult Evangelical Protestant Christians." Unpublished PhD diss., Regent University, Virginia Beach, VA.

Davis, E. B., G. L. Moriarty, and J. C. Mauch. 2013. "God Images and God Concepts: Definitions, Development, and Dynamics." *Psychology of Religion and Spirituality*, 5:51–60.

Dickie, J. R., A. K. Eshleman, D. M. Merasco, A. Shepard, M. V. Wilt, and M. Johnson. 1997. "Parent-child Relationships and Children's Images of God." *Journal for the Scientific Study of Religion* 36:25–43.

Epstein, S. 1994. "Integration of the Cognitive and the Psychodynamic Unconscious." *American Psychologist* 49:709–24.

Exline, J. J. 2002. "Stumbling Blocks on the Religious Road: Fractured Relationships, Nagging Vices, and the Inner Struggle to Believe." *Psychological Inquiry* 13:182–89.

———. 2004. "Anger Toward God: A Brief Overview of Existing Research." *Psychology of Religion Newsletter* 29:1–8.

———. 2011. "Anger Toward God: A New Frontier in the Study of Forgiveness." In *A Journey Through Forgiveness,* edited by M. M. Maamri, N. Nevin, and E. L. Worthington Jr. 29–37. Oxford: Inter-Disciplinary Press.

Fairbairn, W. R. D. 1952. *Psycho-analytic Studies of the Personality.* New York: Basic Books.

Freud, S. 1910. *Leonardo da Vinci and a Memory of His Childhood.* New York: W.W. Norton.

Garzon, F. L. 2007. "Neuroscientific Contributions to God Image Therapy and Theory. In *God Image Handbook for Spiritual Counseling and Psychotherapy: Research, Theory, and Practice,* edited by G. Moriarty and L. Hoffman, 139–155. Binghamton, NY: Haworth/Routledge Press.

Gibson, N. J. S. 2006. "The Experimental Investigation of Religious Cognition." PhD diss., University of Cambridge, Cambridge, England. http://divinity.npsl.co.uk/prrg/people/staff/staff.acds?context=1609849&instanceid=1609850.

———. 2007. "Measurement Issues in God Image Research and Practice." In *God Image Handbook for Spiritual Counseling and Psychotherapy: Research, Theory, and Practice*, edited by G. L. Moriarty and L. Hoffman, 227–46. Binghamton, NY: Haworth/Routledge Press.

Granqvist, P. 1998. "Religiousness and Perceived Childhood Attachment: On the Question of Compensation or Correspondence." *Journal for the Scientific Study of Religion* 37:350–67.

———. 2002. "Attachment and Religiosity in Adolescence: Cross-sectional and Longitudinal Evaluations." *Personality & Social Psychology Bulletin* 28:260–70.

Granqvist, P., and B. Hagekull. 1999. "Religiousness and Perceived Childhood Attachment: Profiling Socialized Correspondence and Emotional Compensation." *Journal for the Scientific Study of Religion* 10:254–73.

Greenberg, J. R., and S. A. Mitchell. 1983. *Object Relations in Psychoanalytic Theory*. Cambridge, MA: Harvard University Press.

Guntrip, H. 1956. "Recent Developments in Psychoanalytical Theory." *British Journal of Medical Psychology* 29:82–99.

Hall, T. W. 2004. "Christian Spirituality and Mental Health: A Relational Spirituality Framework for Empirical Research." *Journal of Psychology and Christianity* 23:66–81.

Hall, T. W., S. Halcrow, P. C. Hill, and H. Delaney. August 2005. "Internal Working Model Correspondence in Implicit Spiritual Experiences." Paper presented at the 113th Annual Convention of the American Psychological Association, Washington, DC.

Hathaway, W. L. 2003. "Clinically Significant Religious Impairment." *Mental Health, Religion & Culture* 6:113–29.

Horowitz, M. J. 1991. "Emotionality and Schematic Control Processes." In *Person Schemas and Maladaptive Interpersonal Patterns*, edited by M. J. Horowitz, 413–23. Chicago: University of Chicago Press.

Jones, J. W. 1991. *Contemporary Psychoanalysis and Religion*. New York: Yale.

Jordan, M. R. 1986. *Taking on the Gods: The Task of the Pastoral Counselor*. Nashville, TN: Abingdon.

Kihlstrom, J. F. 2008. "The Automaticity Juggernaut." In *Are We Free? Psychology and Free Will*, edited by J. Baer, J. C. Kaufman, and R. F. Baumeister, 155–80. New York: Oxford University Press.

Kirkpatrick, L. A. 1992. "An Attachment-theoretical Approach to the Psychology of Religion." *International Journal for the Psychology of Religion* 2:3–28.

———. 2005. *Attachment, Evolution, and the Psychology of Religion*. New York: Guilford.

Kirkpatrick, L. A., and P. R. Shaver. 1992. "An Attachment-theoretical Approach to Romantic Love and Religious Belief." *Personality and Social Psychology Bulletin* 18:266–75.

Levenson, H. 1995. *Time-limited Dynamic Psychotherapy: A Guide to Clinical Practice.* New York: Basic Books.

McAdams, D. 2008. "Personal Narratives and the Life Story." In *Handbook of Personality: Theory and Research*, edited by O. P. John, R. W. Robins, and L. A. Pervin, 242–62. New York: Guilford.

Metcalfe, J., and W. J. Jacobs. 1998. "Emotional Memory: The Effects of Stress on 'Cool' and 'Hot' Memory Systems." In *The Psychology of Learning and Motivation: Advances in Research and Theory*, vol. 38, edited by D. L. Medin, 187–222. San Diego: Academic Press.

Mikulincer, M., and P. R. Shaver. 2004. "Security-based Self-representations in Adulthood: Contents and Processes." In *Adult Attachment: Theory, Research, and Clinical Implications*, edited by W. S. Rholes and J. A. Simpson, 159–95. New York: Guilford.

Moriarty, G. L. 2006. *Pastoral Care of Depression: Helping Clients Heal Their Relationship with God.* Binghamton, NY: Haworth/Routledge Press.

———. 2009. "The Gift of Sin: Modifying Relational Schemas through Relationship with God." Paper presented at the International Congress for the Psychology of Religion, Vienna, Austria.

Moriarty, G. L., and E. B. Davis. 2012. "Client God Images: Theory, Research, and Clinical Practice." In *The Psychology of Religion and Spirituality for Clinicians: Using Research in Your Practice*, edited by J. Aten, K. O'Grady, and E. Worthington Jr., 131–60. New York: Routledge.

Moriarty, G. L., and L. Hoffman, eds. 2007. *God Image Handbook for Spiritual Counseling and Psychotherapy: Research, Theory, and Practice.* Binghamton, NY: Haworth/Routledge Press.

Moriarty, G. L., M. Thomas, and J. Allmond. 2008. "God Image Psychotherapy: Comparing Approaches." *Journal of Spirituality in Mental Health* 9:247–55.

Noffke, J. L., and T. W. Hall. 2007. "Attachment Psychotherapy and God Image." In *God Image Handbook for Spiritual Counseling and Psychotherapy: Research, Theory, and Practice*, edited by G. L. Moriarty and L. Hoffman, 57–78. Binghamton, NY: Haworth/Routledge Press.

Norcross, J., ed. 2002. *Psychotherapy Relationships That Work: Psychotherapist Contributions and Responsiveness to Patients.* New York: Oxford University Press.

Olson, T., G. Moriarty, W. Davis, and T. Tisdale. 2012. "The Effects of a Manualized,

Narrative-Experiential, Group-Psychotherapy Intervention on Client Attachment Tendencies, Narrative Identity, and God Images." PhD diss., Regent University, Virginia Beach, VA.

Phillips, J. B. 1952. *Your God Is Too Small*. Retrieved from http://www.newchurches.com/mediafiles/YourGodisTooSmall-Phillips.pdf.

Propst, L. R. 1997. "Therapeutic Conflict Resolution and the Holy Trinity." In *Limning the Psyche: Explorations in Christian Psychology*, edited by R. Roberts and M. Talbot, 58–73. Grand Rapids, MI: Wm. B. Eerdmans Publishing.

Richards, P. S., and A. E. Bergin. 1997. *A Spiritual Strategy for Counseling and Psychotherapy*. Washington, DC: American Psychological Association.

Rizzuto, A. 1979. *The Birth of the Living God*. Chicago, IL: University of Chicago Press.

Siegel, D. J. 2010. *The Mindful Therapist: A Clinician's Guide to Mindsight and Neural Integration*. New York: Norton.

———. 2012. *Pocket Guide to Interpersonal Neurobiology: An Integrative Handbook of the Mind*. New York: Norton.

Strength, J. M. 1998. "Expanding Davanloo's Interpretive Triangles to Explicate the Client's Introjected Image of God." *Journal of Psychology and Theology* 26:172–87.

Strupp, H. H., and J. L. Binder. 1984. *Psychotherapy in a New Key*. New York: Basic Books.

Suttie, I. D. 1935. *The Origins of Love and Hate*. Oxford: Kegan Paul.

Tan, S. Y. 2003. "Integrating Spiritual Direction into Psychotherapy: Ethical Issues and Guidelines." *Journal of Psychology and Theology* 31:14–23.

Thomas, M. J., and G. Moriarty. 2009. "The Effect of a Manualized Group Treatment Protocol on God Image and Attachment to God." Paper presented at the International Congress for the Psychology of Religion, Vienna, Austria.

Thomas, M. J., G. L. Moriarty, E. B. Davis, and E. L. Anderson. 2011. "The Effects of a Manualized Group-psychotherapy Intervention on Client God Images and Attachment to God: A Pilot Study." *Journal of Psychology and Theology* 39:44–58.

Tisdale, T. T., T. L. Key, K. J. Edwards, B. F. Brokaw, S. R. Kemperman, H. Cloud, J. Townsend, and T. Okamato. 1997. "Impact of Treatment on God Image and Personal Adjustment, and Correlations of God Image to Personal Adjustment and Object Relations Development." *Journal of Psychology and Theology* 25:227–39.

Winnicott, D. W. 1971. *Playing and Reality*. New York: Basic Books.

———. 1975. "Transitional Objects and Transitional Phenomena." In *Through*

Paediatrics to Psycho-analysis, edited by D. W. Winnicott, 229–42. New York: Basic Books.

Wulff, D. 1997. *Psychology of Religion Classic and Contemporary*. Hoboken, NJ: John Wiley and Sons.

Yarborough, C. A., N. Gibson, and G. Moriarty. 2009. "Depression and the Emotional Experience of God." Paper presented at the International Congress for the Psychology of Religion, Vienna, Austria.

Religious Education 8

SALLY MYERS

This chapter will explore the possibilities, challenges, and implications of taking the heart seriously in religious education. The focus will be mainly on religious education within the particular religious tradition of Christianity, and the chapter is written from a Western liberal Christian viewpoint. However, it will also touch on two other approaches: objective inquiry, through critical academic investigation, into faith as a phenomenon and its expression through individual religions; and mission-focused religious education, which seeks to convert learners to a specific religion.

It is perhaps understandable that head knowing has, until recently, largely dominated in religious education. There are, however, good reasons for not ignoring what might loosely be termed "the heart" in religious knowing and learning. First, since the heart might be understood to be a multidimensional and sophisticated information-receiving and meaning-making system, which encompasses instinct, intuition, and emotion, it has the potential to offer insights crucial to the learning process. If the heart is respected and engaged therefore, religious education may become much richer and more meaningful. If on the other hand heart and head knowing is not consciously reflected upon, an individual might be vulnerable to submission, induction, or manipulation in the service of predetermined religious intellectual propositions; or similarly, what simply *feels* right may overwhelm theological reason. Either of these outcomes is potentially disastrous for both the individual and society. As a consequence, it is argued here that it is desirable to try and integrate heart knowing and head knowing in religious learning.

That said, religious education is not for the fainthearted. Religion is about the big questions: What is the meaning of life? What happens when someone dies? What and why is evil? These topics are emotionally demanding and plumb the depths of what it means to be human. Furthermore, teaching and learning about such subjects demands the bringing to consciousness and interrogation of existing, often long buried, yet deeply held beliefs or indeed disbeliefs. Personal ideas about God are not simply discrete mental concepts, but are intimately bound up with an individual's self-image and understanding of the world. Probing them can lead to doubt, distress, and disagreement.

The chapter first examines how religious change and development occurs naturally, and then uses that as a springboard for proposing a formulation of the learning task in the religious life. The second half of the chapter then focuses more explicitly on religious education, looking at the challenges facing both students and tutors.

Religious Development

Before considering the role of heart in religious education it will be helpful to consider how changes in heart generally might occur in the ordinary course of development. A number of psychologists have argued persuasively that people's head understanding of God changes and develops over time. Historically, psychological theories of religious development have focused on head-based understanding of religion, assessed in terms of stages of cognitive development. In particular, Piaget's fourfold account of intellectual development has provided a basis for exploring how children develop in their religion, and several writers such as David Elkind (1961) and Ronald Goldman (1964) have applied Piaget's stage theory of cognitive development to religious development in children (see Spilka et al. 77–86). Children's moral

224

development has been approached in a similar way, especially in the work of Lawrence Kohlberg (1964; 1969). James Fowler (1981) brought together the theories of Piaget, Kohlberg, and Erickson in a general theory of faith development and proposed that, after a brief period of undifferentiated trust, faith advances in a series of six stages:

1. Intuitive-Projective: faith is largely led by imagination and feelings, feelings of powerlessness and attraction to strong images;
2. Mythic-Literal: the beginning of simple thinking about faith, usually in the form of story;
3. Synthetic-Conventional: faith is expressed in relationships and conventional loyalty to like-minded people;
4. Individuative-Reflective: characterized by a moving away from people-centered faith and toward the exploration of ideas, in which emotion and experience are set aside in order to concentrate on meaning;
5. Conjunctive: a renewed sense of mystery and symbolism is employed to hold together paradox; and finally
6. Universalizing: faith is transformed into selflessness and commitment to higher causes, justice, love, etc. According to Fowler this stage is seldom reached.

These stage models of religious development have not been without their critics. Feminist writers, in particular, have argued that stage theories do not adequately consider the broader context of developmental issues, including psychodynamic, emotional, experiential, relational gender, and cultural factors (Gilligan 1982; Slee 2004). Alternative accounts of faith development that try to include more heart knowing have been offered in response to Fowler. Westerhoff (1976) incorporates tacit belief into his account, which separates faith development into four stages: experienced, affiliative, searching, and owned faith. Streib (2001) focuses more on interpersonal relations and describes five religious styles, rather than stages, which are more akin to geographical layers: subjective, instrumental-reciprocal, mutual, individuativesystematic, and dialogical. Slee (2004) focuses on the development of faith in women and, in her interviews, records changes or realizations of heartfelt states, including alienation, awakenings, and relationality in women's faith knowing. Slee's work is consciously centered on women. However, there is nothing intrinsically exclusive about the phenomena she identifies, and further nongender-specific research might be usefully conducted. Each of these alternative accounts seeks in some way to address the balance between head and heart knowing in how faith changes and develops over time. However, cognitive learning theory continues to be the basis upon which thinking about felt knowing is discussed, and comprehension by heart continues to be treated as, at best, a secondary matter, or at worst a distraction from the *real* thinking and learning in which the heart has no place. I suggest that, on the contrary, the heart is not a distraction from religious learning and development, but a crucial part of it.

In finding better ways of approaching the role of the heart in religious development, it may be helpful to consider emotional development. The "emotional heart" is thought to be a consistent aspect of personal identity (Averill and Nunley 1992, 78) even though, for example, the anger of an adult is very different from the temper tantrum of a child, and there is, of course, some change in emotional response and expression over time. Tacit knowing generally in children is thought to be more natural and unmediated; emotions such as delight or distress, for example, are less conditioned by learned control and social niceties. Applied to religion, spiritual knowing in a child is thought to be a form of spontaneous relational consciousness, which is then socialized into religious attachment figures (Nelson 2009, 245–53). It has been suggested this loss of spontaneity, alongside the acquisition of cultural emotional habits and standards, means that religious education loses "reality" somewhere between primary and secondary school (Madge 1965, 112).

Heart learning may involve "reattunement" to (and fine-tuning of) this felt knowing, as a growing consciousness of social context influences people's emotional responses. Life brings many emotional events to deal with, especially in the form of loss and change, providing many opportunities for emotional learning. It has been suggested that one of the consequences of meeting new people is that our mental representations become more complex, so that we are able to integrate more information and viewpoints into our understanding (Suedfeld and Blunk 1993). As social context changes over time, perhaps our heart knowing and felt understanding become, not simply more controlled, but also more flexible, accommodating, and complex. We do not grow and develop in a vacuum, but are faced with different responsibilities, and assume different roles, as our lives unfold. Each of these brings its own challenges and calls for adaptation and readjustment.

Erik Erikson describes eight life stages, each of which presents a specific emotional conflict that needs to be resolved in order to achieve integration of identity (Erikson 1964). Management of the transition through these life stages is the province of the therapist or life coach. However, attention to the emotional processes involved in alerting an individual to the presence of conflict need not be left at the classroom door. The philosophical basis for attention to the affections in decision making generally (that is, not through reason or act of will but out of judgments made in a higher realm of consciousness) is well expounded in chapters 2 and 3. I will now apply this growing understanding of religious development and change to theories of the learning process in religion.

Religious Learning

Piaget's approach to learning remains unsurpassed as a description of how a student might *assimilate their* perception of new material to fit their existing cognitive schema or, alternatively, *accommodate* their existing mental representation to new information, in order to achieve *equilibration.* I suggest that this approach can also be applied to heart knowing. More excitingly, there is a point at which these two strategies for processing information, head and heart, break down and a third method, involving the integration of both head or heart knowing, is required. This threefold taxonomy—head, heart, and integrated—will be explored again from a different perspective in the following chapter on the theology and psychology of wisdom.

When students are confronted with new things to learn, they look for links with what is already known, beginning with existing categories and coding systems. If these are not available, they search for similar patterns in other areas of knowledge. In this latter mode of thinking, students start to "go beyond the information given"; they fill gaps and extrapolate, to try and find a suitable code with which to comprehend the new data (Bruner 1974, 218–37). However, if this proves fruitless, the student has to either ignore the new learning, quarantine it until further evidence appears, or totally review their existing knowing about the subject and replace it with a new schema and pattern of understanding that fits the new presenting reality.

A similar approach has been taken by other scholars concerned with learning theory, including Illeris who identifies four similar types of learning: (1) cumulative, which corresponds to training; (2) assimilative, which involves linking new elements to existing mental schema; (3) accommodative, which requires transcending an existing scheme in order to adapt it; and finally (4) a far-reaching type of learning that has been variously described as "significant" (Rogers 1951; 1969), "expansive" (Engeström 1987), "transitional" (Alheit 1994), and "transformative" (Mezirow 1991), in which changes to knowing are required, which in turn affect personality or organization of the self (Illeris 2009, 1–14). It is in this higher form of knowing that I suggest the heart plays an important role.

Mezirow articulates the centrality of reassessment and resetting of epistemic assumptions of what he calls "frames of reference" in transformative learning. He describes this as less of a change in what is known than as a change in the way of knowing it. He makes the link between transformative learning and what he terms "traumatic learning," which enables transformative growth to come from crisis. He acknowledges the debt owed to Habermas's distinction between instrumental and communicative learning. The former, being concerned with controlling and manipulating the environment relies, on a *hypothetical-deductive* developmental logic, that is, assertions that it is possible to validate by empirical testing. The latter is concerned with the understanding of, and empathizing with, the frame of reference of another and relies on an *analogical-abductive* developmental logic, that is, "best guesses" based upon a multitude of sometimes conflicting evidence (Mezirow and Taylor 2009, 20).

Mezirow's ideas have been taken up by Robert Kegan, who describes transformational learning as "reforming our meaning forming" (Kegan 2009, 45). In fact, Fowler did take from Kegan's early work the notions of "whole ego" and "relational" knowing. He modified his approach to faith development accordingly and began to refer to "constitutive" rather than "constructive" knowing in faith (Dykstra and Parks 1986, 20, 76). However, he did not attend to the wider issues that Mezirow, and later Kegan, raise. Parks, on the other hand, does recognize that Kegan highlights some of the other "neglects" of Piaget: "*cognition* to the neglect of *emotion*; *individual* to the neglect of the *social*; the *epistemological* to the neglect of the *ontological* (or *concept* to the neglect of *being*); *stages* . . . to the neglect of *process*; finally, what is *new and changed* about a person, to the neglect of the *person who persists through time.*" She also draws a connection between Kegan's recognition of the importance of environment and Piaget's theory of equilibration and proposes a link between this and Loder's "paradigm of creativity," (Loder 1989) which elucidates a similar process of conflict, interlude for scanning, constructive act of the imagination, release and opening to wider context, and interpretation of the new shared understanding of reality (Parks 1986, 139).

Traditionally, such transformational "Eureka" moments have been described in purely intellectual terms. However, evidence at this higher stage of knowing suggests an orientation away from purely intellectual processes and toward the heart. It appears to be the case that, as well as exploring intellectual ground, an individual's intuition continues the process of scanning beyond the conscious. That enables it to incorporate a whole realm of unconscious material not ordinarily accessible to the conscious mind, including matters of the heart that are normally suppressed. Bruner came to understand what he called this *left hand* kind of knowing as a continuation and yet transcendence of dialogue, which ultimately results in a rearrangement or transforming of all of the presenting evidence, in order to go beyond it to new insights (Bruner 1962, viii, 82). The essentially epistemological approach to learning taken by Bruner involves interaction in two directions: one outward, between the learner and their environment, and one inward, between existing and new knowing. The former involves a refinement of an individual's understanding of their environment, and the latter a refinement—and perhaps even development—of their understanding of their whole self, including emotions.

Bruner identifies three distinct approaches to teaching and learning, which involve these dynamics, and which might be applied to religious learning. The first is *basic thinking*, that is, teaching the organization and manipulation of information in line with set criteria. This is most effectively achieved by *rote learning*. In this type of learning, there is no search for the unknown, but merely an adoption of, and competency in, a technique for sorting the already known (that is, rejecting or receiving and storing information as it is presented into a given framework). Bruner characterizes the rather mediocre aspiration behind this as "adjustment" and warns that overemphasis on adjustment leads to "a niggling fear of the unusual and the excellent," and an "embarrassment of passion, blandness, standardization and the failure to challenge the full potential of students and by extension human beings" (Bruner 2006a, 24, 28). This sort of teaching and learning corresponds with "closed" religious mental representations, where difference and complexity, if recognized, are actively rejected.

Beyond rote learning is what Bruner describes as the grasp of *trans-*

ference: that is, recognizing and "coming to terms with" the underlying principles and structure of a type of knowledge. This facilitates "continual broadening and deepening of knowledge in terms of basic and general ideas." It is summed up rather nicely by Bruner's comments about teaching myths: "In studying symbolic systems, we want the students to understand myths rather than learn them" (Bruner 2006a, 40, 99). This is comparable to Piaget's formal thought stage, particularly in terms of being able to recognize another's point of view. Piaget notes that "older but not younger children were capable of understanding what another viewer might see, when the other person views it from another perspective" (Holyoak and Morrison 2005, 385). This is a more sophisticated kind of learning that allows, and indeed encourages, a student to look for patterns and connections between new information and what they already know. It provides a stable but adaptable base from which to recognize and integrate new understandings and is much more open and flexible than the first approach. In terms of faith development, this attitude and approach is in line cognitively with Fowler's fourth stage of development. A striking example would be the Golden Rule, which may be summarized as "do to others as you would have them do to you." All major faiths hold this in common, although they have differing ways of presenting it in "law."

However, neither of these ways of teaching and learning is capable of fostering the paradigm leap in understanding noted above. Bruner's answer to this, in educational terms, is *discovery learning*. While he is conscious of the need to grasp the underlying structures, principles, and attitudes of a subject, he is also anxious to capture the even wider connections, not yet thought of, that can then be made. Discovery, he claims, "is in its essence a matter of rearranging or transforming evidence in such a way that one is enabled to go beyond the evidence so reassembled to additional insights." There is of course a need for balance; "unbridled curiosity is little more than unlimited distractibility." Nevertheless he calls for an active encouragement of enquiry. He seeks to foster in a student an attitude of "expectancy that there will be something to find and, once aroused by that expectancy, [s]he must devise ways of searching and finding" (Bruner 2006a, 57, 116, 59). The distinctive characteristic of this way of teaching and learning, compared to the other two, is its attitude of actively looking for difference. Discovery learning involves a search for new codes and presupposes a certain degree of understanding of, immersion in, and engagement with, a discipline. In specific terms, "you don't think about physics, you think physics" (Bruner 1983, 185). It could be argued that only being rooted in a particular religious tradition provides this opportunity in terms of religious knowing. Discovery learning rests upon solid foundations and then engages both "intuitive" and "analytic" knowing to find new insights through an implicit perception of the whole, often with little if any awareness of the process by which new understanding is reached (Olson 2007, 40). It is this kind of knowing that best describes religious experience and might also correspond to the mystical traditions found in all major faiths.

Although, from a pedagogical viewpoint, there are huge advantages to the discovery method, there are some serious problems associated with it for religious education. Preserving a specific religion and passing on the faith does not sit comfortably with the active encouragement of new perspectives. Furthermore, this form of learning is distinctly unsettling: instead of becoming more and more comfortably embedded in certainty, students are fully exposed to the angst of doubt. The second method of learning and teaching outlined above has the advantage of providing a sound and organic basis from which to work. In contrast, the third method of learning rejects even that basis. Nevertheless, this uncomfortable place appears to be comparable with Fowler's later stages of faith development. Bruner himself prefers the discovery method to other approaches to pedagogy. However, importantly, he later added that this method was not just about individual knowledge. Rather, he emphasized that it is best practiced in a community, emphasizing the importance of negotiating and sharing. Indeed the opportunity for this sharing is crucial to growth in knowing generally: "The development of thought may be in large measure determined by the opportunities for dialogue, with dialogue then becoming internal and capable of running off inside one's head on its own" (Bruner 2006b, 97). The key to engaging in the discovery learning described by Bruner above is "connection." He describes myth, the modern novel, and art as all offering a metaphoric means of making connections and fostering an understanding that lies beyond the scientific, encompassing, as it does, instinct and emotion (Bruner 1962, 68). In terms of theological education, the challenge for the tutor is to offer as many opportunities for continuing this dialogue with heart and head as possible, both internally and externally.

Religious Education: The Task of Students

When a student begins a new course of study about religion, they bring with them not only prelearning in the form of facts and mental theories, but also the *felt understanding* of that learning, accumulated throughout their lives so far. This affective knowledge is often difficult for a tutor to ascertain. What is reported is not always the same as what they really believe or feel. Even if a person wants to be wholly honest, tacit knowledge (gained when an individual experiences, engages with, and interprets an event directly) is by no means easy to articulate. Nor is it straightforward to coordinate a person's *felt knowledge* with another to achieve mutual comprehension (Heywood 2004, 57). However, the physical and mental manifestations of emotional arousal that usually accompany any disturbance of heart knowing are a little easier to discern.

For most people, childhood is largely hidden from active memory. However, past incidents that still possess emotional power, when brought to mind, are capable of recreating the feelings, whether positive or negative, that first accompanied them. Indeed, Wynn argues persuasively that especially with religious understanding both perception and conception are infused with feeling (Wynn 2005). If this is the case, then emotions will have a strong influence on how students understand their past and receive new knowledge. Memory is selective. What is remembered most acutely are extremes of emotion, particularly those attached to incidents that made an impact on an individual's self-image or self-understanding. Over time, nuance and peripheral details fade, leaving the "raw" emotional imprint, and since memory is not so much about storage as retrieval, the most emotionally potent memories will be the most influential (Evans 2001, 79ff). Particularly important here are childhood memories of experiences of significant others. Although by no means the only influence, they especially have been shown to have a profound effect on how an individual views God (Kirkpatrick and Shaver 1990).

At the beginning of a course of study, attention grabbing stunts aside, it is widely understood that, in order to engage the student, it is pragmatic to keep learning well inside what Vygotsky terms their "zone of proximal development," that is, to introduce material that they are able to "grasp" easily (Vygotsky 1978, 84–91). This ensures that when a novel piece of information is presented, it is a relatively straightforward task for the student to find a place for it within their existing *cognitive schema or pattern* (way of mentally representing theoretical knowledge about a given phenomenon) and *script* (personal narrative that makes subjective sense of the schema or pattern), thereby building their confidence. However, unless tutors are intent on brainwashing and permanently embedding a specific viewpoint, they will soon want to challenge the student by introducing material that is less easy to deal with. At this point the student has to begin to work harder, and emotion becomes an important clue as to how the new information is impacting their existing felt knowledge.

One of the most serious barriers to learning in theological education is the pain of dismantling existing views about God. If the new learning conflicts with dearly held existing felt knowledge, it will be troublesome to process and will cause confusion. John Hull terms this effect "bafflement" and describes it as a conscious and uncomfortable experience that can be both intellectual and emotional, and yet he claims that it is probably a necessary aspect of religious growth (Hull 1985, 59). When new information conflicts with established mental representations, then it will inevitably cause the cognitive dissonance that has come to be expected between traditional religious belief and academic study (Parks 1992, 201). However, when this also causes doubt to be cast on an abiding understanding of self and personal identity resulting from those representations, it will also cause *emotional dissonance* (Jansz and Timmers 2002, 79–95; cf. Heywood 2004, 66–70).

The presence of heightened emotion may be an indication that a student is having persistent problems with accepting a new piece of information. However, conversely it may indicate that they have really "taken it in," and that tacit rather than nominal head knowing has occurred. When this happens, a student may display a degree of pleasure at the new learning, particularly if it reinforces "good" or displaces "bad" felt knowledge. The level of the emotional response will also be an indication of salience; the degree of relative importance a student places on the learning. A signal that they have grasped a concept might be the emotional release experienced as "the penny drops," and the student adjusts their heart knowing to their new head knowing.

However, in religious learning, deeper heart knowing might occur before head knowing. There are numerous examples both famous and more parochial of people claiming a kind of mystical experience that seems to bypass normal cognition. In terms of learning, this might be described as a *knowing* that precipitates a transformative event and results in conviction (Loder 1989, 153–54), or as a movement from third person to first person expression of understanding; from belief *that* to belief *in* (Astley 2002, 29–30). However it is understood, though, this "I-Thou" (Buber, republished 2004) "connected moment" passes, and a person is left needing to formulate a new cognitive understanding of both themselves and God in light of it.

RELIGIOUS EDUCATION: THE TASK OF TUTORS

Hay and Nye, commenting specifically about children, propose that a teacher has four major responsibilities toward nurturing the spirit, which might just as easily be applied to nurturing the heart at all ages: (1) helping children keep an open mind by encouraging personal freedom and self-confidence; (2) exploring and encouraging new and alternative ways of seeing; (3) encouraging personal awareness by providing "hospitable space" and compassionate concern; and (4) becoming personally aware of the social and political dimensions of spirituality (Hay and Nye 2006, 149).

Peter Jarvis, who is a theologian as well as a learning theorist, suggests that all learning is about a search for an answer to the question: Who am I? He furthermore suggests that all answers to this question take the form of a temporary equilibrium in the relationship between subject and object (Jarvis 2009, 21–35). If religious education has a noble objective, it aspires to a consciousness of relatedness, to self, each other, the environment, and that which might be termed "God." This requires attention to both internal and external exchange and relationship and, I would suggest, is best achieved by enabling, encouraging, and exploring dialogue in both directions.

Various models of theological reflection have been developed in order to try and actively prompt and capture this deeper dialogical learning (Green 1990; Killen and de Beer 1994; Whitehead and Whitehead 1995; Graham, Walton, and Ward 2005). Many of the models are based upon the learning cycle and involve an exploration of both immediate and wider social context and personal response to a specific practice, incident, or phenomenon, whereby the views of both self and the other are investigated and imagined. This might be explored further by positive enquiry in the form of action research (Cameron et al. 2010).

In terms of dialogue with one's self, it is often a matter of bringing to consciousness inner thoughts and feelings in order to try and understand and empathize with them. This inner dialogue might be encouraged by the writing of poems or songs or by simply sharing stories and experience over a coffee. Journaling encourages students to search their hearts and record their feelings and emotional responses to learning. This offers an immediate dialogue with one's own experience and simultaneously facilitates a later dialogue with one's own narrative. In Jungian psychology this might be taken further by practicing meditation on the shadow sides of personality or engaging in "active imagination" (Hannah 1981). Here the student is encouraged to let their imagination roam with as little conscious control as possible, and they are then asked simply to notice what presents in the form of stories, images, or characters. Alternatively, the unconscious might be engaged through play to facilitate the imaginative leap (Loder 1989, 25).

In chapter 2, Malcolm Guite explored the potency of using imagination to "interanimate" heart and head knowledge. Applying this approach to religious education would involve a movement away from any pretense of objectivity or, put another way, a passive response to a receptivity of knowledge about faith, but rather would foster active engagement and wrestling with it. Rather than learning about them, tutors could encourage active dialogue with particular religious traditions, meditation upon, or debate with, their various traditions in writings and liturgy, or active engagement with their metaphors, art, poetry, and music. That is not to say they should encourage students to "lose themselves" in these things, but rather to engage their whole selves, heart and mind, in order to encourage the holistic and deeper kind of learning referred to above. Finally, though of course open to numerous interpretations, dialogue might also be had with God in prayer. All of these methods of engagement with religion move beyond cognitive knowing to a deeper realm of heartfelt knowing.

In religious education, it is essential for tutors to cultivate and maintain a high level of "emotional intelligence." Emotional Intelligence (EI) is now established as an important life skill (Goleman 2006; cf. Seligman 2003). Attention to students' affective traits or dispositions, general moods, and emotional responses to specific stimuli can provide a tutor with insights that will assist them in preparing to teach. For example, it helps to minimize and address symptoms of stress as students settle into a new group or situation, encouraging class cohesion, and facilitating a pleasant and encouraging atmosphere. Tutors may also employ EI as a component of their positive duty of care to students, by being alert to signs of depression or lack of self-esteem, and where appropriate, by offering or arranging suitable support. In short, tutors can promote and model affective competence and management in the learning environment. However, actively assisting students to become conscious of their own felt knowledge (an enterprise that must be undertaken with all of the usual professional caveats of course) can further promote and facilitate learning by helping them to become aware of the influence of past memories on their understanding and habits of response, thereby enabling them to foster a healthy emotional receptivity to new information.

The emotional influence of teachers, good or bad, on subsequent habits of, and attitudes toward learning, cannot be overestimated. They not only teach a given subject intellectually, but also teach a student's heart how best to respond to new information. Early affective memories will therefore be an important factor in a student's enthusiasm for learning about religion. Daniel Dennett puts the cognitive side of this succinctly when he says that, at the simplest level, brains are designed for predicting the future, for "ducking bricks" (Blackmore 2006, 89). This, I suggest, is also mirrored in affective learning. A natural instinct for self-preservation, connected to predicted future outcomes and based on past experience, will determine how keen students are to find out more about God, and will affect their motivation for doing so. Too much or too little enthusiasm inhibits learning. Generally speaking, there is an optimum motivational state for learning, somewhere between very high and very low drive (Bruner 2006a, 14). If a student feels either overly anxious or excited, their ability to comprehend new information is compromised. Religious education tutors might take encouragement from knowing that, according to Bruner, a small degree of boredom is often the most conducive state for new learning! The effects of mood in individuals are magnified in situations where a group of people is sharing emotions. The benefits of belonging to a supportive group of like-minded people are very strong. A child learns at an early stage to recognize the feelings of others and to empathize and adapt their own feelings to generate sympathy or advantage (Dunn 1987, 27). Being part of a group linked by this "heart knowing" reinforces a sense of self, and the shoring up of group opinion also serves to shore up self-esteem. The mood of an individual affects receptiveness to new or conflicting information, with a negative mood narrowing attention and reducing the perception of nuance. In a similar way, the mood of a group acts to consolidate and intensify that affect. A particular religious culture is not just a repository of knowledge but also of emotion, value, and hope. When this is threatened, a protective tribal instinct is never far away, and tutors would be wise to proceed with caution.

One of the major barriers to tutors being able to spend the time and energy necessary to encourage discovery learning and nurture heart knowing is the importance (for very good reason) placed on assessment. Following on from Goleman's work on Emotional Intelligence, Schutte and his colleagues (1998) collected various approaches including assessment of nonverbal expressiveness, attention to feelings, clarity of feelings, and mood repair to produce a thirty-three-item EI scale. However, this is designed to establish baseline EI rather than to assess emotional development. Assessment not only of emotional awareness and management, but of the much more complex skills noted above is very difficult. Indeed, the very validity of assessment in this context has been questioned. However, while there is recognition that it has its problems, it is nevertheless thought necessary (Astley 2000).

As discussed earlier, heart knowing is difficult to articulate, so assessment therefore is going to be very tricky indeed. Formative assessment in terms of nongraded feedback and attention to areas where students have performed less well is not unknown in mainstream education. However, it is an area that is only just beginning to be discussed and researched in theological learning. While journaling and group reflection are fairly well established practices in religious education, they are usually an "add-on" to the more formally academic assessed work, which remains steadfastly cognitively orientated and entangled in accreditation, learning outcomes, and the validating university's ambitions. Even within these constrictions, however, it is possible to introduce, for example, theological reflection on poetry and music or to develop more creative methods of assessment (including portfolios and art). Even if it cannot be included in academic assessment, evaluation of heart learning might be attempted through student self-assessment (or, for the brave, peer assessment) at the beginning, middle, and end of practice-based situated learning, again as part of theological reflection. An oral examination to test how a student might handle certain situations could assess self-awareness, empathy, flexibility, etc. It is certainly an area ripe for research and interdisciplinary dialogue.

CONCLUSION

Not every religious educator will agree with the idea of employing, rather than sidelining, the heart in learning. Opinion about the nature of church, human beings, sin, and evil will guide someone as to the wisdom of such a move, which will be abhorrent to some. This theological educator, however, believes that consciousness of and active attention to instinct, intuition, and intellect together is essential for spiritual and theological development. Combined, they facilitate the paradigm shift required to accept "other" and, I would argue, move from one established religious framework to a higher level of understanding. The active employment and nurturing of the heart in learning also offers a new and refreshing alternative, and perhaps challenge, to a society bound by cognitive chains to particular frames of reference. If the key to accessing heart knowing is imagining how things might be different, then transformative learning becomes essentially about liberation and ethics and begins "denouncing, announcing, prophecy, utopia and dreams" (Freire 2004). Rather than being treated as a distraction or deception, imagine just for one moment a world where people were encouraged to think with their hearts.

REFERENCES

Alheit, P. 1994. "The 'Biographical Question' as a Challenge to Adult Education." *International Review of Education* 40:283–98.

Astley, J. 2000. *Learning in the Way: Research and Reflection on Adult Christian Education*. Leominster: Gracewing.

Astley, J. 2002. *Ordinary Theology: Looking, Listening and Learning in Theology*. London: Ashgate.

Averill, J., and P. Nunley. 1992. *Voyages of the Heart: Living an Emotionally Creative Life*. New York: Free Press.

Blackmore, S. 2006. *Conversations on Consciousness: What the Best Minds Think about the Brain, Free Will, and What It Means To Be Human*. Oxford: Oxford University Press.

Bruner, J. 1962. *On Knowing: Essays for the Left Hand*. Cambridge: Harvard University Press.

———. 1974. *Beyond the Information Given*. London: George Allen and Unwin.

———. 1983. *In Search of Mind: Essays in Autobiography*. New York: Harper & Row.

———. 2006a. *In Search of Pedagogy, Vol. 1: The Selected Works of Jerome Bruner, 1957–1978*. London: Routledge.

———. 2006b. *In Search of Pedagogy, Vol. 2: The Selected Works of Jerome Bruner, 1979–2006*. London: Routledge.

Buber, M. 2004. *I and Thou*. London: Continuum.

Cameron, H., D. Bhatti, C. Duce, J. Sweeney, and C. Watkins. 2010. *Talking about God in Practice: Theological Action Research and Practical Theology*. London: SCM Press.

Dunn, J. 1987. "Understanding Feelings: the Early Stages." In *Making Sense: The Child's Construction of the World*, edited by J. Bruner, 17–26. London: Methuen.

Dykstra, C., and S. Parks. 1986. *Faith Development and Fowler.* Birmingham, AL: Religious Education Press.

Elkind, D. 1961. "The Child's Concept of His Religious Denomination." *Journal of Genetic Psychology* 99:209–25.

Engeström, Y. 1987. *Learning by Expanding: An Activity-Theoretical Approach to Developmental Research.* Helsinki: Orienta-Kunsultit.

Erikson, E. 1964. *Insights and Responsibility Lectures on the Ethical Implications of Psychoanalytical Insight.* New York: W.W. Norton.

Evans, D. 2001. *Emotion: A Very Short Introduction.* Oxford: Oxford University Press.

Fowler, J. 1981. *Stages of Faith: The Psychology of Human Development.* San Francisco: Harper & Row.

Freire, P. 1970. *Pedagogy of the Oppressed,* translated by Myra Bergman Ramos. New York: Continuum.

Gilligan, C. 1982. *In a Different Voice: Psychological Theory and Women's Development.* Cambridge: Harvard.

Goldman, R. 1964. *Religious Thinking from Childhood to Adolescence.* New York: Seabury Press.

Goleman, D. 2006. *Emotional Intelligence: Why It Can Matter More Than IQ.* New York: Bantam.

Graham, E., H. Walton, and F. Ward. 2005. *Theological Reflection Methods.* London: SCM Press.

Green, L. 1990. *Let's Do Theology.* New York: Continuum.

Hannah, B. 1981. *Encounters with the Soul: Active Imagination as Developed by CG Jung.* Boston: Sigo Press.

Hay, D., and R. Nye. 2006. *The Spirit of the Child.* London: Jessica Kingsley.

Heywood, D. 2004. *Divine Revelation and Human Learning: A Christian Theory of Knowledge.* London: Ashgate.

Holyoak, K., and R. Morrison, eds. 2005. *The Cambridge Handbook of Thinking and Reasoning.* Cambridge: Cambridge University Press.

Hull, J. 1985. *What Prevents Christian Adults from Learning?* London: SCM Press.

Illeris, K. 2009. *Contemporary Theories of Learning.* New York: Routledge.

Jansz, J., and M. Timmers. 2002. "Emotional Dissonance When the Experience of an Emotion Jeopardizes an Individual's Identity." *Theory & Psychology* 12:79–95.

Jarvis, P. 2009. "Learning to Be a Person in Society, Learning to Be Me." In *Contemporary Theories of Learning,* edited by K. Illeris, 21–34. New York: Routledge.

Kegan, R. 2009. "What Form Transforms? A Constructive-Developmental

Approach to Transformative Learning." In *Contemporary Theories of Learning*, edited by K. Illeris, 35–52. New York: Routledge.

Killen, P., and J. de Beer. 1994. *The Art of Theological Reflection*. New York: Crossroad.

Kirkpatrick, L., and P. Shaver. 1990. "Attachment Theory and Religion: Childhood Attachments, Religious Beliefs, and Conversion." *Journal for the Scientific Study of Religion* 29:315–34.

Kohlberg, L. 1964. "Development of Moral Character and Moral Ideology." *Review of Child Development Research* 1:381–431.

———. 1969. *Stage and Sequence: The Cognitive-Developmental Approach to Socialization*. Chicago: Rand McNally.

Loder, James E. 1989. *The Transforming Moment*. Colorado Springs, CO: Helmers & Howard.

Madge, V. 1965. *Children in Search of Meaning*. London: SCM.

Mezirow, J. 1991. *Transformative Dimensions of Adult Learning*. San Francisco: Jossey-Bass.

———. 2000. *Learning as Transformation: Critical Perspectives on a Theory in Progress*. San Francisco: Jossey-Bass.

Mezirow, J., and E. Taylor, eds. 2009. *Transformative Learning in Practice: Insights from Community, Workplace, and Higher Education*. San Francisco: Jossey-Bass.

Nelson, J. 2009. *Psychology, Religion and Spirituality*. New York: Springer.

Olson, D. 2007. *Jerome Bruner: The Cognitive Revolution in Educational Theory*. Vol. 3. New York: Continuum.

Parks, S. 1986. "Imagination and Spirit in Faith Development." In *Faith Development and Fowler*, edited by C. Dykstra and S. Parks, 137–55. Birmingham, AL: Religious Education Press.

———. 1992. "Young Adult Faith Development: Teaching in the Context of Theological Education." In *Christian Perspectives on Faith Development*, edited by J. Astley and L. J. Francis, 201–15. Leominster: Gracewing.

Rogers, C. 1951. *Client-Centered Therapy*. Boston: Houghton Mifflin.

———. 1969. *Freedom to Learn: A View of What Education Might Become*. Columbus, OH: Merrill.

Schutte, N. S., J. M. Malouff, L. E. Hall, D. J. Haggerty, and J. T. Cooper. 1998. "Development and Validation of a Measure of Emotional Intelligence." *Personality and Individual Differences*. 25:167–77.

Seligman, M. 2003. *Authentic Happiness: Using the New Positive Psychology to Realize Your Potential for Lasting Fulfillment*. London: Nicholas Brealey Publishing.

Slee, N. 2004. *Women's Faith Development.* Aldershot: Ashgate.

Spilka, B., R. W. Hood, B. Hunsberger, and R. L. Gorsuch, eds. 2003. *The Psychology of Religion.* 3rd ed. New York: Guilford.

Streib, H. 2001. "Faith Development Theory Revisited: The Religious Styles Perspective." *International Journal for the Psychology of Religion* 11 (3): 143–58.

Suedfeld, P., and Blunk, S. 1993. "Changes in Integrative Complexity Accompanying Significant Life Events: Historical Evidence." *Journal of Personality and Social Psychology* 64:124–30.

Vygotsky, L. 1978. *Mind in Society.* Cambridge: Harvard.

Westerhoff, J. 1976. *Will Our Children Have Faith?* New York: Seabury.

Whitehead, J., and E. Whitehead. 1995. *Theological Reflection in Ministry.* New York: Sheed and Ward.

Wynn, M. 2005. *Emotional Experience and Religious Understanding: Integrating Perception, Conception and Feeling.* Cambridge: Cambridge University Press.

PART 4

Integration

Head, Heart, and Wisdom 9

Harris Wiseman

Introduction

In both psychological and theological reflections on wisdom the question of *knowing* is paramount. How does knowing relate to wisdom? What forms of knowledge and which modes of awareness are at the center of wisdom? Psychological reflection here focuses its attention on processes, that is, it aims to provide a metawisdom relating to the underlying cognitive processes that characterize the kinds of knowing epitomized by wise persons. Theological reflection, in contrast, presents a greater diversity of roles for wise knowing and is far broader in its scope. Where theological approaches yield a rich, broad, and deep web of reflections regarding wisdom and knowing, psychological approaches have yielded a series of narrower, yet more focused, models. While theological approaches have yielded penetrating, nuanced, yet unwieldy accounts, psychological approaches have yielded neater, simplified, yet highly workable accounts. The theological accounts have the advantages of depth, a realistic complexity, and a broad diversity within a larger unity; the psychological accounts have the advantages of simplicity, focus, and workability. As such, the two disciplines largely compensate for the weaknesses of the other, the often unwieldy nature of theological wisdom reflection, and the fragmented, often competitive nature of psychological wisdom accounts. It is for this reason that it is of such value to read the two discourses side by side.

The aims of this chapter are twofold. First of all, with respect to theological wisdom reflection (of which the theologies of contemporary thinkers Ford and Kelsey will be taken as the prime exemplars), it will be argued that theological discourse can be advanced by taking a penetrating look at the cognitive processes that underlie its reflections on wisdom. By contextualizing these theological reflections in terms of the various processes that underlie them, this complex and interconnected web of wisdoms can be given new clarity and depth. It will be shown that a broad vision of theological wisdoms sometimes involves antagonistic processes, and it is valuable for pedagogical purposes to be able to distinguish between modes of Christian wisdom in terms of these underlying processes. Secondly, with respect to wisdom psychology, it will be shown that the discourse need not be as competitive or as fragmented as it is. In fact, using a more contextual way of looking at the subject matter—one more characteristic of theological discourse—it is possible to draw together this psychological work into a "wholeness-in-complexity" that is capable of maintaining the profound differences between many of the approaches found in wisdom psychology and which presents them as independently valid models of different kinds of wisdom that serve *particular contexts of application.*

In order to do this, the reflections on wisdom will be divided into three broad approaches, which shall be referred to as a "wisdom of the head," a "wisdom of the heart," and a further wisdom, one of "head and heart," which balances the two very different kinds of knowing that will be associated with head and heart. Before commencing discussion, it is important to clarify what these terms—"head" and "heart"—mean. The idea of knowing with the head is relatively easily and intuitively defined. It refers to predominantly analytic, meta-analytic, and intellectual modes of knowing. This generates an approach to wisdom that is cognitive-heavy and whose focus is largely upon knowledge and expertise, rules and skills, and practical reasoning, that is, applying instrumental intelligence for the selection of wise goals and the production of a greater good. In contrast, the idea of knowing with the heart is rather more difficult to define, because it refers to a kind of knowing that is broader, more holistic, and more embodied in nature. This generates a vision of a wisdom of "being" rather than a "thinking" wisdom; here wisdom is envisaged not in terms of knowledge or skills, but rather in terms of disencumbering oneself of these things in order to promote a more direct, open, and holistic mode of awareness. Finally, once these two very different kinds of wisdom have been presented, discussion will close with a presentation of how they might be brought together into a further wisdom mode, a wisdom of head *and* heart, and what the ideal relationship between these two very different kinds of wisdom might be.

A Wisdom of the Head

In wisdom psychology one finds a variety of models that can be understood as describing a "wisdom of the head." The Berlin Wisdom Paradigm offers the clearest example of such an approach to wisdom. This model is concerned primarily with wisdom insofar as it relates to knowledge and the ability to apply that knowledge in a well-organized and efficient manner. Wisdom manifests through coordinating, organizing, and manipulating bodies of factual and procedural knowledge in ways that either solve problems in one's environment or that generate some larger good. Of course, not all knowledge is relevant to wisdom, rather this "wisdom-related knowledge" is to do with the fundamentals of good living. It is "knowledge and judgment about the essence of the human condition and the ways and means of planning, managing, and understanding a good life" (Baltes and Staudinger 2000, 124). Indeed, the exemplary wise individual in the Berlin group's model is someone who has their feet on the ground, who has the practical know-how to order and successfully manage the important matters of life, mundane as they might be, someone older who has "seen it all," as it were, and who then manifests as the sort of person one would approach for advice in those standard tricky life situations that young persons (and not so young persons) find themselves embroiled in.

This is a view of a very practical wisdom, and wisdom is to be understood here as a "metaheuristic" (Baltes and Staudinger 2000, 122) that organizes and integrates disparate bodies of useful practical knowledge into a workable whole. As a metaheuristic, the ability to form wise judgments is described through the expression of a range of metacognitive thinking skills, such as learning to display various degrees of value-relativism in one's judgments, an ability to take the perspectives of others, as well as a recognition of life's uncertainty and the limited nature of human cognitive capacities (Baltes and Staudinger 2000, 124–27). In terms of affect, wisdom involves evincing a modulated range of emotions (Kunzmann and Baltes 2003, 1104). In this picture "head rules over heart," and wisdom is found where "cooler heads prevail." However, it is not as though feeling is to be detached entirely from these processes. Rather, it is feeling *of a particular sort* that is called for, a more disciplined and educated emotional range. The central terms here are knowledge and skill; feeling is both to inform, and yet be brought to bear under, the supervening powers of meta-analytic and practical modes of reasoning.

In many ways the Berlin model is an attractive picture of wisdom, and it proffers many insights that have theological correlates. The day-to-day administration of life and living is precisely the sort of wisdom that one finds in the book of *Proverbs*. It is the sort of "upbuilding" community work that Paul concerned himself with, and, as such, a pragmatic, day-to-day wisdom is something one finds in many guises throughout theological wisdom accounts. Indeed, both Ford and Kelsey are concerned with developing a contemporary wisdom for persons living their lives now, and a contemporary Christian wisdom is envisaged as something to be interwoven with all aspects of a person's life. Insofar as theological reflection is concerned with day-to-day living, it demands a wisdom (or wisdom*s*) that must engage with all facets of living. Ford writes that there is no scientific formula for deal-ing with challenges of life—raising children, dealing with suffering, trauma, or death; shaping communities and their institutions (Ford 2007, 2). Grappling with these problems in a down-to-earth manner that is true to Christ, scripture, and contemporary society requires pre-cisely the sort of instrumental, problem-solving, and predominantly analytic mode of wisdom that the Berlin model espouses.

Both Kelsey and Ford recognize the need for an intellectually rigor-ous cognitive dimension to wisdom. Ford writes:

> Today it is "still necessary to try to combine knowledge, under-standing, good judgment and far-sighted decision making. The challenges and dilemmas of prudence, justice and compassion remain urgent. . . . The discernment of meaning, truth and right conduct in religion has not become any easier. . . . Choos-ing among possible priorities, each with a well-argued claim, is no simpler today." (2007, 1–2)

Here knowledge and the ability to use that knowledge appropriately are important elements in the idea of "theology as wisdom." Indeed, the promotion of a thorough "learning of the faith" is a necessary com-ponent in producing Ford's wish for "communities of desire and wis-dom" (2007, 225), or in Kelsey's term, communities-in-communion, engaging together in the practice of primary theology for the purpose of shaping the present and future practices of the church. As such, even lay Christians need to have some degree of theological education if their religious practice is to be best oriented toward wisdom. Theology in this view—written, spoken, and lived—is concerned with knowing the very God that is being worshipped and responding appropriately through one's practices as a Christian. As such, this heavily cognitive and discursive element of Christian wisdom is something intended for all lay Christians to have at least some degree of expertise in.

One central feature of contemporary theological approaches to wisdom that is both a great strength and at times a great weakness is its tremendous richness, depth, and the incredibly complex way the various wisdoms in its discourse are interwoven. On the one hand, this "ecology of wisdom" is realistic, natural, and true to the subject matter at hand—wisdom is an extraordinarily complex subject. At the same time, this approach can make theological wisdom reflections rather unwieldy and sometimes too complex to know quite what to do with them. It is here in particular that the neater, more categorical wisdom packages found in the psychology are most valuable. While it is correct to be suspicious of packages of wisdom that are *too* neat, sometimes simplification is the necessary trade-off for attaining a provisional per-spective on wisdom that is workable and which might ultimately lead to valuable pedagogical interventions.

It is true that Ford and Kelsey's reflections for the most part outstrip the neater, more streamlined psychological accounts in both breadth and depth. However, what psychological accounts such as the Berlin model stand to offer here is a way of unifying the vast and complex range of competencies to be found in theological reflections into a more manageable whole. That is, psychological perspectives offer a way of arranging some of the more powerful yet nebulous theological reflections into a higher-level unity. For example, the Berlin group's emphases on metaprocesses, knowledge-integration, and the impor-tance of heuristics in activating one's bodies of knowledge, serve as a way of describing a supervening metacognitive dimension to wisdom that is helpful for making sense of many of the disparate pieces found in the theology. The notions of heuristics and integration function here as a "descriptive glue" that can subtend, provisionally at least, all the seemingly endless reflections one finds in theological reflection. This example is useful when talking about the theological need to balance tradition and innovation in religious practice. Here the notions of heu-ristics and knowledge-integration help describe the manner in which the "generative grammar" of scripture and practices can be expanded in appropriate ways while remaining rooted in the body of scripture and belief that sustains the core identity of a person, or group, as the particular kind of Christian that they are.

Indeed, these considerations point us to a particularly important area of crossover between the notions of wisdom presented here: the importance assigned to the ability to use past knowledge in novel ways. Past learning is often necessary to equip one to handle new situations. Wisdom in the Berlin model is very much a case of activating and reorganizing bodies of tried-and-tested knowledge in ways that yield insights for new or novel situations. Yet the idea of applying tradition to new situations, improvisation, and finding novel expression for an older wisdom is also an important theme found in both Ford and Kelsey's theologies. Indeed, it is an important theme *particularly* for contemporary theological wisdom, a central component of which is the problem of mediating tradition and innovation in a postmodern and pluralistic world. The complexity of applying ancient scripture (a "non-negotiable" basis for the authenticity of a Christian wisdom; Ford 2007, 2) to contemporary problems and modern living is a central element of contemporary theology as wisdom. Reading scripture in this way relies, in Fordian terms, upon balancing both a "wisdom of reserve" and a "wisdom of ramification," that is, the capacity to grasp scripture in ways that are true to the original meanings and intentions while still being able to open up the text in new ways, to improvise on themes, and to nourish the text in ways appropriate to modern concerns. One of the key difficulties posed here resides in avoiding an overly dogmatic literalism without getting lost in an endless stream of interpretation. Improvisation involves a creative freedom, yet it is also a freedom constrained by rules. Taking the Berlin team's notion of wisdom as an organizing metaheuristic is a helpful way of describing how the various interpretive impulses required in this theological scriptural wisdom can be organized to find a best fit between both traditional as well as contemporary concerns.

However, there are also various points of departure between theological reflection and this heavily cognitive "wisdom of the head." It is hard to dispute that knowledge and the ability to manipulate that knowledge plays a broad and important role in wisdom. Yet valid as it is on its own terms, this "wisdom of the head" is not adequate *taken in isolation* for describing a satisfying range of wisdom concerns such as one finds in the broader picture of theological wisdom reflection. For example, perhaps the largest point of departure between the Berlin model and a broader picture of Christian wisdom is this: *the Berlin model is almost entirely preoccupied with knowledge.* It is important to note that there are other important modes of know*ing* that have very little to do with know*ledge per se.* Indeed, for some, wisdom resides not in gathering up more skills and knowledge at all, but the exact contrary, in laying down these things in order to discover another mode of awareness altogether, one less to do with abstractions and concepts and more to do with direct perception of reality, here and now. These considerations have a profound relevance to another kind of Christian wisdom to which we shall presently turn.

A Wisdom of the Heart

It is important to have an understanding of wise know*ing* that goes beyond the notion of know*ledge.* Models that place too much emphasis on knowledge cannot account for those moments in life where wisdom consists not in what facts or procedures one knows, but simply in how one *is*—direct, open, natural, and good. This alternative approach, propounded by psychologists such as Rosch (2009), takes the view that wisdom is more to do with *disencumbering* oneself of knowledge, and returning to a "beginner's mind" state of openness and clarity. This produces an entirely different way of being in and knowing the world. The contrast with a knowledge-centric approach such as the Berlin model could not be more stark. For Rosch, wisdom and the compassion that comes from wisdom are spontaneous results of an unencumbered, direct, and open state of being that has moved beneath the surface levels of mental functioning. Rosch's claim then is that too much knowl-

edge *impedes* rather than assists in wisdom because it is bound up with
the chaotic surface operations of the mind. Rosch writes:

> *People do not need to acquire more information, more logic,*
> *more ego, and more skills to make them wise. What they need*
> *is to unlearn what they have accumulated that veils them from*
> *that wisdom. . . . On the surface is the mind of ordinary con-*
> *cepts, emotions, desires, fears, even boredom—the mind with*
> *which everyone is familiar. Below that is the mind that is more*
> *in contact with basic wisdom and better able to see and act*
> *from it. (2009, 136)*

However, while this open state of being goes beyond know*ledge*, it
still depends crucially on a certain kind of know*ing*—a way of knowing and being present in the world that is very different to the analytic
approach to reality. Such a being-wisdom involves a mode of knowing,
or perhaps better, of "attending" or of "being aware," which is broad
spectrum, receptive, noninstrumental, and nonmanipulative. It is a
way of knowing that resides in a "letting be"—simply allowing the fullness of being to be the fullness of being. At the same time it is *engaged*
with the world in a more immersed and direct, rather than abstract
or intellectual fashion. Rosch is not asserting that knowledge is not
important; rather she is saying that it is a question of "which mind"
one gives priority to. With the Berlin model, feeling was modulated
under the supervening power of the analytic. With Rosch the analytic is
modulated under the supervening power of "the heart"—a direct, open
receptivity and awareness of reality as is. It is this latter "wisdom of the
heart" that is presented by Rosch as primary, leading to "a deeper, more
panoramic, and more immediate wisdom way of knowing, feeling, and
being" (2005, 103). It is "an underlying nascent wisdom mode . . . said
to be always available, half glimpsed, by everyone. . . . A portal into a
radically new (lived) understanding of what it is to know, to be, to act,
and to be an embodied self in time" (2005, 103; 1999, 222).

This idea of a receptive, noninstrumental mode of knowing has many parallels in theological ideas of wisdom and manifests in a variety of sometimes surprising ways. For example, this deeply receptive kind of *attending* resonates most clearly with the more contemplative strands of theological wisdom, an idea perhaps most succinctly expressed by Simone Weil (1951) as "waiting on God." This is a mode of wisdom that involves *clearing a space*, or simply *allowing room* for a deeper wisdom to enter. While the Berlin model focuses far more on an active pursuit of wisdom, an active cogitative "thinking through," in contrast, this idea of receiving, of being acted upon, speaks to the important role the *passive* has to play in wise knowing. Ford's reflections on the story of Job are exemplary here. While an attitude of active searching and questioning are features that all will agree are characteristics of the wise individual, the book of Job indicates vividly the manner in which wisdom often needs to move beyond this active searching and into the passive tense—*being questioned, being searched*. Part of a Joban "wisdom of growth" resides in being willing to let oneself be interrogated, through and through, by new and unprecedented events.[1]

The need for receptivity in this "wisdom of the heart" reveals another important resonance here—what might be termed the "for its own sake" of wisdom. Part of the essence of the kind of wisdom Rosch espouses is that one simply be aware of things as they are *in and for themselves*. This "for its own sake" is a key notion found in both Kelsey and Ford. For example, Kelsey writes:

> *Ad hoc practical wisdom about how to act wisely for the well-being of fellow creatures requires capacities to discern what makes for the well-being of particular fellow creatures in their particular situations. . . . Discernment requires that perceptual, imaginative, and cognitive capacities be disciplined to be capable of paying close attention to particular creatures, to do so intentionally, and to do so in ways that* as far as possible set aside self-interest and the biases it introduces, *in order to*

learn what truly makes for their well-being as creatures. (2009, 353–54, emphasis added)

Ford also, with his characteristic exhortation to "care for those that cry," argues for the necessity of developing a keen receptivity with respect to those that cry out, hearing them *in their particularity*—as the particular individuals or groups that they are, in the uniqueness of their cries. This calls for a kind of wise vision, a certain kind of awareness that is capable of seeing the other precisely as they are, "for their own sake."

Indeed, this kind of self-transcendence, this growth toward a vision of the value of things beyond oneself, is again exemplified in Ford's reflections on the story of Job. The climax of Job's growth in wisdom "towards something more like God's own wisdom" (Ford 2007, 99) comes in the moment God instructs Job to "gird up thy loins now like a man" (Job 40:7, KJV) and questions him in a way that tears him away from and beyond his own concerns toward a sublime vision of creation in and for itself. Job, in the midst of his torture, who had quite under-standably "sucked all of creation into his affliction" (Ford 2007, 114), was shown by God a greater vision: *that there is more to this world than Job and his suffering*—indeed, more to this world than any of us and our suffering. This is a wisdom that moves beyond self-centeredness toward a larger vision—that God, others, and world (*including Job and ourselves*) are precious in and for themselves, to be loved *hinnan*, for nothing, for their own sake (Ford 2007, 100, 113). The key to this kind of wisdom then is that it is *fundamentally other-centered*, and most importantly, it is founded upon a kind of awareness that *engages* with the other *in a relationship of care*. This mode of knowing is one that allows one to move beyond self-centered perspectives, beyond "pro-jections" (Ardelt 2003, 279), and that allows us to become aware of the nature and value of things in their own right.

There is one last point of resonance between a Roschian wisdom and the story of Job, one that shows a very clear contrast between this "wisdom of the heart" and the sort of "head wisdom" espoused by the

Berlin team above. Where the Berlin model relies on using previous knowledge, the tried-and-tested, to deal with novel situations (and this is very important in many contexts), the story of Job shows us that sometimes it is necessary to gain an understanding of things that is *radically new*. Before Job has his encounter with God, he is confronted by his friends who all offer him their advice and views on his affliction. In fact, Job's friends offer him nothing other than the prepackaged answers, the received wisdom of his age—none of which is nearly adequate enough to describe the present reality of Job's situation. While Job's radical questioning vindicates him above his friends, *the irony is that Job's friends were indeed offering him sound wisdom from within the received conceptual bounds.* This ambiguity underscores the difference between the two kinds of wisdom that have been here presented. The Berlin model, the wisdom of the head, epitomizes the ideal of applying received wisdom. In contrast, the Roschian wisdom of the heart represents a kind of wisdom that prizes the "beginner's mind," new and clear vision, which is precisely the sort of wisdom that is required when all received wisdom falters in the face of present reality. Here knowledge systems cannot avail one, and, as in the case of the advice of Job's friends—*good advice* from within the usual paradigms, yet poor advice from the perspective of a larger wisdom—heuristics and received knowledge can actually *hold one back* from growth. Indeed, only something that emphasizes the richness of lived experience, which makes primary the truth of things as they are rather than the way one imagines things should be, or the way one has constructed reality in one's theories, can allow one to transcend in some powerful way the procrustean paradigms that no longer fit with present reality.

So this story of Job and a Roschian wisdom agree on this idea that there are times when past knowledge, while being relevant to a certain kind of wisdom, can be inadequate to present needs, and that sometimes what one already knows can be a hindrance rather than a help. As Ford writes, the wisdom pedagogy of the book of Job is as far away as possible from "packaged" answers. It exemplifies the need and importance of resisting formulaic answers, encouraging uninhibited interrogation of God and God's purposes, acknowledgment that ready-made answers from the past might be inadequate to cope with new developments and trust in God beyond all the received ideas of God (Ford 2007, 174). Job's is a wisdom not caught up with knowledge and procedures, nor is it about sticking to rules, nor previous knowledge, nor even of extending what was previously known, but rather about "going beyond," about perceiving—and receiving—the radically new. "It is a drama about the 'always more' of a wisdom that is genuinely engaged with God, history and creation" (Ford 2007, 99). The mode of awareness one finds at the heart of the Roschian wisdom, one which fosters receptivity, openness, other-centeredness, engagement, and the willingness to transcend the usual interpretations, is key to this growth in wisdom.

Toward a Balanced Account

The contrast between these two wisdoms reveals an important feature about the cognitive processes, and the kinds of knowing, that are the foundations of these two very different kinds of wisdom. Indeed, per-haps the most important assertion that contrasting this head and heart wisdom allows one to make is that *there are two qualitatively different kinds of wisdom that are profoundly antagonistic in terms of the cognitive processes involved in their application*: one that is goal-centered, manip-ulative, problem-solving, based on expertise, knowledge, and rules; and the other which is noninstrumental, open, receptive, and broad spectrum in the mode of awareness it promotes. Yet it has been seen that *both* of these very different wisdoms correlate with elements of the larger picture of Christian wisdom. This yields an important observa-tion: once contextualized with respect to the psychology, one sees very clearly that *the different kinds of wisdom espoused in the theology place very different cognitive demands on the individual*. Thus, one of the problems with the richly interwoven landscape of theological reflection is that it obscures the manner in which the kinds of wisdom that it espouses demand the cultivation of at least two very different kinds of awareness, two very different kinds of wisdom. Yet the situation is even more complex than this. Despite offering two very different, indeed, antagonistic modes of wisdom, there is a case to be made for a further kind of wisdom to be expressed—a wisdom of head *and* heart.

These two wisdoms thus far considered have corresponding strengths and weaknesses. A predominantly analytic kind of wisdom is both strengthened and limited by its reliance on expertise, knowledge, skills, and rules. A wisdom of the head is particularly useful for helping one apply past learning in creative and novel ways. However, while such a wisdom excels with respect to the day-to-day, the practical and the tried-and-tested, this "head" wisdom is a little more abstracted from its subject matter—it has difficulties in handling those circumstances where one's knowledge or expertise is not particularly relevant, or in managing those situations where one needs to go beyond knowledge altogether and see directly. It is here that the more synthetic "heart" models of wisdom, such as Rosch's, have their strengths. They foster a connection to basic reality; they foster more direct modes of engagement with the world, a more holistic sense of the big picture, empathy and connection with others, and they make possible a responsive mode of vision from which one can grow toward a newer and deeper way of understanding things. Yet, as with the analytic kinds of wisdom, the very strength of this more meditative heart wisdom is also its weakness. There are certain circumstances in life where what one requires the most is the advice of someone with broad experience, knowledge, and strong powers of practical reasoning. There are times where an expert's wisdom is needed, and here a reliance upon openness and receptivity simply cannot avail one of the wisdom that one needs.

It seems therefore that the question is one of situation. The two kinds of wisdom that we have here seem to be both antagonistic and complementary. It is hard to dispute that both kinds of wisdom are very important and have their own particular place—depending upon one's context one needs both a wisdom of the head and a wisdom of the heart. *The problem is that we are left over with two very skewed accounts.* Is it possible, despite their antagonism, to draw these two kinds of wisdom together? Is it possible to draw a picture of wisdom wherein these head and heart ways of knowing work more closely and cooperatively together?

A Wisdom of Head and Heart

One common theme found in the theologies of both Kelsey and Ford is the notion of "overcoming the usual dualisms"—theory and practice, interiority and exteriority, cognitive and affective, knowledge and love, the private and the public, the solitary and the corporate, quietude and the feast. Each has their place in the theologies considered, and the full richness of a Christian wisdom requires all of these many things. One requires knowledge, facts, rules, and procedures; yet one needs a mode of knowing where these things are, however temporarily, suspended or left behind; one needs concepts and ideas, yet one also needs a broader connection to the real, to the now; one requires both active and passive, a searching self, and a search*ed* self, an asserting and a receptivity. Indeed, sometimes it is necessary that these opposites be made to interact and build upon each other. Should head and heart be seen as another dualism to be overcome?

There is an important aspect of wisdom in Ford's understanding which involves a kind of knowing which might best be described as a practice of love and desire that is inseparable from learning, knowledge, and truth. For Ford, "faith cannot be disengaged from its relationship with intelligent understanding" (Ford and Stamps 1996, 7), and knowledge and love are presented as "coinherent activities in God" (Ford 2007, 269). As such, this knowing dimension of wisdom might be described as one in which both knowledge and love are found to *overflow* into each other. This speaks to a dual conception of knowing in wisdom. First, there is the knowing associated with know*ledge,* that is, the analytic and conceptual kind one associates with the head. Yet there is also another kind of knowing here more closely associated with the heart, that is, love and desire themselves as ways of knowing.

In combination, these kinds of knowing, "with our whole mind, with our whole heart," take on a highly dynamic and fluid relationship that defies static verbal description. Sometimes loving God in a more intellectual manner is at the fore, as in study and learning; sometimes loving God with a deeper kind of awareness is at the fore, as in practices of prayer or silent contemplation. Both represent distinctive kinds of knowing, yet in neither case is the one to be completely severed from the other. In study, the analytic mode of knowing must be tempered with the imaginative; in prayer, the more subtle and inarticulate modes of knowing, for example, the quiet intuitions of a deeper truth, or the powerful wordless sense evoked by symbols, parables, and metaphors, sometimes seek to be given a voice. They seek to be articulated, spoken, or even cried out, and made the stuff of further reflection. In each case, to varying degrees, there is a dynamic interaction between the two modes of knowing, a back-and-forth, a continuing overflow by which each is deepened with respect to the other. This speaks to an iterative process in which neither analytic nor synthetic modes of knowing are adequate on their own, but rather in which both must work cooperatively in a process of *tempering* that uses both modes alternately in order to articulate a deeper vision of truth.

An insightful way of describing this cooperative relation can be found in Iain McGilchrist's (2009) work on the divided brain.[2] According to McGilchrist, the primary theme of his thesis is *the brain's need for both division and union*. As far as the brain goes, actually, asymmetry is better than symmetry, irregularity better than regularity—the functions of the two hemispheres need to be clearly separated, but they need to work together. Like the two antagonistic kinds of wisdom that have been presented here, the bihemispheric nature of the brain produces two "fundamentally opposed realities, two different modes of experience" where "each is of ultimate importance in bringing about the recognisably human world" (McGilchrist 2009, 3). Like the two wisdoms here presented, the two hemispheres offer *partial but complementary* takes on the world, both of which are essential for the fullness of living. The radically antagonistic yet essentially complementary functions of the hemispheres, and the way they ought to be integrated, serves as an analogue for how a wisdom of the head and of the heart might best be integrated too.

What is to be avoided at all costs here is a *merger* of the two kinds of wisdom. For McGilchrist, the ideal relation between the hemispheres is one of cooperation *but separation*, that is, a bridging but never a melding of their respective functions. Indeed, both hemispheres *need* each other in order to achieve their full potential, in some sense to become fully themselves. Both are necessary, yet they are too distinct to be combined. Precisely the same is true with the modes of wisdom that have been here discussed. The head and heart kinds of wisdom have been presented as deeply antagonistic: they do radically different things, they have corresponding strengths and weaknesses, they rely on radically different ways of approaching the world, radically different ways of knowing the world, radically different ways of being in the world. Insofar as one is looking to describe a wisdom that balances *both* head and heart modes of knowing, *merger* of these processes is not desired. Rather, like the antagonistic powers of the brain's two hemispheres, cooperation and separation is needed, division and union. A wisdom that combines both head and heart must keep the processes distinct in their function, *but they need to interact seamlessly, flipping between strategies in fluid and context-dependent ways.*

In short, a wisdom of head and heart needs to arise from a balanced *betweenness* of these two very different kinds of wisdom. Both modes of knowing are required: one is structured, articulate, clear; the other is more subtle, ephemeral, and broad. What is discerned in one mode is passed to the other, given clearer expression, passed back to the other, and deepened. This is a tempering wisdom, like one tempers a sword, through the heat of embodied care and through the cool of the analytic and intellectual. It is an iterative process, a giving and a receiving; a more specialized kind of attention and a broader more holistic kind of awareness; an active and a passive; an intellectual and an experiential; a being and a reflecting; a subtle intuition of a deeper truth and a making explicit of that which is concealed.

What makes the balanced mode distinctive, then, is the kind of process that is used in its application, the back-and-forth, rather than the predominant reliance on one or other mode. In this back-and-forth between "experiencing" and "digesting," applying as it does these two very different modes of knowing, the product then (what might be called a "refined understanding," a transformative realization of some deep truth) is a full and profound kind of knowing that is neither some "cold" analytic piece of wisdom-relevant knowledge, nor yet a purely direct experiencing of the world—rather it is a truly heartfelt grasp of a deeper truth which motivates the person toward transcendence or growth.

Conclusion

It has been seen that theological and psychological wisdom reflection share many resonances and parallels. I think it would be a mistake to single out any one of the psychological wisdom models as describing "true" Christian wisdom. As has been seen, *each of these visions has a context that is appropriate to them*. As such, I would suggest that these three different wisdoms—head, heart, and balanced—though clearly related, are best preserved as three independently valid, context-appropriate pictures. Head and heart modes of wisdom appear imbalanced in isolation, yet when placed as *options within a larger tapestry of wisdom* represent essential pieces in a larger puzzle. Rather than attempting, on the one hand, to constrain wisdom within a unitary or singular model, or, on the other hand, present an endlessly differentiated ecology of wisdom forms, what is most useful in this context is to provide a descriptive *range* within which wisdom can be cast (using

Kelsey's term) as a "wholeness-in-complexity." The modes of wisdom—head, heart, and balanced—describe interactions at their extremes that are so distinct that, I would argue, they are better off described using three different (though connected) modalities. Certainly it would be a mistake to simply reduce wisdom to the mean. There are occasions that call for the sorts of wisdom the Berlin model describes, some better described in Rosch's terms, and some that fit better with an iterative and cooperative model. The attempts to reduce wisdom to expertise, or to openness, or even to a balanced form of "integrated thought" are all as narrow as the other. While it is true that all modes of wisdom will—to varying degrees—involve some amount of cooperation between head and heart ways of knowing, the attempt to constrain wisdom within a *unitary, singular* picture of "balanced" cooperation is far too narrow to do descriptive justice to the full complexity of circumstances which demand wisdom.

Indeed, keeping these three forms of wisdom separate helps us to discern a further higher-order consideration with respect to wise knowing. Once one understands that there are a variety of useful kinds of wisdom, each of which relates to a certain context, one begins to see that a full picture of wise knowing must include a kind of discernment that is able to appreciate *which situation calls for which particular kind of wisdom.* Here it is no longer a debate between which model better describes wisdom; now it is a question of understanding which strategies to use and when. This is an important contribution: *it poses the psychological wisdom models considered here as no longer competitive but rather as different, situationally appropriate kinds of wisdom, which cater for a complementary set of wisdom needs.*

The issue is one of context. Focusing too heavily on the notion of a "balanced wisdom" falls short in contexts where the wisdom demanded requires a keen skewing in one or other direction. Many examples of such contexts have been described. There are situations that call for the more specialist and expert kind of wisdom that one associates with the head. The day-to-day administration of life and living, circumstances that call for a pronounced ability to think, to discuss, and to negotiate solutions to contemporary concerns and the challenges of everyday living call for the kind of wisdom that is guided by knowledge, that is goal-oriented, and instrumental in nature. With respect to theological reflections, these are all staple components of what it is to be an engaged Christian working to develop contemporary practices with respect to the challenges of modern living. In these contexts one needs efficient means for applying knowledge toward a larger coproductive good. Grappling with these everyday problems in a down-to-earth manner that is true to Christ, scripture, and contemporary society requires precisely the sort of instrumental, problem-solving, and predominantly analytic mode of wisdom that the Berlin model espouses. While the Berlin model is certainly a secular vision of wisdom, the central concerns are common to both disciplines: complexity and uncertainty; managing multiple (and often conflicting) points of view; organizing bodies of facts and procedures; gaining in experience and developing the means for applying that experience efficiently toward a larger good.

Equally there are contexts that call for a more synthetic and open mode of knowing. This "wisdom of the heart" is called for when a profound receptivity is required, or when knowledge is no longer useful, or indeed when knowledge becomes an actual hindrance to seeing the basic reality of what is before one's eyes. Such a receptive wisdom becomes important in situations where a holistic vision is required, where an embodied engagement with the world is most valuable, where a radically new vision is what is called for. Most importantly, this "wisdom of the heart" is called for in circumstances that require engaging with others in a direct and profound relationship of empathy or care. The sort of wisdom one finds in Rosch requires a mode of awareness that is capable of seeing persons and things as they are, and as valuable in and for themselves. These are all circumstances where expertise, skills, and being cluttered with endless concepts can only impede the sort of direct awareness required to engage with these situations in the wisest possible manner. It is a simple "wisdom of being" that transcends instrumental concerns, which calls for a suspension of the usual analytic modes of knowing, however temporarily, in order to clear a space within oneself out of which another deeper kind of awareness can arise.

With respect to wisdom psychology, then, the value of maintaining this threefold distinction within wisdom discourse is that it allows one to retain a rich and unified diversity to wisdom reflection, one that does not reduce wisdom to a series of competitive one-sided accounts, but rather which looks for the particular kinds of context in which the respective models of wisdom best function. *All* of the thinkers about wisdom thus far considered have had something important to say. Accordingly, what is offered here is not a new model of wisdom, but rather a higher-order means of understanding the wholeness-in-complexity of a discourse that is presently unnecessarily fragmented. Admittedly, this threefold approach to wisdom is but a provisional way of reading the discourse. The approach taken here relates to the current state of the discourse as is. Moreover, the question of wisdom is always located to some degree within the context of present needs and concerns. As such, the study of wisdom is a constantly shifting landscape that is continually developing anew. With this in mind it must be noted that the higher-order approach to wisdom presented here is but a provisional *though illuminating* means for unifying a wonderfully rich but highly fragmented discourse.

With respect to the theological reflections, having an understanding of the different cognitive modes that subtend those reflections can only serve to deepen the self-understanding of both teacher and student of wisdom. Whenever one reads (or writes) a theology of wisdom, it can be helpful to keep an eye out for the various modes of knowing which underpin the varieties of wisdom being discussed. One must remain mindful of those aspects which speak toward a receptivity or those which speak toward the more intellectual or analytical; one must be aware of those parts which call for a more engaged or a more modulated emotional stance; aware of those elements which call for more empathy, more direct awareness of other, God, or world in and for themselves; aware of which elements of wisdom require a more active approach, and which require greater surrender or passivity; one must be able to discern what proportion of each mode of knowing, and which process appropriate to that mode of knowing is required in order to find the right balance of these antagonistic head and heart ways of knowing. In short, one has a new "interpretive key" with which to read theological reflections on wisdom. One has to hand a tool for comprehending and discerning within theological wisdom reflection which underlying processes (and which balance of processes) are in play, and which particular mode of awareness is appropriate to the kind of wisdom that is being discussed. What is provided here is a way of seeing the wisdom beneath the wisdom. One must bring to mind that each kind of wisdom is best served by fostering a specific kind of cognitive approach, a specific mode of knowing that is better capable of fostering precisely the kind of wisdom in question.

Thus, given the sometimes nebulous and unmanageable complexity of theological webs of reflection on the subject, contextualizing wisdom theology in this way yields a greater clarity to its contents in a way that is highly practicable. Once one understands the nature of the underlying cognitive processes involved in a particular aspect of Christian wisdom, one is better armed to create interventions to help foster those modes of knowing. Indeed, one can then begin to look at Christian practices with an eye toward developing the sorts of powers that one finds associated with the wisdom in question. For example, a theological practice such as Scriptural Reasoning (see Ford and Pecknold 2006) involves, amongst other things, many of the analytic, meta-analytic, and discursive skills one finds related to the kind of head wisdom that has been described here. In contrast, the sort of "being alongside" and compassionate awareness that is necessitated in members of the L'Arche communities (see Ford 2007) for those with severe learning disabilities might serve as a powerful way of developing the more engaged, direct, and open wisdom of heart. The range of possible practices which might be designed to enhance the qualities that underpin the various kinds of wisdom one finds in theological wisdom reflection is in principle inexhaustible. In this way, *religious practice and the production of religious wisdom in persons and communities can be better harmonized to become a larger coproductive whole.*

Given the vast range of wisdom forms in theological reflection, and given the now apparent antagonism between the kinds of awareness that can be seen to underpin them in so many ways, it becomes very clear that a full theological wisdom education is an incredibly demanding business. Developing some means of harmonizing religious practice with the cultivation of a wide range of wisdom capacities is thus incredibly important. Having a very clear grasp of the kinds of processes that underlie religious practices and religious wisdoms can be of great value in bringing wisdom and practice together—that is, *helping Christians become wiser in the very practice of their faith.*

Admittedly, only the briefest and most general contours of such a harmony has been provided here; the possibilities for bringing wisdom and practice together in this way are too vast to be given an account in such a space. Indeed, this leads the present discussion beyond the question of knowing altogether. Wisdom involves an "ever more" that cannot be adequately captured through the issue of knowing, even in terms of head and heart, but always leads beyond. This is particularly clear in theological discourse where wisdom has faces that are communitarian and even suprapersonal, where wisdom is mediated through practices, scripture, and the Spirit. In the end I must conclude with the theological emphasis on the *mysteriousness* of wisdom. Meditation on the "superabundance" of a wisdom that continually overflows all conceptual bounds serves to remind us that the reality of wisdom and its possibilities are far more complex than can ever be captured in any static model, or any series of models for that matter. While these accounts, both theological and psychological, offer many interesting and valid insights into head and heart knowing in wisdom, we need to be reminded that the workings of wisdom are ultimately a mystery, that no full account can be provided, and it is both beautiful and good that this is so. The wish for an authoritative or fully comprehensive account of wisdom will always be thwarted by the complexity and richness of basic reality. Yet the question of wisdom is so beautiful, so tantalizing, that its final inscrutable complexity ought never to deter us from continuing to seek it out.

Both head and heart are required for this task.

Notes

1. It is important to note at this point that while there are many subtle and enlightening parallels to be found between the Roschian and theological wisdom accounts, the two discourses should not be conflated or too closely identified with each other. Rosch's account is strongly influenced by Buddhist thought and there are many elements that cannot be brought to bear with respect to Christian theological wisdom reflection.
2. For a more complete elaboration of McGilchrist's work, in particular the contrasting powers of the left and right hemispheres, see chapter 6 above.

References

Ardelt, M. 2003. "Empirical Assessment of a Three-Dimensional Wisdom Scale." *Research on Aging* 25:275–324.

Baltes, P. B., and U. M. Staudinger. 1993. "The Search for a Psychology of Wisdom." *Current Directions in Psychological Science* 2:75–80.

———. 2000. "Wisdom: A Meta-Heuristic (Pragmatic) to Orchestrate Mind and Virtue Toward Excellence." *American Psychologist* 55:122–36.

Ford, D. F. 1992. *A Long Rumour of Wisdom: Redescribing Theology.* Cambridge: Cambridge University Press.

———. 1999. *Self and Salvation.* Cambridge: Cambridge University Press.

———. 2007. *Christian Wisdom: Desiring God and Learning in Love.* Cambridge: Cambridge University Press.

Ford, D. F., and C. C. Pecknold, eds. 2006. *The Promise of Scriptural Reasoning.* Oxford: Blackwell Publishing.

Ford, D. F., and D. L. Stamps, eds. 1996. *Essentials of Christian Community: Essays for Daniel W. Hardy.* Edinburgh: T&T Clark.

Kelsey, D. H. 2009. *Eccentric Existence: A Theological Anthropology*. Kentucky: WJK Press.

Kunzmann, U., and P. B. Baltes. 2003. "Wisdom-related Knowledge: Affective, Motivational, and Interpersonal Correlates." *Personality and Social Psychology Bulletin* 29:1104–19.

———. 2005. "The Psychology of Wisdom: Theoretical and Empirical Challenges." In *A Handbook of Wisdom—Psychological Perspectives*, edited by R. J. Sternberg and J. Jordan, 110–36. New York: Cambridge University Press.

McGilchrist, I. 2009. *The Master and His Emissary*. London: Yale University Press.

Pasupathi, M., and U. M. Staudinger. 2001. "Do Advanced Moral Reasoners Also Show Wisdom? Linking Moral Reasoning and Wisdom-related Knowledge and Judgement." *International Journal of Behavioral Development* 25:401–15.

Rosch, E. 1999. "Is Wisdom in the Brain?" *Psychological Science* 10:222–24.

———. 2005. "'If You Depict a Bird, Give It Space to Fly': On Mind, Meditation, and Art." In *Best Buddhist Writings 2005*, edited by M. McLeod, 103–19. Boston, MA: Shambhala Publications.

———. 2009. "Beginner's Mind: Paths to the Wisdom That Is Not Learned." In *Teaching for Wisdom*, edited by M. Ferrari and G. Potworowski, 134–61. Hillsdale, NJ: Erlbaum.

Weil, S. 1951. *Waiting on God*. London: Routledge Kegan Paul.

The Head and the Heart of the Matter in Hope and Forgiveness

10

Liz Gulliford

In the first part of this chapter, knowledge of the head and heart will be examined in relation to a conceptual distinction between optimism and hope. In the second section, head and heart knowledge will be distinguished in relation to the human experience of forgiveness.

Introduction to Hope and Optimism

An important distinction may be drawn between hope and optimism insofar as they relate to the two sorts of knowledge identified in this volume. Optimism represents an orientation toward head knowledge in two clearly identifiable ways. First, as will be shown, the ground of optimism may inhere in potentially calculable probability estimates. Optimistic predictions concerning the economy, global warming, or recovery from a life-threatening illness are based on statistical likelihoods, and as such they represent rational judgments based on objective, external evidence.

Second, it will be argued here that the dispositional traits of optimism and optimistic explanatory style, which have been a focus of recent positive psychological research, locate the ground of optimism in beliefs about personal agency, control of cognitive attributions, and problem-solving strategies. While objective probabilities may exert varying degrees of influence on optimism in different situations, another dimension of optimism is the maintenance, management, and manipulation of cognitive attributions. From a psychological point of view, optimism is construed as a highly *cognized* trait.

Optimism requires confidence that is either grounded in "head knowledge" that concerns objectively calculable and external probabilities, or—as in cognitive therapy—it is grounded in confidence that inheres in the self's ability to exercise control over beliefs. For instance, in cultivating an optimistic explanatory style, accepted and automatic beliefs are disputed and challenged in an attempt to edit the subject's perceived "head knowledge" of the reasons for personal success or failure. It should be noted that in certain contexts there may be potential or actual conflict between the two kinds of head knowledge identified. For instance, an individual might exhibit an optimistic attitude that is "unwarranted," given the statistical probabilities involved.

In contrast to the two kinds of head knowledge that provide the foundation for confidence in optimism, hope is grounded in confidence of a different sort. It is deemed appropriate even in contexts where grounds for optimism may be low, for instance where probabilities are unfavorable, or where the ability to exercise personal agency or control is limited. The final ground of hope involves the heartfelt confidence of trust and, as such, is sustained in communion with other agents. Recent positive psychological models have tended to conflate optimism with hope.

It ought to be noted that while important conceptual distinctions can be drawn between hope and optimism, lay use of the terms may not reflect these contours precisely. Both philosophers and psychologists may privilege their own definitions over lay understandings, but it is important to note that in common parlance people tend not to use these concepts with a philosopher's theoretical rigor or with a psychologist's pragmatic eye toward measurement. It was with a view to tapping lay understandings of hope and optimism that Averill, Catlin, and Chon (1990) attempted a cross-cultural social constructionist analysis of the concepts, mining proverbs and aphorisms for the everyday wisdom about hope and optimism they distill.

For now, suffice it to be acknowledged that though hope and optimism can be distinguished in a careful conceptual analysis, they are frequently conflated in psychological discourse and in everyday life. Thus Rodgers and Hammerstein's "cockeyed *optimist*" Nellie is "stuck like a dope with a thing called *hope.*" People routinely equate optimism with hope, and pessimism with hopelessness. It is perhaps unfortunate this imprecision exists, but no amount of philosophical wishing for greater mundane accuracy will make it so. Nonetheless, there is much to be said for greater clarity in distinguishing concepts that unmistakably share family resemblances, and to strive for a better understanding, informed by a thoughtful and reflective analysis.

Defining Hope and Optimism

First, it will be necessary to address the question of how hope is defined. This will encompass *grounds* for hope and the nature of the confidence upon which it is based. Different species of confidence contribute to understandings of hope and optimism in theological and psychological discourses. The work of psychologist James Averill (1990), Christian existentialist Gabriel Marcel (1962), and philosopher Joseph Godfrey (1987) help clarify issues of definition that surround hope and optimism, providing a background for evaluating theories of hope and optimism and the kind of knowledge (head or heart) they presuppose.

Godfrey (1987) has noted subtle differences in the meaning of "hope" used as noun, adjective, and verb. As a noun, hope generally refers to the *chances of something happening:* "he hasn't a hope." Hope can be deployed as a verb in two ways: "hoping that" and "hoping in." In the first, emphasis is on that which is hoped for (hope's *content*). The second suggests something of the dynamics of maintaining hope (through relationship). The adjective "hopeful" brings another aspect of hope to prominence; the idea of an attitude that can be distinguished from particular things hoped-for or people hoped-in. Positive psychology has tended to focus on hope or optimism as an attitude, trait, or personality disposition that can be measured and inculcated while earlier predominantly psychoanalytic approaches focused on hope more broadly, examining the nature and foundation of hope or optimism.

People may hope for things that are implicitly or explicitly based on potentially calculable likelihoods; reasons for *hoping-that* something may come about, such as a lottery win. People may also invoke optimism when speaking in terms of favorable statistical "odds." Thus the grounds of hoping-that and being optimistic (in the sense of probabilistic reasoning) inhere in facts that are external to the self. That people may legitimately say that they are pessimistic about a future event but nonetheless *hopeful* suggests that hope, while it may be based on reasons for believing a future event probable, can also be grounded in other ways.

Rules of Hope

Averill, Catlin, and Chon's social-constructionist monograph *Rules of Hope* (1990) identified four implicit "rules" governing hope in America and Korea, and in the process acknowledged the existence of both emotional and nonemotional models toward desired but uncertain future events. They demonstrated that hope conforms to implicit criteria people use to assess *emotional* responses. Insofar as hope is deemed difficult to control, to affect thoughts and actions and to motivate behavior, it falls within the contours of responses classified as emotional. In the West the distinction between emotional and nonemotional models is described by hope and optimism respectively. Hope and optimism models engender different kinds of expectation. In some contexts, hope inspires less confidence than optimism because the latter is based on evidence that can be judged in terms of rational criteria. Thus when a clinician gives an optimistic as opposed to hopeful prognosis, it is assumed she is using *evidence* to support her opinion; head knowledge, in this instance, dominates heart knowledge.

Using a self-report questionnaire, Averill and his colleagues scrutinized representative examples of hope in contrast to want, desire, and "forbidden" hopes, identifying four prototypic rules. The "prudential rule" dictates that hope should be realistic.[1] Secondly, the object of hope is circumscribed by what is personally and socially acceptable; people may want and desire things for which they do not hope. This is the "moralistic rule." The "priority rule" describes the gravity with which people hope, a weightiness that surpasses that which they simply want or desire. If sufficiently important, the priority rule may outrank prudential and moralistic rules. Finally, the "action rule" maintains that people who hope should be willing to act appropriately to achieve goals when possible. Participants tended to see things for which they hoped as somewhat, though not completely, under their control.

An element of realism characterizes both hope and optimism; the prudential rule affirms that hope is inappropriate when the probability of future attainment is unrealistically low, though prudential concerns can give way to the priority rule in hope but *not* optimism. On this basis it is perhaps fair to propose that hope involves *possibility*, while *probability* is central to optimism. In hope, the *value* of the event to the subject, not its objective probability, is paramount.

Watts's (2002, 139) reading of Averill's work is that optimism, in contrast to hope, does not carry any specific commitment to action. This distinction is not drawn by Averill himself, and while an attitude of optimism (allied as it is to confident predictions concerning the likelihood of desired events) may suggest a passive attitude to the future, current research on optimism does not support this view. Carver and Scheier (2003) recognize that optimistic individuals *persist* in demanding tasks, while Seligman (2006) maintains that optimism can be learned through *effort*. As was earlier intimated, optimism may involve external probabilities, but this does not rule out some degree of personal investment in a given outcome.

Hope, Optimism, and Existential Involvement

On this question of involvement, hope is always fundamentally "involved" rather than detached in external justifications. While optimism may encompass some measure of personal involvement, it seems to correspond more closely to impartial and objective "head knowledge." In contrast, hope is more directly allied to knowledge of the heart. Gabriel Marcel construed optimism as a "calculating faculty," "a practical little problem of probabilities" (Marcel 1962, 64, 29). On this basis he seems to suggest that an optimistic gestalt can be maintained largely through detached surveillance whereas "he who hopes... seems to himself to be involved in some kind of process, and it is only from this point of view that it is possible to realise what is specific, and ... super-rational, perhaps super-relational, in hope" (Marcel 1962, 35).

It will be maintained here, however, that *in practice* there is some blurring of boundaries between the subjective and emotional model of hope representing heart knowledge, and the nonemotional model of optimism that concerns head knowledge. Marcel seems to overdraw the distinction, perhaps because he identifies optimism *simply* with external probabilities and thus impartial knowledge, whereas recent psychological literature has broadened its scope, constructing optimism on the basis of beliefs about agency and competence. While these beliefs represent a kind of head knowledge, they acknowledge a greater degree of personal involvement than logical, probabilistic reasoning, suggesting that the head/heart distinction may not be so clear-cut in lived experience.

Hope as the Confidence of Heartfelt Trust

In addition to identifying hope as at least potentially transcending rationality (a possibility Averill also acknowledged in his assertion that the prudential rule may be outranked in some instances by the priority rule), Marcel in using the term "super-relational" also hints at what Godfrey (1987) has called the "intersubjective" model of hope. Marcel (1962) develops the idea that hope is characterized by mutuality, a hoping in relationship. A practical example of this is the therapeutic encounter: a person undergoing therapy has *hope in* his or her therapist. This conception of hope relies on confidence understood as trust, in contrast to confidence based on external substantiation (probabilistic reasoning) or confidence that is corroborated by internal validation (beliefs about self-agency, self-control, and self-mastery) that dominate psychological models of hope and optimism. Confidence based on trust may appear to both the externalizing and internalizing optimist as less reasonable or justifiable than confidence based on externally or internally validated "evidence"; both of these represent different kinds of knowledge of the head.

Hope's reputation is tarnished by those who regard it as insubstantial, illusionary, or even fantastical: "the houses hope builds are castles in the air." The work of the psychoanalyst and Roman Catholic priest William Lynch (1974) emphasizes the role of the imagination in hope. Indeed, it might ultimately be argued that he regards despair as fundamentally a failure of imagination. In despair, the vista of the future contracts and a person comes to believe there is no conceivable way out of distress. While hopelessness is characterized by narrowness and a sense of entrapment, hope is typified by breadth and envisages a way out. Hope engages the organ of apprehension that is imagination. There are those who would regard such hoping as irrational wish-fulfillment. However, the view that anticipated goals or hopes are necessarily unreal or illusory represents perhaps too harsh a view of the distinction between what is real and illusory, actual and potential. Much of reality is "transitional,"[2] existing in the tension between these dichotomies.

Imagination must, however, be "realistic." Lynch recognizes that there are many things that are, in fact, hope*less*. For instance, human life must end. Imagination must be tethered to reality; "man has legs but not wings" (Lynch 1974, 61). That which cannot really be hoped-for must not contaminate those things for which it is realistic to hope.

A fruitful distinction may be made between the fixated imagination of the fantasist and a normal, creatively flexible imagination. The fantastic imagination represents a warped attempt to cope with life in a stereotypically rigid way that ultimately and increasingly removes the fantasist away from the real world. It is this desperate sort of imagination that can be identified as irrational.

In order to escape from such an isolating view of the world, it would be necessary for the fantasist to, to use Lynch's words, "put on the imagination of another" (Lynch 1974, 23–24). This, in effect, is what happens in the course of therapy when the patient's imagination and the narrow hopes it entertains gives way, in the context of trust to the influence of the therapist's hope, undergirded by "realistic imagination." There does indeed seem to be something both suprarational and super-relational about hope. If rationality is understood to mean having adequate *justification* for one's beliefs, hope (but not optimism) may go beyond rational "head knowledge." Furthermore, hope (but not optimism) is sustained in empathic communion with others. In the light of this, it is perhaps limiting and even incorrect to construe hope as a purely personal resource since there is an aspect of hope that underscores dependence on and mutuality with others.

Godfrey (1987) identified two kinds of hope in the "will-nature" and "intersubjective" models. In the former, trust is founded on the belief that other agencies or instrumentalities are accessible to realize one's hopes. Conversely, the intersubjective model conceives of trust as a relationship of union, not utilizing. The will-nature model envisages trust in terms of needed instrumentalities. The intersubjective model sees trust as noninstrumental; the other is regarded as *participant* in hoping.

Positive psychological models may accord a role for other people in sustaining hope. Meeting personal goals could involve receiving help from others. Essentially, as will be shown, these models operate within the will-nature paradigm that represents a *hope-that* required resources are at one's disposal, maintaining a focus on hope as a matter of the will acting on nature. This can be contrasted with *hope-in*, corresponding to Godfrey's intersubjective model. In *hoping-in* another person, hope's very essence is relational. Hope exists between persons and is not construed as an internal, personal resource.

That hope is maintained in communion with others is particularly apparent in Kobler and Stotland's (1964) study of a suicide epidemic in an American psychiatric hospital. They demonstrated that expectations of significant others in the therapeutic environment were crucial to whether a patient was able to discern a way out of distress or interpreted their situation as hopeless, leading to their eventual suicide. As more suicides occurred, staff confidence deteriorated and those who had come to the hospital with the hope of being helped found employees increasingly preoccupied with expectations of suicide.

When the future is perceived as devoid of hope and suicide enters the "field," the response of health professionals toward the patient's communication of intent is critical. In conveying suicidal plans, the troubled person attempts to gain assurances from others that hope still exists, but when this meets a response of hopelessness and helplessness, there seems to be but one way out; "suicide occurred in each case when, and only when, all significant and hopeful relationships were broken. The patient, after communicating, testing and searching for hope, then felt that he was alone in an empty world" (Kobler and Stotland 1964, 260).

For hope to be ignited, it must be communicated that there is a way out of despair. Lynch suggests that the means to recovery lies in escaping a solipsistic world by daring to trust the vision of another:

I propose that the sick person is really helpless. . . . For he is operating within his own closed system of fantasy and feeling unable, as a result, even to imagine what is on the outside. He needs another's imagination that will begin to work with his own, and then the two can do it together. He must put on another's imagination in order to rediscover his own. (1974, 77)

Positive Psychological Approaches to Hope and Optimism

Recent psychological study of optimism and hope falls within the remit of positive psychology and includes Seligman's work on "learned optimism" (2006), Carver and Scheier's "dispositional optimism" (2003) and Snyder's "hope theory" (1991; 1994; 2002). These theories tend to extend a narrow concept of hope or optimism that envisages them as essentially *individual* matters of personal agency, will, and self-control. This contrasts with earlier research, such as that of Kobler and Stotland (1964), which acknowledged how hope is affected by significant others within an individual's environment.

Positive psychological models risk reducing hope and optimism to goal-setting, problem-solving, or allied phenomena that emphasize individual agency and control. The element of waiting intrinsic to hope is overshadowed by an almost exclusive focus on planning and projecting. Two of the foremost researchers in positive psychology, Martin Seligman and the late Rick Snyder conceive of optimism and hope, respectively, in terms of planning and personal agency. Seligman's concept of optimistic explanatory style emphasizes the role an individual plays in asserting control over characteristic attributions for success and failure. Snyder advocated a theory of hope that stressed both personal agency and the implementation of strategies to reach desired goals. His model of hope appears to be a composite of self-efficacy and problem-solving that privileges head knowledge in the form of beliefs about personal agency.

Snyder (1991; 1994; 2002) conceived personal hope as consisting of two kinds of thinking: agency thinking (the belief in one's ability to reach goals) and pathways thinking (a problem-solving strategy to generate "pathways" to desired outcomes). The model is primarily cognitive, according emotion the role of setting the initial tenor of agency and pathways thinking and providing feedback that affects continuing effort toward the goal. The adult dispositional hope scale is a self-report inventory consisting of twelve statements (1991, 570–85).[3] Representative items from the scale that tap "agency thinking" include the following:

My past experiences have prepared me well for my future. (9)
I've been pretty successful in life. (10)

Items tapping "pathways thinking" include:

I can think of many ways to get the things in life that are most important to me. (6)
Even when others get discouraged, I know I can find a way to solve the problem. (8)

It should be noted that the two items here that concern "agency thinking" are cast in the past tense and, as such, do not concern genuine expectations for the future, crucial to hope. While one might expect agency thoughts to be influenced by past experiences, the items could be criticized for suggesting that beliefs about the future are wholly determined by such experiences. As a whole, Snyder's agency items overlap almost completely with the construct of self-efficacy (see Bandura 1997). Items that tap "pathways thinking" exhibit a substantial overlap with problem-solving.

In contrast to the emphasis on maintaining internal, heightened self-talk and generating pathways to desired goals, hope also involves waiting. This is not to say hope is incompatible with translating wants and desires into action in the pursuit of goals. However, it does acknowledge that waiting is part of what it means to hope. Not all objectives can be met through our own efforts; willing, wishing, wanting, and implementing plans does not guarantee success, particularly over events where little personal control can be exercised. In the waiting of hope, it is acknowledged that help can come from within and without; in other words, that other agencies may be cooperative with our own in the realization of our hopes.

As noted, confidence may be founded on the head knowledge of probabilistic reasoning or on beliefs about control, or on the heart knowledge that is trust. Indeed, it would seem that confidence understood as trust is perhaps the most fundamental basis of hope, the lack of which has serious developmental repercussions. For instance, the first stage of psychosocial development in Erik Erikson's (1959) scheme is to negotiate the conflict between basic trust and basic mistrust. Hope stems from trust that the infant can depend on his or her mother to meet basic needs. Thus hope can only be sustained where a person has learned he or she can *depend* on others. The consequences of an inability to trust seem to reach far more to the heart of a person's hope than a failure of confidence grounded exclusively in head knowledge.

Optimistic explanatory style also emphasizes personal agency, specifically an individual's control of characteristic attributions for success and failure. Given its focus on cultivating a salutary style of thinking the question arises as to the extent to which it is genuinely oriented toward the future and the degree to which it involves inculcating a protective pattern of self-attributions, representing a more or less stable schema of head knowledge about the self.

In *Learned Optimism* (2006), Seligman shows how a person's "explanatory style" (their pattern of attributions for success and failure) can be modified by systematic intervention. He demonstrates that the characteristic profile of attributions associated with optimism can be emulated so that optimism can be "learned." A person with an optimistic explanatory style makes attributions for negative events that are *external, unstable, and specific*. A pessimistic style for misfortune is marked by opposing attributions (*internal, stable, and global*). Optimistic explanatory style locates the cause of failing an exam *externally*; the examiner set hard questions. In contrast, people with a pessimistic explanatory style identify the cause of failure as *internal* and blame themselves. Optimistic explanatory style involves making attributions for disappointments that are *unstable* or *impermanent*; failure on one occasion does not entail a pattern of repeatedly missing the mark. Conversely, people exhibiting pessimistic explanatory style make attributions for negative events that are *permanent* or *stable*. Finally, people with optimistic explanatory style regard failure as domain specific; disappointment in one area is discrete from the *global* or *pervasive* sense of failure that characterizes its opposite.

Consequently, optimistic explanatory style protects individuals from making attributions for negative events that locate their cause internally, permanently, and pervasively. The opposite pattern characterizes attributions for positive events. While the optimistic person sees their success as internal, stable, and global, the pessimist attributes their success to external causes such as fate or fluke, construing their accomplishments as unstable and specific to particular domains.

Explanatory style is usually assessed with the Attributional Style Questionnaire (ASQ, Peterson et al. 1982), a self-report instrument containing twelve hypothetical scenarios, six positive and six negative. Respondents place themselves in the situations described and decide the one major cause of the event, indicating on a seven-point Likert scale the degree to which the cause is deemed internal, stable, and global.[4] Attributional style therefore grounds what it calls "optimism" completely within the self. The major purpose served by external attributions is to protect the self from internal attributions that locate blame for negative events within the individual.

Future expectancies generated by learned optimism are based on contingencies between making external, unstable, and impermanent attributions for past events and outcomes related to failure and internal, stable, and permanent attributions for success. Learned optimism is based on the premise that future outcomes are related to a particular cognitive schema (a representation of head knowledge) over whose dimensions an individual can exercise a high degree of personal control. The theory shares with the general orientation of cognitive therapy the fundamental belief that cognitions, far from being automatic and inevitable, can be reappraised, shaped, and changed to exhibit more functional patterns.

The ground of optimism in this model is a confidence based on the self's ability to change and manipulate beliefs. It envisages optimism as largely under an individual's control, fundamentally cognitive and thus amenable to conscious modification. Optimistic explanatory style concerns how adaptive beliefs are and is more concerned with utility than with truth: "the question to ask yourself is not 'Is the belief true?' but 'Is it functional for me to think it right now?'" (Seligman 2006, 223). From a positive point of view, this accentuates what an individual can do to alter his or her reading of circumstances. However, carefully controlling perceptions to avoid negative self-attributions could be criticized for shielding the self from taking responsibility when appropriate.

The focus of optimistic explanatory style and hope theory is how the individual can either construe the future more favorably or instigate problem-solving strategies alongside heightened self-belief to attain desired objectives. Thus the foundation for these theories of hope or optimism is different from the hope derived from trust. The latter represents a hope maintained collectively and that involves relationships of warmth and affection with others. In contrast, the theories of hope and optimism reviewed above represent a species of personal head knowledge where hope or optimism is construed in terms of personal goals, objectives, and pathways toward which the self determinedly strives. Both assert the self's reliance on itself and are characterized like all essentially cognitive therapies by control. In contrast to self-determined striving grounded in individual cognitive flexibility, hope grounded in heart knowledge of trust involves a degree of dependence on others.

Optimistic explanatory style or "learned optimism" represents a *style of thinking* that describes how an individual has explained causes of events in the past and is based on the assumption that these character-istic patterns of attribution are applied in the future unless systematic efforts to change habits of thought are undertaken. While previous events play a part in constructing expectations for the future, too heavy an emphasis obscures a vital dimension of hope and optimism; namely that the future is potentially radically different from the past.

Seligman asserts that an individual's future can be different from their past because optimistic explanatory style can be learned but conceives the *future itself* as following an essentially predictable and unchanging course. It could be argued that optimistic explanatory style is a protective, potentially modifiable pattern of attribution that is indifferent to the objective future and emphasizes the individual's positive subjective attitude across time. Within the model, expectations for the future (optimistic or pessimistic) are grounded in the ability to control one's way of thinking (head knowledge) of the future. Where hope is grounded in relationships of heartfelt trust with other agents, the salience of individual control is reduced.

This raises an issue that seems to further differentiate between the head knowledge of optimism (and also Snyder's "hope" theory) and the heart knowledge of hope. Optimistic predictions about the future tend to rest on the assumption that the future will in many respects be similar to the present. Predictions, whether based on external cal-culable likelihoods or beliefs about the self, are possible only where the contours of the future are predict*able*. But whereas people may be optimistic within a known and predictable order, people can and do *hope* for radically new futures that transcend all present expectations.

In the positive psychological approaches examined thus far, "hope" and optimism are characterized by a narrowing toward particular personal goals, the attainment of which emphasizes planning and/or personal agency. Snyder's theory incorporates both "agency" and "pathways" thinking that combine in aspiring to attain personal objec-tives. Optimistic explanatory style is less involved with goals *per se* and represents a more general means of buoying up control and mastery of attributions that could be detrimental to future success. Essentially, it is a method through which agency beliefs may be substantially enhanced.

Carver and Scheier's (2003) "dispositional optimism" constitutes another positive psychological concept in this domain that focuses on how individuals are motivated to reach goals. In common with other psychological theories, it centers on specific and personal objectives. However, in contrast to other theories reviewed here, Carver and Scheier distance their approach from models that emphasize agency, self-efficacy, or control, asserting that the confidence on which optimism is founded may depend on sources that lie beyond purely cognitive resources and the associated manipulation of head knowledge and cognitive schemata.

Dispositional Optimism

Carver and Scheier (2003, 75–76) regard optimism as a trait; "optimists are people who expect good things to happen to them; pessimists are people who expect bad things to happen to them." They locate their model within the broader category of expectancy-value theories of motivation. These theories combine goals, "actions, end states, or values that people see as either desirable or undesirable," with an individual's expectancy, defined as "a sense of confidence or doubt about the attainability of the goal value." Confidence is essential in maintaining both initial and ongoing efforts toward the goal. Doubt hampers such efforts. The motivating power of the goal depends on its degree of importance to the individual. While goal importance is a significant factor, so too is degree of confidence; "when people are confident about an eventual outcome, effort continues even in the face of great adversity."

Dispositional optimism and pessimism describe two self-regulatory mechanisms through which goals are approached. Optimistic individuals confidently hold that objectives can be achieved and maintain persistence in pursuing desired outcomes. Conversely, pessimistic beliefs are characterized by doubts about goal attainment. Carver and Scheier envisage a place for personal agency, as "persistence" suggests. However, their model allows confidence to be founded in sources other than personal agency such as luck, divine blessing, and other people. They explicitly distance dispositional optimism from constructs that cast hope or optimism *entirely* in terms of personal agency or self-efficacy. Thus it can be argued that dispositional optimism is potentially broader in scope than dispositional hope or optimistic explanatory style because the confidence that undergirds it inheres in a wider array of possible sources.

It has been shown that in positive psychology, the orientation toward future desired goals has been expressed both in terms of hope (Snyder et al. 1991; 1994; 2002) and optimism (Carver and Scheier 2003; Seligman 2006). However, this seems to be merely a semantic difference, for these paradigms share a good deal of common ground. All three are based on identifying fairly narrowly conceived goals. The objectives associated with these theories tend to be personal and individual goals whose realization comes about through confidence based on the agency of the self to either generate routes to desired goals or by boosting self-efficacy beliefs more generally. The species of hope and optimism that these models embody seems to be largely a composite of problem-solving skills and beliefs that enhance perceptions of control of future outcomes. These psychological approaches may be helpful in equipping people to identify personal goals and find ways of realizing them. Enhancing peoples' self-belief and confidence as they strive to attain their aspirations is to be commended, provided that it does not obscure the reality that believing in oneself is not sufficient to attain all types of goals. Not all objectives are controllable.

Positive psychological models of hope and optimism exemplify the self-determined side of hope. They emphasize building strategies to reach goals and facilitate means of construing an unknown future more favorably. This ignores the dependent and relational aspects of hope acknowledged in an earlier psychological tradition. Erikson (1959), Lynch (1974), and Kobler and Stotland (1964) assert that in part hope consists in being able to depend on others, with the expectation of receiving from, not solely acting on, one's environment. The focus in positive psychological approaches to hope and optimism is personal goals and the meeting of such objectives through marshaling internal resources. Hope and optimism are construed within this literature as internal, largely cognitive processes. The models do not speak to situations where people have little personal control over things for which they hope, such as recovery from serious illness or rescue from a collapsed mine.

CONCLUSION

In the first part of this chapter it has been shown that there is some blurring of head and heart knowledge in models of hope and optimism. Optimism can represent simple "head knowledge" when it is construed purely in terms of objective and external probabilities about future events. However, when optimism is taken to include some investment of the self in a personally held attitude toward the future that involves agency or the will, it is more internalized and perhaps incorporates some elements of the existentially involved knowledge of the heart. Optimism is not without a degree of emotional involvement; "Optimism . . . implies that the expected event is positive and in some way personally relevant" (Averill, Catlin, and Chon 1990, 96n2).

Similarly, hope is not purely wishful thinking; hope should be realistic, as both Averill (1990) and Lynch (1974) have noted. There are elements of both knowledge of the head and of the heart in optimism and hope, though the former maps more closely onto head knowledge, whether represented by objective probabilistic reasoning or cognitive schemata that may be subject to active management strategies. While hope-that represents knowledge of the head that also invokes probabilities, hoping-in conveys trust. As such, hope-in is relational and is based on a species of confidence that incorporates the heart. Furthermore, such hope may be kindled by the imagination, a resource that inspires hope beyond the detached justifications of probabilistic reasoning.

The conceptual clarity Averill sought to introduce to this domain has received only scant acknowledgment in the literature, and existing questionnaire measures do not operationalize the particular characteristics of hope or optimism identified by this earlier research. Ostensibly, Carver and Scheier's (2003) focus is optimism, not hope. However, the "expectation through confidence" that they define as characteristic of optimists might perhaps be better construed as hope. When confidence inheres in trust rather than the head knowledge of external probabilities or self-agency, it may come closer to the heart knowledge of hope than to optimism.

Forgiveness

The second part of the chapter contrasts forgiveness of the heart with forgiveness of the head as it pertains to both appropriating forgiveness oneself and extending forgiveness to others. In the case of receiving forgiveness, people may objectively know they have been forgiven without feeling this forgiveness subjectively, perhaps because of a keen sense of shame or guilt. In this volume, Zahl, Sharp, and Gibson (chapter 4) bear witness to a disconnect between propositional knowledge *about* God and experiential knowledge *of* God. Zahl, Sharp, and Gibson note that "the individual who 'knows' in his head that God loves him but doesn't feel loved by God may hold propositional knowledge of God as loving; however, this knowledge may evoke feelings of guilt or frustration because of its apparent conflict with his actual experience."

Similarly, Moriarty distinguishes between God concepts and God images: "God images are the personal, emotional, and relational understandings of God whereas God concepts are the abstract, intellectual, and theological understandings of God" (chapter 7). These "head" and "heart" understandings might not be in alignment with one another. By way of example, he introduces us to Martin, a forty-two-year-old Caucasian male who graduated with a master of divinity from Princeton Theological Seminary when he was twenty-five. In spite of years of prayer and study, Martin's emotional experience of God seems stuck; "he *knows* God has forgiven him, but he *feels* like God is upset with him for falling short." Moriarty suggests that God images may be influenced subconsciously by early patterns of attachment and his chapter is dedicated to how people like Martin can learn to experience grace and forgiveness *emotionally* (in their heart) through careful self-examination and reflection.

There may be a similar lack of alignment between *deciding to forgive* an offender and *feeling genuinely forgiving* toward them. An individual may sincerely desire to transform their feelings toward a person who has wronged them yet be "blocked" by resentment or anger. While forgiveness of the head is not to be disparaged, truly transformative forgiveness is likely, at least eventually, to involve forgiveness of the heart.

Defining Forgiveness

It is important to differentiate forgiving from pardoning, excusing, condoning, and forgetting. Many therapeutic interventions take such contrasts as their point of departure. For instance, a "pardon" is given by a person who has jurisdiction over a law or laws that an offender has violated. As such, it may be bestowed by a judge or monarch. Forgiveness, on the other hand, describes the overcoming of offence in an interpersonal relationship rather than within a legal or social arrangement. It is the offended party, not a representative, who has any "right" to forgive.

Secondly, forgiveness must be distinguished from excusing or condoning, which constitute attempts to explain why something occurred and how, within a given context, it was understandable. When an offence is condoned or excused, it has been dealt with *without* the need for forgiveness. Finally, while forgetting may be a "symptom" of forgiveness, we do not need to forget in order to forgive, especially where hurt runs deep.

Distinguishing forgiveness from the above concepts is a helpful first step toward circumscribing it. However, when it comes to positively defining forgiveness, differences of emphasis emerge. As I have noted elsewhere (Gulliford 2004, 84), "Whether forgiveness is conceptualized primarily as a change of emotional tone or behavioral change towards an individual has a bearing on models of forgiveness, on the putative psychological mechanisms underlying these interventions, and on measures of success and failure in realizing forgiveness." In relation to the present reflection on head and heart knowledge, the question arises as to whether forgiveness is primarily concerned with a renewed appraisal of an offender (which would identify forgiveness with head knowledge) or whether it also involves an emotional rehabilitation of feelings toward a transgressor, a transformation of the heart.

While a number of definitions of forgiveness focus on abandoning or foreswearing resentment, it is suggested here that forgiveness should also involve an increase in positive feelings as well as the reduction or elimination of negative affect. Enright, Freedman, and Rique (1998, 46–47) offer the following comprehensive definition: "a willingness to abandon one's right to resentment, negative judgment, and indifferent behavior toward one who unjustly injured us, while fostering the undeserved qualities of compassion, generosity, and even love toward him or her." This definition encompasses cognitive, affective, and behavioral components. It also emphasizes that forgiveness is a free choice on the part of the victim of wrongdoing, a willingness that represents its conative aspect. A number of therapeutic approaches to forgiveness that will be reviewed here, including those of Smedes (1988) and Enright (2000; 2001), stress that forgiveness should be voluntarily undertaken by the forgiver. People should not be coerced to forgive.

Forgiveness is not simply reducing *unforgiveness*, a "combination of delayed emotions, including resentment, bitterness, hatred, hostility, anger and fear, that develops after a transgression and can motivate desires for retaliation against or avoidance of the offender" (Worthington and Wade 1999). Indeed, it has been empirically demonstrated that people can lower unforgiveness without actively forgiving someone (Wade and Worthington 2003). On the basis of this observation, Worthington has used the terms "decisional" and "emotional" forgiveness. The former is "a behavioural intention statement to forswear one's revenge and avoidance (unless it is unsafe to interact with the offender) and to release the offender from the social debt incurred by the wrongdoing" (Worthington 2005, 424).

In contrast, the latter represents "the replacement of negative emotions with positive, other oriented emotions" (Worthington 2005, 424). Wade, Worthington, and Meyer (2005) note that while researchers may endorse the view that complete forgiveness involves *both* reduction of negative feelings and an intensification of positive emotions, frequently only a reduction in *unforgiveness* is measured. It should not be assumed that an increase in positive emotion necessarily occurs as a result of a reduction of negative sentiments toward an offender. Though there is likely to be a correlation between these factors, they represent separate systems, as Wade and Worthington have shown (2003).

The sincere desire to forgive may not always be matched by *feeling* forgiving toward someone. Paul Coleman (1998, 83–84), a marital and family therapist, notes that the decision to forgive is not contingent on actually *feeling* forgiving: "Ultimately, forgiveness is a decision. I inform people that they must *choose* to be forgiving. If they wait until they *feel* forgiving before they choose to forgive, it may be a long and arduous wait." Similarly, I have indicated elsewhere that in many instances the desire to forgive may be all an individual can muster toward the final goal of forgiving someone.[5] In time it may be possible for a heartfelt emotional forgiveness to develop.

Deciding to forgive someone must be differentiated from "pseudo-forgiveness." In the latter case an individual merely gives the impression of having forgiven someone while maintaining anger or bitterness toward them. There is no real desire or commitment to truly forgive. By contrast, in deciding to forgive there is a genuine intention to forgive fully, though this may be fraught with emotional difficulties such as continued resentment that it is hoped will be eliminated in the fullness of time.

Appropriating the forgiveness of another also incorporates two dimensions; a person may objectively *know* that they have been forgiven yet feel no accompanying emotional release, perhaps due to continued feelings of shame or guilt. In some instances and over time, it may be possible for cognitive and affective elements of accepting forgiveness to come into closer or even complete alignment. Thus far it has been established that both appropriating forgiveness and extending forgiveness to another may involve both head and heart. While in some cases instant feelings of forgiveness may be present, in others the commitment to forgive may not be matched in the moment by such emotion.

It is suggested here that the distinction between decisional and emotional forgiveness may reflect the operation of different mechanisms through which forgiveness might be reached. As will be shown, some therapeutic approaches seem to emphasize the head while others turn more centrally on the heart. For instance, within psychology, a number of interventions to promote forgiveness incorporate cognitive reframing as the crucial turning point that enables attributions of blame toward an offender to be loosened. This represents the recalibration of "head knowledge" concerning an offender's behavior. Akin to optimistic and pessimistic explanatory styles that were the focus of the previous section, such an approach grounds forgiveness in revisiting and reworking cognitive appraisals. Whereas optimistic and pessimistic explanatory styles involve self and other attributions for personal success and failure, reframing, as will be shown, is largely concerned with attributions of culpability and responsibility.

In contrast to predominantly cognitive approaches, Worthington's "Pyramid model" ascribes the definitive moment toward forgiveness as mediated by empathy, a transformation that comes about primarily through a *change of heart* toward a person who has wronged another.

Reframing

A number of approaches to the question of how forgiveness might be effected have centered on the idea of "reframing," "reappraising," or seeing the offence with "new eyes" (Smedes 1988, xiv). Essentially, these techniques aim to widen the perspective of the victim of wrongdoing so that the actions of the wrongdoer are placed within a framework that expands the narrative of blame to see what might have led the offender to behave in a hurtful way. The process of reframing takes account of both proximal and distal causes of the offending behavior that might lead the injured party to see the wrongdoer in a different light. The theory is that if attributions concerning blame and responsibility are reworked, forgiveness might be facilitated.

The process of causal attribution underlies social and self-perception and psychological epistemology (the way we construct our worlds). Fritz Heider (1958), the father of the theory of attribution, has called it "naïve psychology" since it is the type of psychology we all engage in when involved in the task of interpreting the causes of behavior. Of key significance in the field of attribution is the question of whether events are attributed to personal (internal) or environmental (external) factors. It has been found that subjects are more likely to attribute the behavior of strangers to characterological or internal dispositions rather than external or situational factors, unless they are explicitly made aware of mitigating factors that might explain the stranger's actions (Weiner et al. 1991). The fundamental motivation for making attributions is to gain a purchase on the world, to be able to predict outcomes and gain a sense of control.

It is almost inevitable that in the wake of interpersonal offence an attribution of blame will occur. However, this attribution will be influenced by the biases noted above and will also be shaped by perceptions of the offender's power, influence, and responsibility. In view of this, there may be therapeutic value in examining attributions in the light of awareness of such systematic biases in interpretations of blame. When a person is seeking to forgive, it is likely that attributions of blame have helped swell a rising tide of anger. Examination of attributions may reveal that anger is overblown, thereby facilitating forgiveness.

Reframing is deemed "the most crucial stage in the whole process of forgiveness" in the theoretical model advocated by North (1998, 23). It stands at the seventh stage of a nine-stage paradigm and follows a decision to try to forgive the wrongdoer. According to North the process of reframing attempts "a fuller understanding of the wrongdoer, putting his actions in perspective." In North's view, this contextual understanding of the wrongdoer enables the injured party to separate offenders from their behavior. In terms of attribution theory, reframing enables attributions to become situational rather than internal, that is to say, pertaining to the person's character.

Support for North's theoretical model and the role of reframing may be found in Enright and colleagues' (2000; 2001) empirically validated, twenty-stage process model. Within this model, "reframing" the wrongdoer emerges at stage twelve and is the catalyst through which empathy for the offender is generated. A five-phase process of forgiveness in marital and family therapy, also involving reframing, is envisaged by Coleman (1998), who describes reframing as "the dialogue to understanding" that leads to forgiveness and letting go.

Lewis Smedes (1988, xiv) introduces a fourfold scheme of forgiveness that involves seeing things with "magic eyes," a metaphor for the process of reframing: "You cannot change the past, you can only heal the hurt that comes to you from the past. And you can heal it only with the vision of the magic eyes." He notes that in the process of seeing things with new eyes, "the story is not usually about an innocent lamb and a bad wolf. Most of us have to do our forgiving while we are being forgiven" (Smedes 1988, 7). Smedes highlights that reframing not only gives us a new perspective on the offender, but it also affords a new insight into ourselves.

An early reframing approach to forgiveness may be found in the sermons of the Anglican bishop Joseph Butler. While Butler saw a place for the passion of resentment, he noted that it could become exaggerated. The injunction to love one's enemies does not preclude resenting them "but when this resentment entirely destroys our natural benevolence . . . it is excessive, and becomes malice or revenge" (republished 1970, 84). Butler's suggestion that individuals seeking to forgive place themselves at a due distance from the offence is remarkably similar to the reframing stage advocated by Enright, North, Coleman, and Smedes, as is Butler's evaluation that we may put the offence down to "inadvertence and mistake" rather than malice and scorn, with the result that the indignity or injury lessens in its force:

> *To make allowances for inadvertence, misunderstanding, for the partialities of self-love and the false light which anger sets things in; I say, to make allowances for these, is not to be spoken of as an instance of humbleness of mind, or meekness and moderation of temper; but as what common sense would suggest, to avoid judging wrong of a matter before us. (1970, 87)*

Butler's approach to forgiveness is not entirely based on his view that attribution of blame is inevitably due to faulty cognitions in our perceptions of offences, though clearly this plays a major part in his argument. Though Butler seems to emphasize "head knowledge" in his approach to forgiveness, he later points out that while those who cause injury, injustice, and oppression are naturally the objects of our resentment, they are also the objects of our *compassion*, highlighting the role of the heart. It is with this in mind that attention is turned to those approaches to forgiveness that emphasize empathy and compassion. While reframing may play a key role in "decisional forgiveness," loosening bonds of resentment that may stem from attributional biases, it seems likely that approaches to forgiveness that major on fostering compassion for others may expedite "emotional forgiveness," or forgiveness of the heart.

EMPATHETIC APPROACHES TO FORGIVENESS IN PSYCHOLOGY

Worthington (1998) has emphasized the importance of empathy in the forgiving process. While he is aware of the important cognitive factor of "perspective-taking," he envisages this occurring *as a result of empathy* (sympathy, compassion, and tenderness) on the part of the injured party toward the wrongdoer. His "Pyramid Model" of forgiveness requires that the forgiver complete five stages of recovery (REACH): Recall the hurt; Empathize with the one who hurt you; Altruistic gift; Commit to forgive; Hold onto forgiveness.

According to Worthington, difficulties in forgiving arise through "fear conditioning" rather than through anger or resentment, the blocks to forgiveness assumed by reframing models that aim to loosen attributions of blame. He writes, "Because fear conditioning is an emotional response, we combat it to some degree by creating cognitive and emotional conditions that activate other emotional systems within the brain and body" (Worthington 2002, 118). He therefore advocates a forgiveness strategy that aims at "emotional reconditioning" based on the view that unforgiveness is rooted in fear (Worthington 2002, 121). Empathy for the offender is fostered by placing oneself in the offender's shoes and by imagining what they are feeling in the wake of their behavior. As a result of this phase, the injured party moves toward the third stage (offering the altruistic gift of forgiveness); "the person identifies with the experience of the offender (through empathy) and sees the other as needy" (Worthington 2002, 125).

Once this stage has been reached and the injured party has forgiven the offender "in his heart" (Worthington 2002, 125), he or she moves toward a verbalization of forgiveness to cement the commitment to forgive. This may take the form of a letter or confrontation with the offender, reinforcing the internal "emotional forgiveness" experienced. Finally, in stage five, the forgiver must "hold onto forgiveness" in order that he does not regress to the fear-conditioned response of earlier days; fear is still present and it is inevitable that hurt will be experienced at some future time, though this does not negate or devalue commitment to forgive. Worthington suggests that using emotion management techniques such as imagining or remembering good times with the offender may help to stabilize forgiveness when it is threatened by negative emotions. Thus in relation to the current concern with head and heart, Worthington acknowledges that there may be some dislocation between head and heart knowledge of forgiveness with the potential for them to slip out of alignment from time to time.

That empathy may be generated toward an offender as the mediatory factor in forgiveness is consonant with research concerning a variety of prosocial phenomena, such as cooperation, altruism, and inhibition of aggression, all of which have been shown to be facilitated by empathy (Batson 1990; 1991; Eisenberg and Fabes 1990). The practice of empathy reduces the relative salience of the hurtful actions of the perpetrator:

> Regardless of the pathways by which empathy for the offending partner develops, we posit that once it has exceeded a certain level, the perceptual salience of empathy for the offender overshadows the perceptual salience of the offending partner's hurtful actions, leading to the set of motivational changes that we have defined as forgiving. (McCullough, Worthington, and Rachal 1997, 323).

McCullough, Worthington, and Rachal also suggest that apology facilitates empathy since it signifies clearly the offender's distress "in much the same way that recognition of the distress of a person in need may facilitate empathy in other social situations" (1997, 328). An apology, therefore, not only serves the function of helping the forgiver to reframe the offender from an attributional point of view (the shift from characterological to external causes), but it also is effective at the emotional level of producing the empathy crucial to forgiveness.

Thus far two approaches to how forgiveness might be brought about have been considered. The first technique makes use of a process of reframing and is advocated by North, Enright, Coleman, Smedes, and in a "pretherapeutic" form by Joseph Butler. Reframing is primarily an interpretative endeavor focused on revisiting causal attributions of an offender's behavior. The point at which reframing intervenes in forgiveness is, therefore, at the level of understanding, of head knowledge about the interpersonal offence and the perpetrator. Viewing the offender's actions in the context of proximal and distal causes for their behavior such as their current stress or developmental history, may facilitate forgiveness, though it should be noted that for particularly heinous violations it may be impossible to "get one's *head* around" an offence by such reasonable and reasoned means. Furthermore, there is a risk that it may in practice collapse forgiveness into excusing or condoning behavior; "to understand all is to forgive all."

In most reframing models empathy is envisaged as the affective result of having reframed the causes that led to the other's actions. There is some support for the view that empathy is determined by perceptions of responsibility, justice, and causality (see Heider 1958). However, in the second approach to forgiveness, empathy is generated directly to mediate forgiveness. The role of the head in understanding is not stressed as the primary factor in forgiveness, as in reframing approaches, and a heartfelt response of compassion toward the offender is promoted.

It would seem that there are weaknesses with both types of approach; if one assumes the priority of empathy over explanation and understanding, there may be huge obstacles in the way of identification with the offender, especially if that person has behaved in an inhuman or unfeeling way. On the other hand, the cognitive approach of reframing is not without difficulties. While a process of reattribution enables one to separate offenders from an act or acts of wrongdoing, so that their offensive behavior is no longer their defining characteristic, it may constitute an overly intellectual approach to forgiveness that assumes that once faulty cognitions concerning blame have been reappraised, affective and behavioral change will necessarily occur. Such an assumption may not be justified in cases where Worthington's observation of a lingering and occasionally recurring bitterness is evident. What is more, there may be instances where such a reasonable approach as reframing seems inadequate to elucidate the utter *in*comprehensibility of particularly monstrous violations.

Psychological interventions tend to espouse the view that forgiveness, whether driven primarily by the head or by the heart, takes place in stages. However, people may have a sudden awareness that they have finally forgiven someone for a long-standing transgression. Though it is likely that sudden forgiveness, akin to an unexpected conversion might have a period of what William James called "subconscious incubation," it is perhaps the case that the stepwise forgiveness envisaged in psychological models is simply too rigid a scheme for all instances of forgiveness. A person may feel empowered to forgive by a sudden (and perhaps inexplicable) upsurge in magnanimity. While too rapid a forgiveness may signal the operation of a defense mechanism, too much of an emphasis on a rational process of forgiveness may eliminate a sense of ardent benevolence, compassion, and humanity.

Reframing may not be an appropriate forgiveness strategy to employ in isolation for persons prone to excessive rumination. It may, however, be useful, especially in the initial stages of forgiveness since it affords another perspective on the offender. It should not be assumed that reframing is a *necessary* precursor to empathy, as most models imply, nor should it be assumed that it is appropriate for all situations where forgiveness is sought. Indeed it would seem that using *both* types of intervention (primarily empathic or predominantly cognitive) might afford the most holistic approach to forgiveness incorporating both head and heart.

Forgiveness of the Head and of the Heart in Hebrew and Greek

Interestingly, three words used to translate forgiveness in the New Testament seem to reflect a distinction between forgiveness of the head/ decisional forgiveness and forgiveness of the heart/emotional forgiveness. The Greek word most often used to express forgiveness is the verb *aphiemi* and its cognate noun *aphesis*. The word's usual meaning is simply "to leave, abandon" and the word is used in this sense in the New Testament.[6] However, *aphiemi* is also used in relation to sin, which is described as somehow "abandoned" when a person comes to participate in the coming kingdom. This specialist use of *aphesis* may also be found in the Septuagint and in the writings of Josephus.

Forgiveness is also expressed by the verb *apoluo*, which means to "release." Once again, this may be used in a literal sense of release from captivity. However, like *aphiemi* it is also used metaphorically to convey the idea of release from sin. Thus both *aphiemi* and *apoluo* signify release, casting off, or letting go. In this sense, they echo those approaches to forgiveness that emphasize deciding to "let go of" or "loosen" resentment.

On the other hand, and focusing more on people rather than on sin objectively cast off, is Paul's use of the verb *charizomai*, which in essence means "to behave graciously toward." It is most often used to describe God's bestowal of gifts on God's people (see 1 Corinthians 2:12 and Romans 8:32), but it is also used interpersonally to translate forgiveness in 2 Corinthians 7, 10, and 12:10. There can be no doubt that *charizomai* connotes a more empathic forgiveness of the heart than either *aphiemi* or *apoluo*, though all three describe kinds of forgiveness.

The distinction between these two sorts of forgiveness is redolent of the differentiation between two types of forgiveness in Judaism, *mehilah* (a forgoing of indebtedness) and *selihah*, described by Blumenthal (1998, 80) as "an act of the heart. . . . It is achieving an empathy for the troubledness of the other."[7] Furthermore, it would also seem that these different emphases on remitting wrongdoing and warming compassionately toward another are reflected in different theories of the Christian understanding of the atonement. Substitutionary theories of the atonement such as Anselm's focus rather cerebrally on the casting off of debts of sin, while Abelard's interpretation of the atonement emphasizes the emotional influence of Christ's inspirational love.

DEVELOPMENTAL FACTORS

Clearly, the capacity for forgiveness is mediated to some degree by cognitive competencies. In order to understand the nature of forgiveness, a person must have reached a certain stage in the developmental process (Coate 2004, 137). An individual must have the cognitive capabilities to recognize that forgiveness involves an interpersonal violation for which the offender is responsible and perhaps also culpable, yet also requires that the forgiver set aside resentment and the desire for retaliation. Both Piaget (1932) and Kohlberg (1968) have examined the development of moral judgment, observing that children's moral reasoning tends to begin with a preoccupation with rules and authority, passing through revenge and punishment to cooperation and the abstract ideal of justice. Coate (2004, 137–38) suggests that the change from "crude reciprocity" ("give as good as you get") to the maxim of "do as you would be done by" at the stage of formal operations is the basis for "articulated compassion and forgiveness."

However, in addition to possessing the necessary cognitive capabilities to comprehend the concept of forgiveness, it is also the case that over the course of development, this "head knowledge" must be accompanied by an emotionally transformative *experience* of forgiveness. To understand that forgiveness involves the withholding of punishment and ill will toward another, a child must have experienced its caregiver's holding back from punishing his or her transgression and to have received their forgiveness.

Atkinson (1982) approaches forgiveness from a Kleinian perspective, evaluating it alongside the related concept of *reparation*. He stresses the importance of parental forgiveness in the development of concern for the other in very young children. Following Melanie Klein, Atkinson puts forward the view that the "depressive position" marks the beginning of infant concern that he or she has hurt the "good object" with the hostile feelings that characterized its treatment of the primary caregiver in the previously experienced "paranoid schizoid" position. As a result of splitting, the good object (usually the infant's mother) is perceived as two persons, "good" and "bad." It is only with the advent of the "depressive position" at around five or six months that the infant becomes able to regard the primary caregiver as a "whole" object, capable of being *both* good and bad. As the infant grows out of the "paranoid schizoid" position, he or she feels the precursors of guilt, depression, and sadness as he or she perceives that his or her hostile feelings have caused hurt to the good object. These feelings of concern, according to Kleinian theory, represent the beginnings of the human capacity for empathy and the desire to make reparation for one's wrongdoings.

However, as Atkinson indicates, forgiveness by the parent has to come first in order for the infant to understand reparation; "before the child can come to understand this peculiar life-drive which we call reparation to be reparation and not another thing, forgiveness has to come from the mother as a gift towards the 'wrong' which helps interpret the child's own desires to himself" (1982, 20). "Grace" therefore precedes repentance, and forgiveness is appropriated before it is extended. There are therefore developmental elements of forgiveness that involve affective experience in addition to the cognitive capacities upon which a complete understanding of forgiveness depends. Head and heart knowledge are therefore intertwined in a developmental understanding of forgiveness.

The Role of Liturgy in Forgiveness

If the experience of having been forgiven by another person for a particular transgression is powerful, for many people the experience of being forgiven by God is even more potentially transformative. However, while many Christians may profess belief in divine forgiveness, there may be a lack of alignment between believing oneself to be forgiven, at the propositional level, and really feeling this forgiveness in one's heart, as the articles by Moriarty and Zahl, Sharp, and Gibson in this volume show. In view of this disjunction, it would seem that liturgy and ritual has an important role to play in bringing head and heart knowledge of forgiveness into closer alignment with one another.

There are three sacraments through which forgiveness may be experienced and reexperienced in the life of the church. In the rituals of baptism, confession, and Holy Communion, head knowledge of forgiveness is combined with actions that may help heart knowledge of forgiveness to be perceived more deeply, though it might be argued that the sacraments differ in the degree to which they bring head and heart knowledge of forgiveness into harmony.

For example, adult baptism affords an opportunity for the propositional knowledge of forgiveness to be enacted bodily and powerfully relived, while such a possibility lies beyond the scope of infant baptism. Interestingly, the case against infant baptism is usually stated in propositional terms (an infant cannot give rational assent to the creed), though it could also be suggested that the emotionally transformative effect of the ritual is also absent in infant baptism. It must be emphasized, however, that while rituals may be subjectively experienced, the transformations they mark have objective effects; whether adult or child, the rite of baptism represents a sacrament of incorporation into the body of Christ.

The ritual practice of confession and absolution may also bring head and heart knowledge of forgiveness into closer alignment. While some individuals may find confession helpful in dealing with guilt, it may be the case that we now inhabit a more shame-oriented than guilt-oriented culture, such that the sense of being liberated from the burden of specific transgressions no longer affords the feeling of release it once did (see Watts 2001). For this reason, the rite of the Eucharist may be better able to convey the movement from separation and sin to forgiveness and reconciliation, as Grainger (2004, 75) has noted. This raises the question of whether an analogous form of secular ritual may be helpful to potentiate forgiveness of the heart outside a specifically religious context. Grainger (2004) offers some suggestions for how this catharsis might be enacted.

Sacramental rites such as these enable people to transform heart knowledge of God holistically, engaging mind and body. Moriarty (this volume) offers helpful suggestions for how heart knowledge of God can be transformed when harmful God images are overcome through a guided process of pastoral counseling. While this work is undoubtedly beneficial to individuals like Martin, helping them to "learn to experience the God they believe in," it is rather cerebral and does not engage the whole person in the same way sacramental rituals and their secular analogues might afford.

Conclusion

The process of forgiveness encompasses both head and heart knowledge, though these dimensions may not always be in harmony with one other. There is an aspect of forgiveness that seems to center on foreswearing or "letting go" of resentment and the cognitive attributions that sustain it, alongside an interpretation of forgiveness that centers on the transformation of emotions and behavior toward an offender. The former, sometimes referred to as "decisional forgiveness," seems to correspond to head knowledge, while the latter ("emotional forgiveness") is identified here with knowledge of the heart.

Although a decision to forgive may take a while to bear emotional fruit, it should not be disparaged since it represents a significant step toward an anticipated goal of complete forgiveness. Likewise, acknowledging one has been forgiven by another may precede genuinely *feeling* forgiven, a state that may be potentiated by engaging in ritual acts that bring head and heart knowledge into closer alignment.

SUMMARY

In the first part of this chapter it was argued that hope and optimism rest on different conceptual foundations. Optimism or *hoping-that* appear to be grounded in head knowledge based either on external and rationally calculable probabilities concerning the likelihood of anticipated future events or, as in recent positive psychological models, on internal cognitive schemata and beliefs about agency and self-control that may be subjected to conscious moderation. *Hoping-in*, on the other hand, was shown to be based on a different species of confidence, a confidence that stems not from head knowledge based on what is externally or internally "known" to the subject, but in a heartfelt communion of trust with another. It was suggested that this kind of confidence may be more fundamental to mental adjustment than a confidence that inheres in probabilities, or beliefs about personal agency, control of cognitive attributions, and problem-solving strategies.

However, it was also suggested that in practice a clear distinction between hope and optimism in relation to head and heart knowledge is perhaps difficult to delineate. While optimism that is based entirely on probabilities may be identified almost completely with knowledge of the head, in the case of optimism construed as beliefs about agency and competence, there is some investment of the self in a personally held attitude toward the future that merges with elements of the existentially involved knowledge of the heart. Similarly, hope should be realistic and is not antithetical to reason, as in purely "wishful thinking."

Turning to forgiveness, it was shown that knowing and feeling forgiving or forgiven may not be in complete harmony with one another. People may objectively "know" they have been forgiven without feeling this subjectively. Similarly, they may sincerely desire to transform their feelings about an offender but be prevented at the emotional level by feelings of anger and resentment. While "decisional" forgiveness or forgiveness "of the head" should not be denigrated, it seems that complete forgiveness also involves emotional transformation and *metanoia*, a fundamental change of heart.

NOTES

1. "By definition, almost, hope involves future uncertainties; but the uncertainties should not be too great. When the probability of attainment is unrealistically low, hope is inappropriate" (Averill, Catlin, and Chon 1990, 33).
2. The notion of the "transitional" was first entertained by D. W. Winnicott (1980).
3. Initially, respondents completed the questionnaire on a four-point scale, though this has more recently been expanded to a continuum ranging from one to eight. Of the twelve items in the scale, four reflect agency thinking and four reflect pathways thinking. There are four distractors.
4. 1 = external/unstable/specific and 7 = internal, stable, and global.
5. "Learning to Love your Enemies," *Church Times*, January 16, 2009, 19. Interview by Rebecca Pavely.
6. For example, Luke 4:38ff, where a fever "leaves" Peter's mother-in-law after her healing by Jesus.
7. Cited in Schimmel (2004, 20).

REFERENCES

Atkinson, D. 1982. "Forgiveness and Personality Development." *Third Way* 5:18–21.
Averill, J. R., G. Catlin, and K. K. Chon. 1990. *Rules of Hope*. New York: Springer Verlag.
Bandura, A. 1997. *Self-efficacy: The Exercise of Control*. New York: Freeman.
Batson, C. D. 1990. "How Social an Animal? The Human Capacity for Caring." *American Psychologist* 45:336–46.
———. 1991. *The Altruism Question*. New Jersey: Hillsdale.
Blumenthal, D. R. 1998. "Repentance and Forgiveness." *CrossCurrents* 48:75–81.

Butler, J. 1970. "Upon Forgiveness of Injuries." In *Butler's Fifteen Sermons*, edited by T. A. Roberts, 80–89. London: SPCK.

Carver, C. S., and M. Scheier. 2003. "Optimism." In *Positive Psychological Assessment: A Handbook of Models and Measures*, edited by S. J. Lopez and C. R. Snyder, 75–89. Washington DC: APA.

Coate, M. A. 2004. "The Capacity for Forgiveness." In *Forgiveness in Context: Theology and Psychology in Creative Dialogue*, edited by F. Watts and L. Gulliford, 123–43. London: T&T Clark International.

Coleman, P. 1998. "The Process of Forgiveness in Marriage and the Family." In *Exploring Forgiveness*, edited by R. D. Enright and J. North, 75–94. Madison: University of Wisconsin Press.

Eisenberg, N., and R. A. Fabes. 1990. "Empathy Conceptualisation, Measurement and Relation to Pro-social Behavior." *Motivation and Emotion* 14:131–49.

Enright, R. D. 2001. *Forgiveness Is a Choice*. Washington, DC: APA.

Enright R. D., and R. P. Fitzgibbons. 2000. *Helping Clients Forgive: An Empirical Guide for Resolving Anger and Restoring Hope*. Washington, DC: APA.

Enright, R. D., S. Freedman, and J. Rique. 1998. "The Psychology of Interpersonal Forgiveness." In *Exploring Forgiveness*, edited by R. D. Enright and J. North, 46–62. Madison: University of Wisconsin Press.

Enright, R. D., and J. North, eds. 1998. *Exploring Forgiveness*. Madison: University of Wisconsin Press.

Erikson, E. H. 1959. *Identity and the Life Cycle*. Madison, CT: International Universities Press.

Godfrey, J. J. 1987. *A Philosophy of Human Hope*. Dordrecht, Germany: Martinus Nijhoff.

Grainger, R. 2004. "Forgiveness and Liturgy." In *Forgiveness in Context: Theology and Psychology in Creative Dialogue*, edited by F. Watts and L. Gulliford, 69–82. London: T&T Clark.

Gulliford, L. 2004. "Intrapersonal Forgiveness." In *Forgiveness in Context: Theology and Psychology in Creative Dialogue*, edited by F. Watts and L. Gulliford, 83–105. London: T&T Clark International,.

Heider, F. 1958. *The Psychology of Interpersonal Relations*. New York: Wiley.

Kobler, A. L., and E. Stotland. 1964. *The End of Hope*. New York: Macmillan.

Kohlberg, L. 1968. "The Child as a Moral Philosopher." *Psychology Today* 2 (4): 24–30.

Lynch, W. F. 1974. *Images of Hope*. North Bend, IN: University of Notre Dame Press.

Marcel, G. 1962. *Homo Viator: Introduction to a Metaphysics of Hope*, translated by Emma Crauford. New York: Harper and Row.

McCullough, M. E., E. L. Worthington, and K. C. Rachal. 1997. "Interpersonal Forgiving in Close Relationships." *Journal of Personality and Social Psychology* 73:321–36.

North, J. 1998. "The 'Ideal' of Forgiveness." In *Exploring Forgiveness*, edited by R. D. Enright and J. North, 15–34. Madison: University of Wisconsin Press.

Peterson, C., A. Semmel, C. von Bayer, L. Y. Abramson, G. I. Metalsky, and M. E. P. Seligman. 1982. "The Attributional Style Questionnaire." *Cognitive Therapy and Research* 6:287–99.

Piaget, J. 1932. *The Moral Judgement of the Child*. New York: Harcourt, Brace Jovanovich.

Schimmel, S. 2004. "Interpersonal Forgiveness and Repentance in Judaism." In *Forgiveness in Context: Theology and Psychology in Creative Dialogue*, edited by F. Watts and L. Gulliford, 11–28. London: T&T Clark International.

Seligman, M. E. P. 2003. *Authentic Happiness*. London: Nicholas Brealey.

———. 2006. *Learned Optimism: How to Change Your Mind and Your Life*. New York: Vintage Books.

Smedes, L. 1988. *Forgive and Forget: Healing the Hurts We Don't Deserve*. San Francisco: Harper and Row.

Snyder, C. R. 1994. *The Psychology of Hope: You Can Get There from Here*. New York: Free Press.

Snyder, C. R. 2002. "Hope Theory: Rainbows in the Mind." *Psychological Inquiry* 13:249–75.

Snyder, C. R., C. Harris, J. R. Anderson, S. A. Holleran, L. M. Irving et al. 1991. "The Will and the Ways: Development and Validation of an Individual-differences Measure of Hope." *Journal of Personality and Social Psychology* 60:570–85.

Wade, N. G., and E. L. Worthington Jr. 2003. "Overcoming Unforgiveness: Is Forgiveness the Only Way to Deal with Unforgiveness?" *Journal of Counseling and Development* 81:343–53.

Wade, N.G., E. L. Worthington Jr., and J. E. Meyer. 2005. "But Do They Work?: A Meta-analysis of Group Interventions to Promote Forgiveness." In *Handbook of Forgiveness*, edited by E. L. Worthington Jr., 423–39. New York: Routledge.

Watts, F. 2001. "Shame, Sin and Guilt." In *Forgiveness and Truth*, edited by A. McFadyen and M. Sarot, 53–70. Edinburgh: T&T Clark.

Watts, F. 2002. *Theology and Psychology*. Aldershot: Ashgate.

Watts, F., and L. Gulliford, eds. 2004. *Forgiveness in Context: Theology and Psychology in Creative Dialogue*. London: T&T Clark International.

Weiner, B., S. Graham, O. Peter, and M. Zmuidinas. 1991. "Public Confession and Forgiveness." *Journal of Personality* 59:281–312.

Winnicott, D. W. 1980. *Playing and Reality*. Harmondsworth: Penguin.

Worthington, E. L., Jr. 1998. "The Pyramid Model of Forgiveness: Some Interdisciplinary Speculations about Unforgiveness and the Promotion of Forgiveness." In *Dimensions of Forgiveness: Psychological Research and Theological Perspectives*, edited by E. L. Worthington Jr., 107–37. West Conshohocken, PA: Templeton Foundation Press.

———, ed. 2002. *Dimensions of Forgiveness: Psychological Research and Theological Perspectives*. West Conshohocken, PA: Templeton Foundation Press.

———, ed. 2005. *Handbook of Forgiveness*. New York: Routledge.

Worthington, E. L., Jr., and N. G. Wade. 1999. "The Social Psychology of Unforgiveness and Forgiveness and the Implications for Clinical Practice." *Journal of Social and Clinical Psychology* 18:358–415.

Conclusion
Head and Heart in Cultural Context

Fraser Watts

This last chapter will put issues about head and heart in broader context, especially in cultural and historical context. Though we have been concerned in this book with head and heart in religion specifically, it will be suggested here that the current issues about head and heart are much wider. Indeed, it would not be too much to say there are cultural wars about head and heart, cultural wars that have been developing through the course of the "modern" period, or at least since the Enlightenment.

In sketching the story of the changing balance between head and heart in recent centuries, a particularly helpful source is *The Master and His Emissary* by Iain McGilchrist (2009). Other chapters in this book (Watts, chapter 5; Savage, chapter 6; Wiseman, chapter 9) have drawn on the masterly account of the functioning of left and right brain in part 1 of that book. In part 2, McGilchrist goes on to attempt a reinterpretation of cultural history, particularly of the last few hundred years, in the light of the relative emphasis of left and right brain through each period. What he says about left and right brain can be translated into the relative roles of head and heart. Though he doesn't himself use the terminology of "head" and "heart," he effectively provides, in other terms, a history of head and heart in recent centuries. (In summarizing his account here, I will use the terminology of "head" and "heart," even though his terminology is that of left brain and right brain.)

McGilchrist's narrative is one of gradually increasing reliance on the "head," punctuated by counterreactions toward the "heart." To present his complex narrative in broad and simple outline, he sees the Renaissance as a period in which head and heart were well-balanced and working fruitful harmony. But that was succeeded by the Enlightenment period in which there was an overemphasis on the head, on a few simple principles that could be articulated clearly and defended rationally. In the Romantic period there was a reaction against that, with a reversal to a broader way of understanding things, in which the heart and the imagination played a crucial role (as discussed by Geoff Dumbreck in chapter 1 and Malcolm Guite in chapter 2 of this book). However, as McGilchrist sees it, the Industrial Revolution marks a return to the predominance of the head, something that has continued through the period of "late modernity" and been taken further than ever before. The Industrial Revolution and Romantic Movement proceeded concurrently for a period, with Romanticism making an increasingly explicit protest against industrialization, for example by William Blake, in his "Jerusalem" and elsewhere.

I am aware that I am summarizing here in a few sentences a story that McGilchrist tells at much greater length, though he admits that even his account is a cursory summary of a story that ought to be told more fully. His cultural history has much in common with other accounts of the intellectual life of this period, especially Charles Taylor's *Sources of the Self* (1989). What McGilchrist adds is a mapping of cultural movements on to the functioning of left and right brains. He is well aware of how controversial terms like "Enlightenment" and "Romanticism" are, as they raise questions about the events they are trying to summarize. He is also aware of the many complex twists and turns in this story, and that trends which at first appear to point in one direction can end up pointing in the other. However, I believe that his basic narrative of an oscillation, but one that is going in the underlying direction of increasing dependence on the head, is sound.

There is a fruitful convergence to be explored between McGilchrist's narrative and the argument of Gordon Rattray Taylor in *The Angel Makers* (1974), which takes the vantage point of social and cultural history. They cover many of the same cultural twists and turns, but Taylor maps them on to changes in socio-developmental psychology rather than neuropsychology. It seems that the periods in which head and heart were relatively balanced (such as the Romantic period, in which McGilchrist sees the right brain as having significant influence) are, in Taylor's terms, more "matrist" periods, in which the ego is more "thin walled." In contrast, periods in which there is an overdominance of head are, for McGilchrist, heavily dominated by the left brain and, for Taylor, more "patrist," with a "thick-walled" ego. It is beyond the scope of this chapter to explore how these different accounts might be integrated, but it is worth noting that more than one approach to psychology may be relevant to understanding the twists and turns of the intellectual history of recent centuries.

The Religious Head and Heart in Cultural Context

Though this cultural warfare about head and heart is much broader than religion, religion has been massively affected by it. Fluctuations between head and heart have been hugely important for religion; it has been at the center of the culture wars of recent centuries.

Religion has often been carried along by the cultural tide toward reliance on the head. In periods when general culture has been dominated by the head, that has often been true of religion too. However, religion has particular reasons to challenge the domination of head and, as Geoff Dumbreck made clear in chapter 1, it has often done so. Sometimes, when there has been a growing cultural emphasis on the "head," religion has deliberately taken steps to strengthen a counterbalancing emphasis on the religious "heart," such as in the Catholic development of devotions focused on the "sacred heart of Jesus," which seem to have been an explicit counterbalance to the intellectual aridity of the Enlightenment. Religion, more than most things, can't be content with an exclusive focus on the head; religion must always be about the transformation of the whole human person.

Religion is also pivotal to the cultural wars about head and heart in a broader sense. McGilchrist argues that there is an urgent need for society to find a way to rebalance its present overvaluation of the head. Religion, McGilchrist acknowledges, is one of the sources from which such a rebalancing might come, precisely because religion has often wanted to resist the increasingly prevalent domination of the head. However, the critical question is whether religion itself has been so much affected (and distorted) by the predominant overreliance on head that it will be unable to play this crucial role in contemporary culture effectively.

Though religion has, in many ways, been one of the arenas of cultural life most concerned with the importance of "heart," McGilchrist argues that it has not remained uninfluenced by the prevailing emphasis on the head. Indeed, he suggests that even religion and art, the two cultural arenas most likely to stand outside the general movement toward "head," have in fact been so much influenced themselves by the prevailing trends that they are no longer able to provide an escape from the increasing emphasis on "head." McGilchrist argues at some length that art has been distorted by a growing emphasis on the head. However, it is clear from brief remarks that he extends the argument to religion as well, and Sara Savage (chapter 6) has set out that case in some detail.

McGilchrist is concerned about this, not so much because he cares about the distortion of religion that it represents, but more because he regrets that religion is now too weakened and distorted to make the significant impact on these general culture wars that he wishes it could make. He thinks the excessive dependence on head is very dangerous for humanity, from many points of view, and he regrets the inability of religion to put up effective resistance. That is not only because religion now has less general cultural influence, but also because religion has itself become increasingly affected by the dominance of the head.

It is interesting that someone such as McGilchrist, who has no personal religious commitment, ascribes such a potentially important role to religion in the development of human culture. However, it is also dismaying that he thinks that religion is already so disabled that it is unlikely to be able to play this role effectively. The mood of his view of religion is rather reminiscent of C. G. Jung, who thought that religion was the custodian of archetypal symbols of great importance for humanity, but regretted that it had such little awareness of the nature and significance of these important symbols that it was unable to do anything useful with its inheritance. Such views of religion represent an interesting challenge to the religious community. McGilchrist's challenge is to nurture a form of religion that holds heart and head together in a balanced way, rather than one that is carried along by the general cultural bias toward head.

One place in which one can discern an attempt at a counterbalancing emphasis on the heart is in the rapidly growing Pentecostal and charismatic forms of Christianity. Indeed, one of the most interesting ways in which current forms of Christianity differ among themselves is where they stand on the head/heart issue, and it cuts across some widely accepted distinctions.

For example, different kinds of evangelicals take a very different stance on head/heart issues. On the one hand there are conservative evangelicals, who often veer toward fundamentalism, and who seem to be strongly influenced by the current cultural emphasis on the head, which they are importing into Christianity. In contrast, charismatic forms of evangelicalism place a much stronger emphasis on the heart, and indeed may often go too far in that direction. If charismatic Christianity focuses too much on the heart and ignores the head, it will have too little engagement with rational reflection and will then have little potential to facilitate the integration of head and heart. There is also a tendency for charismatic religion to attend more to short-term feelings and not enough to the development of sustained dispositions. There are some signs of charismatic religion beginning to make a contribution to systematic theology, as Dumbreck noted in chapter 1. That is very much to be welcomed, but so far they have been rather limited.

Our culture is not going to be helped by forms of religion that simply do not engage with our culturally predominant rationality; neither is Christianity going to be true to itself, if it simply emphasizes heart rather than head. Referring back to the theological figures discussed in chapter 1, it needs the kind of integration of head and heart seen in people like Newman, rather than the rejection of the head represented by people like Bushnell. Charismatic religion can easily fall into being simply a rejection of the rational aspects of modernity, rather than the healing of modernity for which David Ford has called (2007).

Similarly, the significant appeal of Buddhism in the West is linked to the widespread view that Buddhism offers helpful religious practices without the "metaphysics" of Christianity. It may indeed offer religion without supernaturalism (though there are mystical forms of Christianity that do that too; like *The Cloud of Unknowing*, which says that God can be known by love but not by thought). However, Buddhism actually has a rich and elaborate intellectual tradition, especially about the human person. When probed in a full and balanced way, it also has the potential to integrate head and heart and does not eschew intellectual formulations as much as is widely assumed by adherents to Western Buddhism.

What religion, at its best, may be able to offer our contemporary culture is a form of rationality that is fully integrated with the heart, and which helps to integrate the whole person. The implicit plea of this book is not for forms of religion that emphasize either head or heart to the virtual exclusion of the other, but for a form of religion that holds them in balance. I hope we have shown here how the religious life can be an arena in which head and heart can be integrated. Religion is potentially well placed to become a laboratory in which the proper integration of head and heart is explored, practiced, and propagated.

Religion faces some stark choices here. It can become a victim of the prevailing cultural emphasis on the head, in a way that distorts and diminishes its own tradition, or it can swing to the other extreme and embrace a form of religion that is largely emotional and has little intellectual integrity. Alternatively, despite the cultural pressures, it may be able to hold to a more balanced approach to head and heart, and indeed set an example of how to do so. That would both be more faithful to its own tradition and also make a valuable corrective contribution to what, as McGilchrist sees it, is one of the most serious current cultural problems facing humanity. It is a challenge that affects every faith tradition and every tradition of Christianity, albeit in somewhat different ways. None is unaffected by current pervasive problems in integrating head and heart, but all have the potential to get this right if they inhabit their own tradition in a balanced way.

The Fragmentation of Religion

Religion tends to fragment in a way that leads people to focus on particular aspects of religion rather than on all its facets, creating problems for the integration of head and heart in religion. A series of leading figures in the study of religion have commented on this fragmentation (see Hood et al. 2009, 8–12). For example, Glock and Stark (1966) divide religion up into its experiential, ideological (i.e., religious beliefs), ritualistic, intellectual (i.e., knowledge about religion), and consequential (i.e., the effects of religion on attitudes and behavior) aspects, and it has become increasingly apparent that these different facets have only weak interrelationships.

There are also similar issues about morality. Empirical studies of moral functioning show that morality tends to fragment (Wright 1971), with little connection between different areas of moral functioning such as moral norms, resistance to temptation, and reaction to transgression. More recently, Jonathan Haidt (2012) has made a similar argument for multiple moral systems that are relatively independent of one another. It is clear that knowing the difference between right and wrong has little impact on whether people actually behave in a moral way.

The study of morals has perhaps been too much dominated by philosophical ethics that, though interesting in itself, has little relevance to whether people take moral principles to heart deeply enough to be influenced by them.

The fragmentation of both religion and morality is perhaps, in part, a product of the failure of our society to hold head and heart together, though it no doubt has deeper roots. Unfortunately, this fragmentation of religion and morality makes it easy for people to connect with just one aspect of the tradition and to ignore others; they can focus entirely on Bible, or meditation, or good works, or whatever has particular personal appeal. Such partial engagements with religion will not allow it to realize its potential to integrate head and heart.

The issues that arise here are rather like those that have often been debated about religious experience, which also has head and heart aspects. The relationship between experience and doctrine is rather like that between head and heart, as noted in chapter 4 by Bonnie Zahl et al. There are those, like William James in his *Varieties of Religious Experience* (1902), who have claimed that experience is the foundation from which doctrine and religious institutions have been built. In similar vein, and more recently, Nancey Murphy (1990) has suggested that theology is essentially a scientific research program, with religious experience its raw data. Others, such as Nicholas Lash in *Easter in Ordinary* (1988), have emphasized that any experience can be counted as "religious," provided that it is interpreted within a religious frame of reference.

My own view is that there is a to-and-fro between personal experience and cultural context, including received intellectual traditions. I recognize, with Lash, that William James makes exaggerated claims for the priority of personal experience, but it seems misleading to go to the opposite extreme. Culture shapes individual experience, but it is also in turn shaped by the personal experiences of particular individuals. Doctrine shapes experience, but it is equally true that experience shapes doctrine.

Equally, classic cases of religious experience have both a distinctive experiential aspect and employ a religious interpretative framework. I suggest that it does not do justice to religious experience to place exclusive emphasis on the heart aspects (i.e., the distinctive sense of unity) or the head aspects (i.e., the interpretative framework). Head and heart have the potential to come together in religious experience, though it is perfectly possible to have secondary cases of religious experience characterized by just one or the other.

Personal Integration of Head and Heart

The challenge of integrating head and heart faces different people in different ways. Psychology always has an interest in how people differ among themselves, and the issues about head and heart with which we are concerned here are not only broad cultural issues; they also affect particular individuals in ways that have far-reaching personal significance. Integrating head and heart is part of the personal challenge of each individual religious person. How these issues arise for particular individuals depends on where they started in their religious life and what initial contact with religion they had.

Particular issues arise for individuals when there are discrepancies between their head-level and heart-level engagement with the religion. The most common situation is a discrepancy between head-level doctrine and heart-level experience, as discussed by Zahl et al. (chapter 4) and Moriarty (chapter 7). Moriarty's particular concern there is with the problems that arise when people's heart understanding of God is imbalanced, leading them to feel a degree of anger or guilt toward God that would not arise if they relied more on their correct head-level view.

Certainly, there is a tendency for people to be somewhat unbalanced in how they experience religion, though it is perhaps not always the head that is the best guide. There is considerable evidence that people's memories are biased by their mood-states; the more depressed people are, the more they tend to selectively recall negative memories that are congruent with their mood (Teasdale and Barnard 1993). It is likely that people's assimilation of religious teaching is open to bias in a similar way. For example, people who tend to feel guilt are likely, as a result, to have a strong emphasis on the judgment of God, whereas people who have better self-esteem are likely to emphasize being accepted by God. These effects will be felt at the heart level in the first place, but they may in turn affect head-level doctrine.

There can also be quite broad cultural shifts in how religion is formulated and experienced. It has often been remarked that there are some cultures that are predominantly guilt-oriented and others that are predominantly shame-oriented (e.g., Watts 2001), and this has far-reaching implications for the religious outlook in particular periods. There are also probably similar fluctuations between relatively melancholy and relatively optimistic cultures, something that McGilchrist touches on. It is an interesting research task for intellectual historians of religion to track these oscillations and to explore their implications for religion.

More broadly, it would be interesting to map changes in religious doctrine on to the changing emphasis on head and heart in recent centuries. For example, there has been a striking shift from the strong emphasis on eternal punishment in hell of the period before the First World War to a contemporary theology that, for the most part, shies away from that, and instead puts the emphasis on the love, acceptance, and forgiveness of God. In some ways that movement may have been helpful to people at a psychological level, and it has probably been influenced by a general movement toward a culture that has embraced the values of psychological counseling. However, there is a danger, as Garrison (1982) has pointed out, that an official theology that neglects the judgment of God will fail to connect with the personal "shadow" that is an important part of many people's personal experience.

There seems to be a hard-wired tendency for the more linguistic left brain to be relatively melancholy (McGilchrist 2009). That would result in a tendency for people's heart-level religious experience to be more guilty and angry than their more linguistic, official faith. (Equally, it is possible to have an official, articulate religion that emphasizes sin and guilt, which can coexist with good self-esteem at the intuitive level.)

People can deal with these discrepancies in various ways. They can allow head and heart religion to coexist, with little connection between them. Alternatively, they can work toward integration, which can proceed in either direction. For example, if people have heart-level religion that is more downbeat, they can work at bringing their more downbeat religious experience under the influence of more balanced doctrine. Alternatively, they can stay with their rather downbeat religious experience, what John of the Cross called the "dark night of the soul" (May 2005) and work through that to an articulate faith that really is grounded in intuitive religious experience.

The predominant mode of initial contact with religion varies from one culture to another and is probably changing quite rapidly, as "secularization" unfolds. Until recently, the predominant mode of contact with religion was probably as a body of teaching and set of religious institutions. That is still probably true of relatively religious cultures like the United States, though it is ceasing to be true of Western Europe, where there is a rapidly growing ignorance of the intellectual tradition of Christianity.

If people engage with religion first as a body of teaching and set of institutions, then the personal task of religious adherents is to take the faith they have received "to heart" and to make it their own in ways that are meaningful and transformative for them, as discussed by Myers in chapter 8. Christianity has long been concerned with that task, as is seen in the thinking of people like Newman (see chapter 1). The process here is of starting with a body of teaching and collective religious practices and working with it sufficiently richly until it affects the heart, as well as intellectual belief and public religious practice. For example, as Liz Gulliford explains in chapter 10, people do not only need to *believe* that they are forgiven, they need to take that to heart and actually *experience* forgiveness.

Religion is by no means the only arena in which such issues arise. Another is psychotherapy and counseling (about which McGilchrist says surprisingly little, despite his professional background in psychiatry). As Watts and Williams (1988) point out, there is an interesting distinction in the literature on psychotherapy between "intellectual" and "effective" insight, which seems, in effect, to be a distinction between insight at the level of head and of heart. It is recognized that intellectual insights are often achieved quite early in psychotherapy, but have little therapeutic benefit until they have been "taken to heart." Much of the work that goes on in psychotherapy is devoted to taking insights to heart in a way that makes them effective, and it is similar to the process of taking religion to heart.

Sometimes things go the other way round, and people have an experiential engagement with religion (or "spirituality") before they know much about it. As societies become more secular, that is likely to happen increasingly, as the studies of religion and spirituality in Kendall in the United Kingdom illustrate (Heelas et al. 2005). So people may initially engage with religion through practices like meditation, which primarily affect their experience rather than what they know or think. Meditation may then start to affect their assumptions about religion and life in ways that are, at first, largely implicit, but which can then become increasingly explicit. That in turn will start to challenge the implicit metaphysical assumptions of an increasingly secular society.

Religion is probably less experienced at providing resources to help people make the journey from heart to head than it is at helping people to take intellectual teaching to heart. However, it seems that this is likely to be an increasingly common pathway and one that deserves attention. There are actually advantages in approaching things this way round, partly because of features of the structure and function of the human brain to which McGilchrist has drawn attention. The intuitive "heart" knowledge of the right brain shows a natural tendency to collaborate with the more articulate ways in which the left brain knows things. However, the left brain seems to show less interest in enriching its head knowledge by connecting with the intuitive approach to knowing of the right brain.

There is a danger that if people are presented at the start of their religious journey with head-level systematizations of belief that are the proper end point of that journey, they may either simply reject them or may not be able to move beyond them. It is an interesting feature of the way in which most faith traditions emerged that the initiators and their immediate followers did not have the option of approaching things that way round. For example, Jesus's initial followers seem, on the gospel record, to have followed him with little idea of who he was and where he was taking them. That may, in some ways, have been an advantage. As the process of secularization proceeds, an increasing number of people are likely to encounter religion in an experiential way, rather than initially through the head. There may be advantages in that, though it remains important to move toward a mature integration of head and heart.

People can enter religion by various different routes, leading to different conversion types, such as intellectual, moral, and social (Thouless 1971). Whichever route people follow, there is a task of broadening the initial engagement with religion out to include other aspects. It is worth noting that intellectual conversions are relatively rare; people don't often enter religion through the head and then need to engage the heart. It is more common for people to enter by some other route that affects the heart in the first place, but which leads on to a subsequent phase of more intellectual engagement.

Religious education has generally been too head-orientated, and there is now a need to move toward a mode of religious education that integrates head and heart better, as Sally Myers advocates in chapter 8. The tactic for promoting integrative complexity in young Muslims, described by Sara Savage in chapter 6, is another valuable approach to religion that connects with heart as well as head and has the subtlety and complexity that comes from that. The notion of "wisdom" is central to integrating head and heart. There can be approaches to wisdom that focus on head or heart separately, as Harris Wiseman shows in chapter 9, but the approach that captures the essence of the religious notion of wisdom most adequately is one that synthesizes the contributions of head and heart.

CONCLUSION

The dominance of head in our society, and its impact on contemporary religious life, affects every individual on any kind of religious path. The options are threefold: to engage with forms of religion that reflect the prevailing dominance of head; to react against that and engage with forms of religion that arise from the heart, but fail to engage with the prevailing rationality of our culture; or to forge forms of religion that integrate head and heart. I suggest that the latter is both more faithful to the religious traditions themselves and more helpful to the people who engage with them.

REFERENCES

Ford, David F. 2007. *Christian Wisdom: Desiring God and Learning in Love.* Cambridge: Cambridge University Press.

Garrison, Jim. 1982. *The Darkness of God: Theology after Hiroshima.* London: SCM Press.

Glock, C. Y., and R. Stark. 1966. *Christian Beliefs and Anti-Semitism.* New York: Harper & Row.

Haidt, Jonathan. 2012. *The Righteous Mind: Why Good People Are Divided by Politics and Religion.* Pantheon.

Heelas, P., L. Woodhead, B. Seel, B. Szerszynski, and K. Tusting. 2005. *The Spiritual Revolution: Why Religion Is Giving Way to Spirituality.* Oxford: Blackwell.

Hood, Ralph W., Peter C. Hill, and Bernard Spilka. 2009. The Psychology of Religion: an Empirical Approach. New York: Guilford Press.

James, W. 1902. *Varieties of Religious Experience.* New York: Longmans.

Lash, Nicholas. 1988. *Easter in Ordinary: Reflections on Human Experience and the Knowledge of God.* London: SCM Press.

May, Gerald. 2004. *The Dark Night of the Soul: A Psychiatrist Explores the Connection Between Darkness and Spiritual Growth*. San Francisco: Harper.

McGilchrist, Iain. 2009. *The Master and His Emissary: The Divided Brain and the Making of the Western World*. New Haven, CT: Yale University Press.

Murphy, Nancey. 1990. *Theology in the Age of Scientific Reasoning*. Ithaca, NY: Cornell University Press.

Taylor, Charles. 1989. *Sources of the Self: The Making of Modern Identity*. Cambridge: Cambridge University Press.

Taylor, Gordon Rattray. 1973. *The Angel Makers: A Study in the Psychological Origins of Historical Change, 1750–1850*. London: Secker & Warburg.

Teasdale, John D., and Philip J. Barnard, 1993. *Affect, Cognition and Change: Re-Modelling Depressive Thought*. Hove, UK: Lawrence Erlbaum Associates.

Thouless, R. H. 1971. *An Introduction to the Psychology of Religion*. 3rd ed. Cambridge: Cambridge University Press.

Watts, F. N. 2001. "Shame, Sin and Guilt." In *Forgiveness and Truth*, edited by A. McFayden and M. Tarot, 53–69. Edinburgh: T&T Clark.

Watts, F. N., and M. Williams. 1988. *The Psychology of Religious Knowing*. Cambridge: Cambridge University Press.

Wright, D. S. 1971. *The Psychology of Moral Behaviour*. Harmondsworth: Penguin.

About the Contributors

THE EDITORS

Rev. Canon Dr. Fraser Watts is reader in science and theology, and director of the Psychology and Religion Research Group, Faculty of Divinity, University of Cambridge (PRRG). He is a fellow of Queens' College, Cambridge, chief research officer of the Cambridge Institute for Applied Psychology and Religion, and a former president of the British Psychological Society. He is the author or editor of many books, including *Theology and Psychology* (Aldershot: Ashgate, 2002).

Dr. Geoff Dumbreck is a former research associate in PRRG. He is the author of *Schleiermacher and Religious Feeling* (Leuven: Peeters, 2012). He is now training for ordained ministry in the Church of England at Ripon College, Cuddesdon.

THE CONTRIBUTORS

Dr. Nicholas Gibson was formerly director of the Religious Cognition Research Lab and university lecturer in social psychology at the Department of Social and Developmental Psychology, University of Cambridge. He is now with the John Templeton Foundation.

Rev. Dr. Malcolm Guite is chaplain of Girton College, Cambridge. He is the author of *Faith, Hope and Poetry: Theology and the Poetic Imagination* (Aldershot: Ashgate, 2010).

Dr. Liz Gulliford is a research fellow at the Jubilee Centre for Character and Values at the School of Education, University of Birmingham. She previously worked for the Psychology and Religion Research Group, coediting *Forgiveness in Context* with Fraser Watts (London: T&T Clark International, 2004).

Dr. Glendon L. Moriarty is associate professor at Regent University's School of Psychology and Counseling. He is the author of *Pastoral Care of Depression: Helping Clients Heal Their Relationship with God* (Binghamton, NY: Haworth Press, 2006), coeditor of the *God Image Handbook for Spiritual Counseling and Psychotherapy: Research, Theory, and Practice* (Binghamton, NY: Haworth Press, 2008), and editor of *Integrating Faith and Psychology* (Downers Grove, IL: InterVarsity Press, 2010).

Rev. Sally Myers is a program leader at the School of Theology and Ministry Studies in Lincoln, acting principal of East Midlands Ministry and Mission Training Course, and a doctoral student at the University of Cambridge.

Dr. Russell Re Manning is the Lord Gifford Research Fellow in Natural Theology at the University of Aberdeen and the Isaac Newton Teaching Fellow in Theology at St. Edmund's College, Cambridge. He is the editor of the *Oxford Handbook of Natural Theology* (Oxford: OUP, 2013). He was formerly a research associate in PRRG and a lecturer in the Faculty of Divinity, University of Cambridge.

Dr. Sara Savage is a senior research associate in PRRG. She is the author of *Joseph: Insights for the Spiritual Journey* (London: SPCK, 2011), coauthor of *Conflict in Relationships* (Oxford: Lion, 2010), *The Human Face of Church* (Norwich: Canterbury Press, 2007), *Making Sense of Generation Y* (London: Church House Publishing, 2006), and

Psychology for Christian Ministry (London: Routledge, 2002), as well as chapters and articles on fundamentalism and radicalization.

Dr. Carissa Sharp completed her doctorate at the University of Cambridge in the Department of Social and Developmental Psychology. She is currently a postdoctoral research associate at the Culture and Morality Lab in the University of Oregon's psychology department. Her research interests include the application of social cognitive findings and techniques to the study of religion.

Mr. Harris Wiseman is a research associate in PRRG and is completing a doctorate in the Faculty of Divinity at the University of Cambridge. His latest research project examines virtue engineering and moral augmentation through biologically based interventions.

Mrs. Bonnie Poon Zahl is a doctoral student in the Department of Psychology at the University of Cambridge. Her primary research interest is in the relationships between cognition, emotion, and religious belief.

Index

....